Les Icariens

Statue of Liberty–Ellis Island Centennial Series

Board of Editors

Roger Daniels, *Chair, University of Cincinnati*
Jay P. Dolan, *University of Notre Dame*
Victor Greene, *University of Wisconsin–Milwaukee*

*A list of books in the series appears
at the end of this volume.*

Robert P. Sutton

Les Icariens

The Utopian Dream in Europe and America

University of Illinois Press · Urbana and Chicago

Publication of this book was made possible in part by a grant
from the Ellis Island–Statue of Liberty Foundation.

This book is printed on acid-free paper.

Library of Congress Cataloging-in-Publication Data

Sutton, Robert P.
    Les Icariens : the utopian dream in Europe and America / Robert P.
Sutton.
        p. cm. — (Statue of Liberty-Ellis Island Centennial series)
    Includes bibliographical references and index.
    ISBN 0-252-02067-7
    1. Icarian movement—History.   I. Title.   II. Series.
HX632.S87 1994
335'.02—dc20   93-8609
                                                                    CIP

To my wife, Jill

For the wise man did easily foresee, this to be the one and only way to the wealth of a commonalty, if equality of all things should be brought in and established.

—Thomas More, *Utopia* (1551)

... in the generation after 1815 the United States was discovered by the common man ... and the Europeans ... did not hesitate to call the land a Utopia. ...

—Marcus Lee Hansen, *The Atlantic Migration*

Contents

Acknowledgments

It hardly seems worth mentioning, but a book on the Icarians, covering almost a century in time and two continents in scope, accumulates countless obligations. I owe a long-standing debt of thanks to Pearce S. Grove, former director of the Foundation Libraries of the Colonial Williamsburg Foundation, who as director of Western Illinois University Libraries in 1976 saw the need for, and worked successfully to create, the Center for Icarian Studies. Without the Center and the Icarian materials now stored there this history could not have been undertaken. I am also indebted to the staff of the Archives and Special Collections of Western Illinois University Libraries, especially Gordana Rezab, university archivist, and Marla Vizdal, archives specialist, who have kept up with the steady pace of the Center's accessions over the past seventeen years. John C. Abbott, former director of the Lovejoy Library of Southern Illinois University–Edwardsville, and the staff of the Iowa State Historical Library in Des Moines were early, and crucial, supporters of my investigations. I cannot express adequately my appreciation for the help offered by the officers and members of the National Icarian Heritage Society, especially its executive director Lillian M. Snyder.

More recently, a number of individuals have offered their time and expertise to assist my labors. John Hoffman, head of the Illinois Historical Survey of the University of Illinois at Urbana-Champaign, led me to and through the vast Robert Owen Correspondence. Wayne Wheeler, director of the Institute for Icarian Investigations at the University of Nebraska-Omaha, sharpened my understanding of the Icarian experience by his critical observations on my work and publications. Jacques Rancière of the Université de Paris VIII graciously assisted my research in France in the spring of 1990. Bruno Verlet guided me in the intricacies of getting access to the manuscripts at the Archives Nationales (Centre d'Accueil et de Recherche des Archives Nationales) and the Bibliothèque Historique de la Ville de Paris. Ms. Mieke Ijzermans of the Information Department of the Internationaal Instituut voor Sociale Geschiedenis, Amsterdam, was so accommodating as to have all of the folders of the Archief Cabet pulled from storage and ready for me to use upon my arrival. And Kees Rodenburg, head of the French Section of the Instituut, freely gave of his knowledge of their Icarian holdings. Then, too, the staffs at the Bibliothèque Nationale and the British Museum both welcomed me to their collections and quickly facilitated the necessary procedures required to gain admission to them.

Western Illinois University, in addition to its long-term commitment to the Center for Icarian Studies, helped my efforts in other ways. In the 1979–80 academic year a sabbatical leave of absence allowed me to complete the first English translation of Cabet's *Voyage en Icarie*. Then, in 1989–90, another sabbatical gave me the opportunity to travel in Europe to complete my research on this project. Of course, a thank-you must be extended to my typist, Allene Jones, for the painstaking job of turning my handwritten material into legible copy, and to Rulon N. Smithson, professor of French at Western Illinois University and a specialist in early French socialism, for his careful proofreading of the manuscript.

Introduction

The story of the Icarians is a fascinating chapter in utopian socialism, a significant episode in nineteenth-century European immigration, and a saga of one of America's longest-lived utopian experiments. But up to now it has been a history told only in bits and pieces. One of the first historians to tell it was Jules Prudhommeaux, who in *Icarie et son fondateur, Etienne Cabet* (1907) presented Icarianism essentially as a biography of its creator. Consequently, he left much of the story unexplored (whenever Cabet moved off center stage in the action) or undeveloped (after Cabet died in 1856, more than a half-century before the demise of the last Icarian community). Prudhommeaux had too much empathy with Cabet and offered little explanation, let alone a critical understanding of his motives and actions. Since the appearance of *Icarie et son fondateur,* a good deal of new information about Cabet the man, his role in the movement he organized, and the American communities he launched has been uncovered.

Christopher H. Johnson attempted a partial revision of Prudhommeaux in *Utopian Communism in France: Cabet and the Icarians, 1839-1851* (1974). He showed, as Prudhommeaux did not, that "Icarianism drew its following overwhelmingly from the urban working classes, above all from among distressed artisans whose livelihood was threatened less by the direct impact of machinery than by concentration of ownership, increasing division of labor, and generally more efficient modes of organization in their still largely handicraft occupations."[1] Johnson's treatment of Cabet and his followers and their place in the labyrinth of French politics is solid. Unfortunately, he cut off his narrative at the point when the Icarians embarked to America.

Johnson's work has its weaknesses. He overworked Icarianism as a political phenomenon and wrote off the importance of Cabet's contribution to the ideology of labor history, stating that an analysis of the man's thought "hardly seems worth doing."[2] Perhaps. No one can argue for Cabet's originality, but originality is not the sole criterion by which to judge a contribution to the history of ideas. Some gods in the pantheon of

American intellectual history, Jefferson for example, would be thrown out according to that standard. Cabet's dream of a utopia should be dealt with in terms of how his ideas captured the workers' imaginations, lifted their expectations, and, consequently, became useful symbols of their ultimate hopes and commitments. Jacques Rancière has suggested as much. In *La nuit des prolétaires* (1981) he presented a comprehensive reappraisal of the hopes and fears of working-class Frenchmen. His final chapter, "Le Voyage d'Icarie," is a penetrating exploration of Icarian ideas and their relevance to the European labor movement.[3]

Johnson also focused exclusively on continental events and made no effort to identify those elements of Cabet's utopianism that had crucial bearing upon the American side of the story. In fact, there is no definitive treatment of the American Icarian communities. Over a hundred years ago Albert Shaw, who had interviewed Icarians at their Iowa utopia, published *Icaria: A Chapter in the History of Communism.* A short sketch, it had no footnotes and rested almost entirely on newspaper accounts and anecdotal information. Shaw all but ignored the European background of Icarianism and, because his book appeared in 1884, he had nothing on the Icarians up to the dissolution of their last colony in 1898. Other scholars have investigated segments of the Icarian story in America, and their findings, appearing as chapters in books or articles, are mentioned in the bibliography at the end of this book.

Why has a thorough treatment of the Icarians not been done? Part of the problem, for many scholars of American history, is that most of the sources are in French. Then, too, the Icarian holdings were not easy to get at. Until recently they remained scattered, largely uninventoried, in libraries and private hands across Europe and the United States. Recognizing the problem of accessibility, Western Illinois University in 1976 established the Center for Icarian Studies with a mission to gather in one place all of the extant materials on or about the Icarians. By 1990, the overall goal of the Center had been largely, though by no means conclusively, accomplished. And it was upon the extensive materials housed there that I was able to begin my research.

My journey to discover the facts about the Icarians took me to collections in St. Louis, Chicago, Southern Illinois University–Edwardsville, the University of Illinois at Urbana-Champaign, the Iowa Historical Library at Des Moines, and Cloverdale, California, just to mention a few of the most important American locations. No thorough investigation of the Icarians could be done without perusal of the large manuscript and print holdings in Paris (at the Archives Nationales, Bibliothèque Nationale, and Bibliothèque Historique de la Ville de Paris), Amsterdam (at the

Internationaal Instituut voor Sociale Geschiedenis), and London (at the British Museum).

What, then, have I discovered? Icarianism was built upon a utopian dream created by Cabet's fertile imagination in the *Voyage en Icarie*, a romantic novel published in 1839. The book depicted a society without private property or money, devoid of political corruption, unemployment, immorality, and crime. The Icarians believed that if they created the society depicted in the book, they could eliminate these and all other evils.

Such utopian ideas, of course, were by no means new. Thirty years before Cabet wrote his novel the French socialists had called for a restructuring of society. Charles Fourier (1772-1837), a reclusive, almost neurotic bachelor, thought that capitalism was fatally hostile to the innate passions of mankind and had spawned a nation of millionaires and tramps. The alternative lay in evolving toward "universal harmony" through stages built upon model communities that Fourier called phalanxes, where human passions could be expressed in complete pastoral freedom. Here sexual activity could be liberated and marriage delayed until late in life. Here men and women could move from one task to another and eliminate boredom and dullness.

More widely known than Fourier, Count Claude Henri de Saint-Simon (1760-1825) likewise wanted to save France from the consequences of the industrial revolution. He proposed a new system of rational management under a national board of directors that would administer wealth and property and coordinate all production to achieve the same goal that Fourier desired, "harmony." But he added a veneer of mysticism, a "New Christianity," to his social science and tried to convert Frenchmen to a lifelong commitment to "faith, love, and labor." His followers even adopted a red, white, and blue costume, developed rituals, and laid plans for a communal organization, but nothing concrete ever developed.

By 1840, though, the Fourierists and Saint-Simonians had disbanded, in large part because of continuous rivalry between the two. Each side condemned the other for apostasy: the Fourierists were ridiculed as naive, atheistic mathematicians; the Saint-Simonians were condemned as propagandists for a naive, phony religion. And both groups faced other severe problems. The French middle class saw utopian socialism as dangerously radical. The French workers found Fourier's scientific planning too complicated and intellectual, if not irrelevant to their most immediate concerns about stable wages and shorter work days. And they had little time for Saint-Simon's pie-in-the-sky promises of noble work and opaque idealism.

Cabet simplified Fourier's environmentalism into a dramatic picture of utopian life that workers easily understood. At the same time, he changed

Saint-Simon's preachy mysticism into an equally appealing—to skilled artisans at least—Christian morality of brotherly love and the daily application of the Golden Rule. Unlike Fourier or Saint-Simon, Cabet applied his theories in actual community building. Although he could achieve nothing like the grandiose utopia described in the *Voyage en Icarie,* he nevertheless tried to create the *communauté de biens* or the "community of goods" in the United States. In 1849 he led a group of loyal Icarians to Nauvoo, Illinois, to replicate Icaria and to create there one of America's most successful nonreligious communal experiments. Despite mistakes and personal flaws, he instilled in his followers a vision of perfectionism that endured for almost a half-century. After Cabet died in 1856, dedicated Icarians—at four more sites in Missouri, Iowa, and California—held to their dream that if the community described in the book were created then they would have economic abundance, political equality, and social fraternity. And in every community Cabet's *Voyage en Icarie* was as much a guide to the Icarians as the Bible was for the Puritans of Massachusetts Bay.

The Icarian colonies took shape in an America already alive with communal experiments. In some aspects they resembled the Fourierists at Brook Farm, the North American Phalanx, the Wisconsin Phalanx, and the Owenites at New Harmony. They all expected to create a model for a new social order. They shared common assumptions about voluntary membership and some form of communal property. They condemned the same perceived evils of industrialization. They shared an optimistic faith in the improvement of human institutions. But the Icarians, more than the other experimenters in perfectionism, persisted in following the communal plan dreamed of by Cabet and set out in the *Voyage en Icarie*. Whether or not they realized their dream or even came close, or why and how they fell short of the mark, is the subject of the following pages.

ONE

Origins

The French Revolution was in embryo on the first of January, 1788, when Etienne Cabet was born in Dijon, the commercial center of the Burgundian wine trade, in the district of Côte-d'Or. His father, Claude, and his grandfather were coopers, a respectable and secure craft in that part of France.[1] During the years of the Directory and Consulat he attended the Dijon public schools, helped in the barrel shop, and was expected to follow in the family trade. Young Cabet's interests, however, were academic and he showed no inclination to become a master craftsman. And his horizons were considerably broadened during adolescence by Joseph Jacotot, the director of the Dijon lycée, who cultivated in this bright and serious student an avid enthusiasm for the Revolution's ideals of liberty, equality, and fraternity.[2]

After completing the lycée Cabet entered the University of Dijon intending, he said, to study medicine. But he soon found the curriculum too tedious. Besides, he was drawn to grand ethical questions of history, economics, and law. So, at the age of twenty, he switched to his lifetime avocation, jurisprudence. Moving over to the Dijon law school, he came under the influence of another powerful mentor, Victor Proudhon, dean of the law school. Like Jacotot, Proudhon was an ardent republican who in the first decade of the nineteenth century shifted his allegiance to become a supporter of Napoleon Bonaparte. He took a strong paternal interest in this intense, myopic student, even to the point of offering him room and board. In May 1812, at the age of twenty-four, Cabet graduated from the law school.[3]

He had hoped to stay on at the university as a member of the faculty, but when no invitation was offered he opened a private practice in town. His popularity as a successful advocate caused him to be chosen legal counsel to local Bonapartist officials who had been arrested for sedition during the conservative crackdown after the fall of Napoleon. At the Piogy Trial, named after the Dijon major who was one of the officials, Cabet received wide acclaim for his eloquent defense, and the men were acquitted of all charges. "It was a noble day for my country," he wrote, "a noble day for me." "From that moment my comrades said to me," he recalled, "you will be the deputy from Côte-d'Or." He believed them.[4]

But Cabet's political career would have to wait. The trial left him almost blind and, to add to this adversity, he was disbarred for one year on bogus charges of malpractice, brought by Dijon royalists in retaliation for his victory in the trial. Rather than stay in Dijon and fight to retain his legal practice, he left for Paris. He arrived there in the late spring of 1820 with more courage than money and was hired as a personal secretary to one of the city's prominent lawyers, Félix Nicod. He held this position for several years while he became more and more involved with the Society of the Charbonnerie.[5]

The Charbonnerie, although divided into two quarreling factions, plotted the destruction of the Restoration monarchy. One faction, directed by Marie-Joseph Lafayette, wanted to recreate the republic through constitutional reform and statutes, essentially imitating what had happened in America between 1776 and 1787. The other group, led by Jacques Antoine Manuel, wanted a coup d'état and a strong central government that by fiat would establish democracy.[6]

Cabet sided with Manuel and became his lackey, running hither and yon on errands to take care of petty details. One Charbonnier, Paul-François Dubois, described young Cabet as an ardent, orderly, efficient bureaucrat, "politically inclined, restless, impassioned, narrow-minded." "Austere in personal habits," Dubois wrote, "he started each day with a bowl of milk and slice of bread. . . . At night, after the errands were done, Cabet could be seen in some little out-of-the-way restaurant like a simple worker, a veritable political ascetic."[7]

In 1827, this Dijon ascetic revealed what he had been up to during those lonely hours by himself. He had written a short tract entitled *"Exposé d'une révolution nécessaire dans le gouvernment de France,"* in which he put forth some of the ideas that later became integral parts of his Icarian utopia. He abandoned all hope of monarchy, even a constitutional one, and argued that France needed a temporary dictator who would eventually create a republic.

Cabet was quite specific on the sequence of his revolution. The temporary dictator would convene a national assembly, establish freedom of the press, replace all bureaucrats with young patriots like himself, and provide the "popular classes" with enough work to be comfortable. But Cabet was no socialist or communist. "If men will be content to renounce personal independence in order to unite in society, to form a nation, to submit to laws . . . and promise to obey [them]," he wrote, "it is necessary . . . to assure their liberty, their equality, [and] their property."[8]

Soon after writing the *"Exposé"* Cabet's career began to founder. He started to feel uncomfortable under the thumb of Manuel and found another job as a broker in a commercial exchange. But it collapsed early in 1829 and left him broke. Desperate, he joined a Parisian publishing house as Director of Collections of General Jurisprudence but quit within a year because he found it too boring.[9]

By that time opposition to the government of Charles X was reaching a crescendo. Newspapers such as *Tribune des Départements, Jeune France, Révolution, Patriote,* and *National* all pressed for the king's abdication and the resignation of his hatchet man, the Prince de Polignac. When in the spring of 1830 the Chamber of Deputies turned against the government, Charles arrogantly dismissed it and called for new elections. To the king's chagrin the liberals won, and Charles, on the advice of Polignac, issued the July Ordinances that dissolved the Chamber and imposed strict censorship of the press, among other things. The barricades went up in Paris and the Revolution of 1830 was on.

Students and workers demanded the creation of a republic. But the aging Lafayette declined the offer to head a new government, and liberal deputies, recalling the rampant violence of the first French Revolution, pulled back. They hated Charles, but they feared chaos even more. Consequently, France emerged from its second revolution with a constitutional monarchy, not a republic, when the deputies on August 7 voted to offer the crown to Louis Philippe, Duc d'Orléans.

Ten days earlier Cabet had sent a letter to Louis urging him to get a national plebiscite to approve him as the new monarch. When Louis ignored the advice and accepted the invitation of the legislature, Cabet reversed himself, writing a brochure entitled *Au duc d'Orléans,* in which he sanctioned the whole procedure. Crassly opportunistic, he wanted a job in the new government, and he got one almost immediately. Through the influence of Nicod, his former employer, he was appointed Procurer General of Corsica. Gratified, Cabet considered the position "the logical stepping stone" toward his heart's desire, to be elected one day to the Chamber of Deputies. Besides, the appointment, however far removed it might be from Paris, was preferable to no work at all.[10]

Cabet left for Corsica on October 15, 1830, and arrived by steamboat at Bastia, its capital, ten days later. In a letter to fellow Charbonnier Dupont de l'Eure, he described his pleasant accommodations—the most beautiful house in the city, with a charming terrace, from which he could see the island of Elbe and Italy itself. He confided to Dupont, however, that he was constantly homesick and his ardent "patriot soul" thought "always about his country."[11]

Shortly afterward he heard disturbing news from Paris. Louis Philippe was much more conservative than the Charbonnerie had expected him to be. He had dismissed liberal leaders like Dupont (who had led the Chamber to give Louis the crown) and had removed Lafayette from his position as commander of the National Guard. Most alarming of all, the king appeared to back the repressive measures of Casimir Périer, head of the new ministry, to restrict suffrage and to revive police surveillance of political organizations. Dupont, hoping to solidify his strength in the legislature, encouraged Cabet to become a candidate for the Chamber of Deputies from his home district of Côte-d'Or. As an incentive Dupont assured him of the support of political action groups, such as the *Aide-toi*, to help in the campaign.[12]

Cabet needed no incentive to leave Corsica. On April 7 he mailed a statement of his political principles to Dijon and had it published in that city's newspaper. He stated that even though the July Revolution must command the honor and respect of the voters, citizens should applaud the "generous efforts of the people who have taken up arms for the cause of their liberty."[13] He stated that a "great man" or an "immortal genius" was needed. Louis Philippe, he said, did not fit the bill.[14] On May 17 he wrote to a friend in Paris that he was eager to begin the fight for preservation of first principles. "Nothing equals in my eyes," he said, "the peace of conscience." "I prefer my absolute independence and my liberty," he proclaimed.[15] Two days later he boarded a steamboat and headed for Dijon, a city second only to Lyons as a bastion of opposition to the July Monarchy.[16]

Cabet's opponent, the Marquis de Chauvelin, was a prominent former deputy. But Cabet shrewdly posed as the candidate of "the people," a poor, honest public servant, unlike the wealthy and arrogant marquis. He was also a native son, the child of a local artisan, who had demonstrated courage in the Piogy Trial as the champion of individual liberty. The *Aide-toi* distributed posters that stressed his recent opposition to the oppressive Bourbon regime. Covering all angles, Cabet tried to appeal to moderate voters as well. In a June 6 letter he said that while he opposed royal abuse under the Bourbons he was not a radical and could support a legitimate constitutional monarch. He was a monarchist and republican! On July 6, he won a majority of the 439 votes of Côte-d'Or. So, by the circuitous route of Dijon to Paris to Corsica to Dijon, Cabet at the age of forty-three thought he had achieved his destiny.[17]

The Paris that Cabet entered in late 1831 had become something of a political theater: ardent conservatives, moderate republicans, and radical utopian socialists all vied for popular support. The last group, relative newcomers on the scene, rallied around the ideas of Fourier and Saint-Simon. Fourier as a young man had stumbled onto a massive theory of restructuring all political and social institutions. Later, in retirement as a solitary bachelor in the Bourse district of Paris, he spelled out a detailed critique of what he called civilization: it was corrupt from top to bottom, and all institutions must be replaced by "universal unity" based upon laws of "universal harmony." In his brooding, Fourier claimed to have solved all of the fundamental problems that had plagued mankind for eons.

Put simply, Fourier condemned a culture based upon fraud and exploitation that had evolved unchallenged through stages of what he called savagery, patriarchy, and barbarism. He saw the contemporary world as mired in institutional vices such as "priestly superstition," the degradation of the "wage system," the hypocrisy of the "isolated household," and the rapacity of the "commercial system." Nevertheless, civilization could be rescued through "competitive individualism" and "cooperation" wherein mankind would progress through gradually improved stages of "Guarantism" and "Simple Association" to the ultimate level of "Harmony." This last stage, he assured everyone, would endure for sixty thousand years and would bring about "mature happiness." A final ten-thousand-year period of decline, though, would ultimately return everything to primitive beginnings. But mankind need not endure the two stages preceding Harmony; it could move immediately to utopia by creating phalanxes.

These phalanxes, the essence of Fourierism, permitted the flowering of the basic human passions that were so frustrated and twisted in civilization. Set in serene, bucolic environments, each phalanx would contain 1,620 individuals from all classes. Each member would receive an income based upon his or her labor in a rotational work plan that allowed people to change from one job to another and to develop those talents best suited to their unique passions. Eventually, the tensions and competition of civilization would be replaced by a harmonious network of mutual interests and feelings. Sexual passion would be liberated from the frustration of the isolated household in the open enjoyment of fraternal promiscuity. Once two million phalanxes were established around the globe, Fourier predicted, national boundaries and identities would disappear. The world, in equilibrium, would see humans sporting "long and useful tails," living in an "Italian climate," surrounded by docile, cuddly animals.

Count Henri de Saint-Simon emphasized a similar restructuring of society, but with a different emphasis. A soldier of fortune (he had fought with Washington at Yorktown), bank speculator, and sometime politician, he spent his retirement years as Fourier's neighbor in the Bourse, developing the "New Christianity." In pamphlets and discussion groups at the Ecole Polytechinque he identified the villains and spelled out the new order that would eliminate them. Contemporary society was debauched by industrial capitalism, he said. Frenchmen must pull together in a classless community where workers, skilled artisans, and engineers could maximize economic productivity and social selflessness. He shared Fourier's confidence in reason and science to create a utopia, but he also emphasized love, family, and "public sermons" to arouse the nation. By 1829 costumed Saint-Simonians were seen around Paris talking about the creation of an autonomous community of true believers. That year they experimented outside the city at Menilmontant with a monastic community devoted to manual labor and love. But bickering and governmental investigations into charges of "sexual freedom" brought the colony to an end in a couple of months.

Although the Fourierists and Saint-Simonians squabbled with each other, by the time Cabet arrived in Paris the two sides had fused temporarily into a cadre of missionaries led by Victor Considerant, Jules Lechevalier, Hippolyte Renaud, and Charles Pellarine. In a weekly newspaper, the *Phalanstère,* they tried to distill Fourier's complex theories and Saint-Simon's mystical ethics into a plan of action to save France. The editors of the *Phalanstère* weeded out Fourier's ideas on sexual freedom. They eliminated his laborious technical phrases and used direct language to convey their ideas. They discarded Saint-Simon's costumes and rituals. They described the pleasant daily life to be enjoyed in their pastoral utopia.

In 1832 they announced the construction of the "Societary Colony" at Condé-sur-Vesgre, some thirty-five miles southwest of Paris. As originally planned, the phalanx was to be located on a 750-acre farm that would be capitalized at 1,200,000 francs and would house and feed 600 colonists. But nothing ever happened. Soon the utopian socialists again fell into vicious recriminations between what Carl Guarneri has called the "cosmopolitan theorists" and the "pragmatic provincials."[18]

By this time the July Monarchy was in a confrontational mood. The Périer ministry was determined to suppress both the outrageous ideas of the socialists as well as the carping of the republicans. Louis Philippe, too, was now more than ever convinced that he should never submit to the shackles of a constitutional monarchy. As a member of the republican coalition in the Chamber of Deputies, Cabet never lived up to what Dupont had expected of him. His speeches, when he gave them, were long, rambling tirades against the ministry that impressed his listeners, at best, as tedious lectures.[19] At times his opponents ridiculed and heckled him. Conservative deputy P. F. Dubois later recalled Cabet as pathetically erratic and comical in diatribes that "singularly fatigued the Assembly." Cabet, he wrote, "in a tremulous voice, with harsh and menacing gestures ... with insults, invectives, ... [ran] from one end of the speaker's platform to the other ... while advancing his arm and forefinger." "A goodly number of brave Center members," Dubois recounted, "shuddered from head to toe believing themselves to be looking at some hyena." Feeling rebuffed, Cabet receded into the shadows, into petty, routine organizational tasks.[20]

Meanwhile, in Paris and other cities, newspapers told of growing frustration and hopelessness. The people had supported Louis Philippe, the feeling went, yet to what purpose? The king, once enthroned, seemed oblivious to the problems, needs, and aspirations of those who had placed him in power. In Lyons the National Guard brutally crushed an uprising of silk weavers. Violent clashes erupted between the police and republican political societies. Then in Paris in June 1832 students and workers demonstrated and Périer again brought in the National Guard to keep the peace.[21] While Cabet tended his assigned duties in the Chamber, he privately crafted a response to these events. Finished on October 11, 1832, it appeared that month as his first book, *Histoire de la Révolution de 1830.* The editor of *La Tribune* called it the "patriot's manual," and it undoubtedly raised Cabet's stature far above the almost buffoon-like Deputy he had become.[22]

The book purported to be an objective chronicle of the French Revolution, of Jacobin patriots and their espousal of the natural rights of man, and an analysis of the causes of the ascension of Louis Philippe. Actually, under the guise of historical scholarship, it indicted the king and his perfidious ministry. Cabet showed that the original aim of the 1830 Revolution had been to reestablish a true republic, based on universal suffrage, that once was found in the Jacobin Constitution of 1793. A second aim had been the liberation of the continent and the extension of republicanism to all reactionary monarchies of Europe. A third objective had been the alleviation of the suffering of the working people.

But Louis Philippe had accomplished none of these things. Cabet condemned the king for not calling a constituent assembly to draft a new constitution based on universal suffrage. He denounced his support of other repressive European governments and their total disregard of popular discontent. As far as the king's interest in the working class was concerned, Cabet listed the specific policies that the king should, but would not, adopt to relieve their misery: creation of jobs for the unemployed, establishment of old age and health benefits, abolition of all taxes except those on luxuries, and institution of a national education program.[23]

Encouraged by the response to his book, Cabet jumped into radical politics. As chairman of a committee of the *Association pour la Liberté de la Presse,* he investigated and exposed illegal actions against republican newspaper editors. He put out a succession of attacks on governmental suppression in pamphlets such as *Nécessité de populariser les journaux républicans, Procès du propagateur du Pas-de-Calais, Procès du journal républican "Le Patriote de la Côte-d'Or,"* and *Arrestations illégales des crieurs publics du "Populaire,"* all distributed in 1833. And in November of that year he traveled to Dijon to help personally in the defense of the editor of the *Patriote de la Côte-d'Or.*[24]

About the same time he was chosen Secretary General of another society, the *Association Libre pour l'Education du Peuple.* Organized in 1830 by Parisian students, it had quickly grown into an agency led by professors and was repressed in a crackdown in June 1832. It was revived, but with a strict governmental license to concern itself only with academic matters. A rift soon developed between those who were content with this official halter and those, history professors for the most part, who wanted to head back into politics. The two sides asked Cabet, as secretary, to be a compromise leader, a peacemaker. So in February 1833 he assumed that responsibility and took on the editorship of the society's newspaper, *Le Fondateur.*

He soon expanded the list of members to over two thousand and enlarged the society's legitimate course offerings in Paris and other cities. Most significantly, he secretly disseminated what the police called "republican propaganda" under the "cover of innocent lessons in spelling, art, and arithmetic." That same winter he published a full account of the events of the previous year in *Faits préliminaires au procès devant la cour d'assize contre M. Cabet.* He protested against statutes that "put Paris in a state of siege," that were nothing more than "bloody and tyrannical laws." He denounced the hauling of honest citizens before what amounted to military tribunals, a procedure, he said, that "could be only a veritable assassination." Then Cabet launched his own newspaper, *Le Populaire.*[25]

On June 24, while working as editor of *Le Fondateur,* Cabet mailed out the prospectus of the new paper. This was not just another society newsletter, he said, but a publication committed to defending the people against oppression. The prospectus, in which he printed the names of the first subscribers such as Dupont and Lafayette, announced a weekly edition dedicated to the political interests, welfare, and morals of the people. It reiterated and emphasized the themes of *Histoire de la révolution de 1830:* the first revolution, founded on universal suffrage, had overthrown oppression to create a republic dedicated to the rights of all men. That victory was lost with the return of the repressive Bourbon monarchies who reinstated rule of the minority over the majority. What to do?

Cabet stated that *Le Populaire* would push for the essential reforms that would give the majority, once again, the power to make laws. Universal suffrage, he claimed, was indispensable to a republic. In addition, Frenchmen must demand improved working conditions, a change he thought could be accomplished by machines. The paper would feature biographical sketches of famous men who had served the cause of republican principles and goals. All these goals, Cabet concluded, could be accomplished—the republic restored and the people assured their rights —without violence, "by discussion, by persuasion, by conviction, by the power of public opinion." The success of *Le Populaire* was colossal by contemporary standards of French journalism: its circulation within months shot to over twelve thousand copies.[26]

Cabet, whose essays in *Le Populaire* castigated the king and the ministry, soon got into serious trouble. On January 12, 1834, in an article *"La république est dans la chambre,"* he argued that Louis Philippe was responsible for the oppression of the people. In a second piece, appearing the following Sunday, he charged the king with being involved in a plot to execute patriotic Frenchmen. Entitled *"Crimes des rois contre l'humanité,"* it labeled Louis as the most reactionary monarch of Europe, a man who would, if he thought it necessary, "have Frenchmen shot, gunned down in the streets."[27]

This was sedition and Cabet knew it. The French penal code, as well as laws passed by the Chamber of Deputies after 1819, made it a felony to print any material that was an "affront to the king [or incited] hatred and contempt of the government." Such action was punishable by a fine of up to one thousand francs and imprisonment of five years. Not only was Cabet clearly conversant with the legal consequences of his writings, he was also well aware of the fact that the Périer ministry had enforced the laws to the limit; over 500 press cases had been brought to trial in Paris alone. The editor of the *Tribune,* for example, had appeared in court 111 times and received a sentence of five years in prison and a fine of twenty thousand francs.[28]

These two articles appear more audacious in light of the other writings Cabet had published during the previous autumn. In October he had composed a twenty-page brochure called *La république du populaire.* Here he embraced the likelihood of a revolution through a violent coup. More than just a different tone had entered Cabet's propaganda: a change had taken place in his thinking. Up to this point he had always meandered back and forth between various degrees of republicanism, sometimes embracing popular sovereignty and the interests of the people, at other times proclaiming his confidence in a constitutional monarch. Now, he saw the need for a violent overthrow of the government to create a republic in which the citizen would at last be liberated. In almost mystical language he wrote of Frenchmen united in a glorious uprising to create the perfect republic. He proclaimed that "if it [the united citizenry] existed as a people for a single day, a single hour, its powerful hand or its voice alone would at once resuscitate its rights, and force would then be acting only to assure the triumph of justice."[29] The next month, in *Moyens d'améliorer l'état déplorable des ouvriers,* he advocated the creation of a national union of craft workers. Such a union would organize workers and support their demands for governmental programs to deal with unemployment and declining wages. It would make them feel proud of themselves. "Instruct yourselves, sense your dignity as men," Cabet wrote, "make yourselves respected, do not endure insults, humiliation and aggression."[30]

By 1833 Cabet had not only escalated his attacks and changed his ideas and propaganda tactics; he acted in a much more open and defiant manner. He now associated publicly with members of the *Société des Droits de l'Homme,* a radical organization notorious for its seditious ideas. At a banquet in Dijon held in his honor by the *Société* he praised their goal of having all citizens know "their rights and duties as well as the political and moral ideas that ought to distinguish a free man."[31]

By the early winter of 1834 the authorities had *had* their fill of Cabet's antics. In January, the Procurer General of the Court of Paris asked the Chamber of Deputies to indict Cabet for sedition. On February 8, a shouting match erupted on the floor of the legislature over the indictment, in which Cabet charged the Minister of the Interior, the Comte d'Argout, under whose jurisdiction the Court of Paris operated, with treason to the republic and burning the tricolored flag in 1814. Outraged, Argout, in the midst of the uproar, challenged Cabet to a duel. Cabet accepted, crying out, "If my death were able to bring about the triumph of the cause of the people I would require point blank combat by pistol!" Before the time and place of the duel could be arranged, however, the request for the indictment was put to a voice vote. Cabet lost.[32]

He stood before the Assize Court of the Seine on February 28, 1834, and his trial took place on the first of March. His two lawyers, both personal friends, were ineffective. Also of no consequence were the sixty deputies who came to the trial and one by one shook Cabet's hand. Even an attempt to scare the jury fell flat—or perhaps backfired. An attaché of the Austrian embassy in Paris reported that "everything was done to intimidate the jury—including the drawing of a skull and crossbones on their houses."[33]

The decision came quickly: acquitted of sedition in the first article, guilty in the second one. In this article the key phrase was Cabet's charge that the king would fire on citizens if he thought it necessary to save himself. The court sentenced him to two years in prison, a fine of 4,400 francs, and forfeiture of all political rights, that is, voting and publishing, for four years—an unprecedentedly severe judgment in such civil cases. His friends were shocked, especially at the sentence of civil death. His enemies gloated: "That will deliver us of him."[34]

Initially at least he wanted to accept the stiff sentence. He said that the jail time would have allowed him solitude for more writing. Furthermore, in the relatively comfortable accommodations for political prisoners permitted in Cabet's time, he would have been allowed regular visits by friends. But his friends urged him to ask for the alternative offered under French law, five years in exile. They promised Cabet that if he went abroad they would raise an annual pension of four thousand francs to support him. There were also private matters pressing Cabet to accept exile. He had a mistress, Delphine Lesage, and an illegitimate daughter, Céline, and Delphine wanted to keep Cabet out of jail. She was so upset, he later wrote, that she "suffered a brain fever."[35]

Cabet decided that he had little choice but to leave France. It was just as well, because his friends really wanted to get rid of him. Alone among republican editors hit by the government's recent crackdown, he had become outspoken to the point of recklessness. Moreover, it was evident that he was fast abandoning moderate republicanism to encourage, if not embrace, violent revolution. To many republicans like Dupont and Lafayette he had passed the pale of credibility. Maybe Cabet believed the police were ready to gun down honest patriots in the streets, but most of his republican colleagues in the Chamber of Deputies did not. In a word, his emotional outbursts and polemical exaggerations had made him a political liability to the republican cause. Pathetically, he seemed not to have recognized his predicament until much later.[36]

By the time Cabet left France he had come a long way, intellectually and emotionally, from the early days among the Charbonnerie. No longer the terrier-like sycophant, he had passed from moderate republicanism to the edge of socialism. He had accepted its concern for the misery of the working classes, although he still did not believe that the whole social order had to be reorganized. But soon after he left France for a five-year exile in London, he changed his mind.

TWO

Icaria Conceived

On his way to London in the spring of 1834 Cabet stopped off in Brussels, by then a familiar haunt of French political exiles, where his host was a liberal member of the Belgian government. No sooner had he arrived in the capital, however, than an article in the *Gazette de Frankfort* charged that he had come to overthrow the monarchy. "Imagine what that is going to do to peace and quiet," the editor warned. Two weeks later, on April 14, the head of King Leopold's Council of Ministers, a son-in-law of Louis Philippe, ordered him out of the country. Cabet arrived in London on May 1.[1]

Only a small amount of information survives about his London years, but it reveals a man who accepted his fate. A number of times he wrote that life in London was not bad at all. Indeed, he found the early months a welcome relief from the turmoil he had just gone through. A letter to his mother dated September 4, 1834, for example, refers only to the "inconveniences" of exile. Then, too, his personal life stabilized. In that first summer his mistress and daughter crossed over to London. Soon afterwards Cabet and Delphine were married. The couple found comfortable lodgings at Cirencester Place with a Dr. Berrier-Fontaine, a twenty-nine-year-old physician and co-founder of the *Société des Droits de l'Homme,* who himself had escaped to London in July of 1835.

Cabet was also cheered by visits from other continental refugees such as Armand Marrast and Godefroy Cavaignac and the two aides de camp of Louis Bonaparte, colonels Vaudrey and Montauban. He was pleased with arrangements he had made for running *Le Populaire* by appointing as the new editor a colleague from his early days in the Chamber of Deputies, Etienne Garnier-Pagès. In September 1834 he told his mother that he was "feeling very good right now" and the city of London was "superb," as "rich and beautiful as Paris."[2]

Eventually, though, the darker side of Cabet's nature took over. In a January 1836 letter to Nicod he cursed his fate and moaned about the great "gloom in his soul."[3] London, he complained, was "one vast prison" and more than ever he saw himself as a "forlorn soul." His financial situation by then only made things worse. His republican friends in France who pledged him a four-thousand-franc annuity had reneged. Probably the amount would not have been enough to maintain his family in any reasonable standard of comfort. But it was never paid regularly, as Cabet should have expected, had he clearly understood the motives behind his friends' recommending exile. He felt betrayed and humiliated. He saw himself sliding downward into the milieu of the poor, unskilled working class, a grave indignity to a former National Deputy.[4] He managed to compose just one short pamphlet, published in Paris in February 1835, called *La justice d'avril,* in which he condemned police brutality against the press. The recent laws enacted against republican editors were, he said, "an unmerciful system" sustained by "the iron collar and the gag."[5] Otherwise he went each day to the Reading Room of the British Museum. There, at his assigned desk, he studied, pondered, and contemplated (often for eighteen hours a day) what had happened to him and to France. By the spring of 1837 he began to write.

By early 1838 he had finished the *Histoire populaire de la révolution française.* A huge, four-volume work of 2,313 pages, it appeared in Paris the next year and was reprinted in two subsequent editions in 1846 and 1851. In an elevated and forceful style Cabet dramatized the rise and fall of one man, Maximilien Robespierre, in a story with plot, setting, theme, and character development. Robespierre, the unsung hero of the Revolution, delivered democracy to France, that is, "the power of the whole People in exercising it in the interest of everyone . . . the principle of fraternity and equality, without exclusion, no oppression of anyone." The Revolution under Robespierre created a "political system most favorable to the dignity and perfection of mankind, to public order, to respect for the laws and to the happiness of all of the citizens, in providing for them the basics of education and work."[6]

Robespierre embodied democracy. He was the force behind the decision of the Committee of Public Safety and the Convention to proclaim a commitment to equality, freedom of religion, free public education, and the abolition of misery. To Cabet, the Reign of Terror was a necessity: the end justified the means. A temporary dictatorship was essential to run the true course between the extreme violence of Marat and Lafayette's reconciliation with the aristocracy. Robespierre was faultless except in his precipitous move toward communism. This one excess, Cabet claimed, caused the Thermidor Reaction and the twin calamities of Robespierre's execution and the end of the democratic revolution.[7]

Robespierre was the Great Man, the person without ambition, willing to sacrifice his life for his country. He was "the man who personified the

Étienne Cabet, age 51, at the time
of the publication of the *Voyaqe en
Icarie.* Center for Icarian Studies,
Western Illinois University.

people, the man who defended equality against all the powers on earth, against the court, against the nobility, against all the clergy, against all the aristocracy, against all the aristocratic bourgeoisie, against all the privileged, against all the schemers, against all the ambitious, how could that man, I say, not have managed to have been slandered?"[8] Although Cabet criticized Robespierre for moving too fast in abolishing private property, nevertheless, as he wrote these lines, he had himself traveled rapidly from republicanism to his own utopian dream of a society without property or money. He called this society the *communauté de biens,* or the "community of goods," and he described it at great length in his third book, *Voyage en Icarie.*

Cabet conceived the *Voyage en Icarie* about the same time he was drafting the *Histoire populaire.* He stated as much in the conclusion of the *Histoire:* "When one looks at all the revolutions since 1789, all the corruption, all the treason . . . is there no other remedy than an entire reordering of society and its politics?"[9] Both books connected the goals of the French Revolution with what had to be done in France in the mid-nineteenth century—to establish complete equality. And both the *Histoire* and the *Voyage* have benevolent dictators as central characters: Robespierre and the the "good Icar," founder of Icaria.[10]

In constructing his fictional *communauté de biens* Cabet drew upon French history and a myriad of social critics and political theorists. Among the most apparent influences were François Fénelon's *Aventures de Télémaque,* Morelly's "heroic poem" the *Code de la nature; ou, le véritable esprit de ses lois,* the egalitarian ideology of Gracchus Babeuf, the utopianism of Thomas More and Louis Mercier, and the environmentalism of Robert Owen.

Joseph Jacotot, Cabet's teacher in the Dijon lycée, had given him a copy of Fénelon's description of the fictional La Betique and Salente, in which the author showed how countries corrupted by militarism could be regenerated by the elimination of private property and money. Then, in his twenties, Cabet read Morelly's *Code,* a poem about how man's essential goodness had been perverted by modern institutions. All evils disappeared, Morelly claimed, when these institutions were eradicated and the human family recreated in a "community." Cabet was well acquainted with Babeuf's abortive 1796 "Conspiracy of Equals" that had tried to topple the Directory. Babeuf's trial for treason produced a three-hundred-page transcript in which he testified that no democracy was possible without economic equality. To achieve this equality the government must control all production and distribution of goods. It must gather the nation's wealth in state warehouses and allocate it to every citizen according to need.[11]

Cabet acknowledged Thomas More as the paramount inspiration for the *Voyage en Icarie.* He said that he discovered More's *Utopia* in the British Museum and experienced an almost religious awakening. The communist system, Cabet wrote, "struck me in such a manner that after the first line, I closed the book to plunge in deep thoughts which led me to the most complete and firm belief. . . . [I then] adopted my plan and started to write."[12] More showed how property, the quintessential moral evil, was the source of all selfish behavior and the root cause of political dissension and war. So his utopia eliminated property and, consequently, all vice. Everyone worked for six hours each day to produce the necessities of life that the government then placed in common warehouses located, convenient to every citizen, in quarter-sections of every city. Each person simply took what he or she needed (never purchased, for there was no money) from these warehouses.

From the vast amount of eighteenth-century French utopian literature Cabet selected the ideas of a little-known academic from Bordeaux, Louis Sebastian Mercier. In 1795 Mercier had published *L'an deux mille quatre cent quarante,* an imaginary tale of a man who goes to sleep in 1790 only to wake up in Paris 650 years later and see all around him a marvelous utopia. Mercier described in detail all the physical surroundings of an exciting new Paris—promenades, gardens, homes adorned with flowers, hospitals, public theaters, and libraries. There are "aromatic baths to reinvigorate the bodies of those who are grown rigid by age."

Outside the city, one finds productive agriculture and hears the "fertile plains rebound with songs of joy." The government now "rational," "made for man," had been created by a revolution brought about "without trouble" by "the heroism of one great man . . . a philosophic prince." France is democratic. Each province elects representatives to a legislature that meets every two years and enacts all laws by a simple majority. The "philosophic prince" had stayed on after the revolution but does not rule; he only supervises "the execution of the laws." "Politics," Mercier wrote at the end of the book, "does not now ruin but unites and enriches the citizens."[13]

Just after Cabet settled in London he read Robert Owen's recently published *New World Order.* Whether or not the Frenchman was the conquest of the Scots philanthropist, as Pierre Leroux claimed, Cabet later confessed that Owen's principles were "perfectly the same" as his own. Both of them, he said, thought it necessary to construct a "heavenly city" from the ground up. In this book Owen reiterated his philosophy that one must change the physical surroundings to improve man's political and moral condition. Through "permanent education" society could increase personal happiness and promote the common good. Owen renounced trade unionism in favor of total community ownership of property. Still, Cabet did not accept everything that Owen advocated. He lamented that Owen had "too much confidence in the goodness of Sovereigns and Aristocrats." Owen wrongly assigned "too short a time to the realization of hopes which are not yet realized." Lastly, Cabet faulted Owen for not trying hard enough, for attempting only "partial and too-small communities that could never succeed."[14]

Cabet all but neglected the writings of Fourier and Saint-Simon. Although he cited some of their ideas in the second section of the *Voyage* and believed that their "work might be attractive," he condemned Fourier for conceiving of "a defective community." Cabet had no time for his "passionate attraction" and never thought that free play of passion created social harmony. Cabet had some affinity with Saint-Simon's writings on Christian brotherhood and his commitment to "equality and Community . . . the infinite perfectibility of man . . . fraternity and association." Still, he rejected the concepts of a hierarchy of talent and genius that would lead the new society. And, most significantly, unlike either socialist, Cabet wanted the elimination of all private property and money.[15]

Cabet did not just *think* in London, he lived there. Pierre Angrand, in analyzing Cabet's exile, stated that his participation in the daily life of the London poor was instrumental in his conversion to communism.[16] He saw the impact of English capitalism on the average worker. He observed confusion in the labor supply: too many men in some jobs and not enough in others. Chaos reigned in production as well: one year too much of one product was made, and the next year there were shortages. The cycles of business depression caused disruption and hardship to entrepreneurs and workers. Insecurity and suffering abounded. All of these woes were only exacerbated by the serious economic depression that hit Europe in the spring of 1836.[17]

One aspect of English capitalism, however, Cabet did not criticize: its advanced stage (compared to anything he had known about in France) of mechanization. He was amazed at factories whose machines put out, he thought, ten times the country's needs. Here he saw *how* communism could work. Mechanization could immediately eliminate drudgery and shorten the workday to six hours. Factory management could be chosen from among the workers, since they would know from experience with the machinery how to administer production. If the factories, controlled by the workers, standardized output by mechanization, then waste and scarcity would disappear.

All of these influences, intellectual and circumstantial, changed Cabet. Before the exile he had been preeminently focused upon political problems, fixed in France in place and time. He had been an effective journalist who popularized such reforms as universal suffrage and freedom of the press. By 1836 he had shifted ground. He had become a working-man's philosopher.

Cabet wrote the *Voyage en Icarie* as a romantic novel for a combination of reasons. More had described his utopia in a fictional travelogue, and subsequent imitators, such as Mercier, had depicted a journey to some sensational make-believe place where the traveler discovered a superior civilization. Also, Cabet had sound political reasons for choosing fiction. He had been arrested for violating earlier press laws, and the ones in place in 1838–39, called the September Laws, were even harsher. A novel, he thought, might not be covered by the same restrictions as a political treatise on the "community of goods."[18]

The choice of the name Icaria is something of an enigma. Some historians think it refers to the mythical Icarus, who ignored the advice of his father, tried to fly with wax wings too close to the sun, and perished. But there is no evidence that Cabet had the story of Icarus in mind. Sylvester Piotrowski believed that he based the title on a slogan from the time of the French Revolution, "*Ça ira*" or "it will succeed," and a more recent student of Icarianism has endorsed this explanation. But again, there is only circumstantial evidence to support it. Cabet's explanation might have to suffice. He told his readers that the people of that mythical country adopted the name of Icaria out of their esteem for the hero who had established the republic in the year 1782, the "immortal Icar," the "regenerator of the Native Land."[19]

Voyage en Icarie is a long book, over eight hundred pages in eight-point type, in which Cabet describes in minute detail all aspects of daily life in the utopia. Through the persona of Lord William Carisdall, an English visitor to Icaria, Cabet tells the reader everything there is to know about the nation's history, politics, geography, economy, education, recreation, family life, and religion. In the last section of the book he presents a long line of witnesses, both historical and contemporary, who endorse in their own words the legitimacy of the "community of goods."

*

Cabet introduces Carisdall on the first page and immediately transports him by ocean steamer to Icaria. During his four months' stay in the utopia, located somewhere off the coast of east Africa, he is continually "astonished," "surprised," "amazed," and "delighted." Carisdall soon develops a close friendship with his young Icarian guide, Valmor, and then falls in love with Dinaïse, Valmor's girlfriend. The Englishman is particularly enthralled with the Icarian historian, Dinaros, and his tale of the founding of the ideal society. Dinaros tells his visitor that the nation was created in 1782, the year of the "great revolution." Before then, barbarians had overrun the island and established a cruel and oppressive monarchy. But about the year 1600 an uprising, led by the aristocracy, started a series of upheavals in which several forms of government were tried: monarchy, theocracy, finally a dictatorship. In 1772, the last of the dictators, old Corug, was finally deposed by a man Cabet calls Lixdox and his queen Cloramide. Both of them, unfortunately, were personifications of treachery and evil.

Ten years later, the people, now led by Icar, revolted against Lixdox and Cloramide. On June 14, after two days of bloody fighting, they chose Icar as their benevolent dictator by popular acclamation. Icar set to work. He "proposed to his fellow citizens social and political equality, the good community, and a democratic republic all attainable after a transition period of fifty years." In 1798 Icar died. By 1812, far ahead of schedule, Icar's goals were realized. Icaria became a democracy with full equality for all citizens.[20]

Icaria is the antithesis of Louis Philippe's France. A two-thousand-member legislative assembly, chosen every three years by the adult men, makes the laws. The same electorate annually chooses an executive council and a president, both of which are subservient to the Assembly and only carry out its policies. To enact such measures the Assembly appoints fifteen committees, each with a specialization. No political parties are necessary. The Assembly, on the advice of the committees, governs all aspects of daily life: transportation, education, housing, food production and distribution. The people "willingly obey" all statutes. If they do not like a particular law they call a referendum "to approve or reject its propositions." Thus, government is all-powerful but not tyrannical. It is based on unanimous consent, on the "general will" in Cabet's terminology. "Our political organization," Dinaros tells Carisdall, is "therefore a democratic republic and even an almost pure democracy." "Everywhere, in a word," he brags, "you will see here equality and happiness."[21]

Icaria is a beautifully proportioned country, symmetrically divided into 100 provinces, each subdivided into ten equal communes. The provinces and communes have their own capital in the exact center of the unit. The city of Icaria, the national capital, is located in the middle of the nation and is accessible by river on ocean steamers and bisected by the waterway. It is a model of urban planning. The National Palace, the seat of government, stands on a small island in the river. Each city block has sixteen houses on both sides of the street and a public building at either end. Trees shade the walkways in front of the homes, and in their backyards the Icarians cultivate family gardens. Carisdall is overwhelmed with the geometric order of the countryside. All roads, paths, and even ditches run in a straight line and are intersected at right angles. The fields are rectangular. Everywhere he sees the environment, urban and rural, organized to produce uniformity with variety in order to perpetuate what is necessary and useful. Faced with such perfect harmony Carisdall's friend Eugène, a French visitor, cries out: "Happy women! Happy men! Happy Icaria! Unhappy France!"[22]

Its economy is absolutely egalitarian. Icarians abjure private property and money. The government controls all production and distribution. The committees of the Assembly supervise the highly mechanized workshops, each one turning out a single product. All able-bodied men and women tend the machines. Conditions are ideal. No one is sent to a factory by his or her family until the age of seventeen (for girls) or eighteen (for boys). Sick leave and maternity leave are provided, and retirement is fixed at fifty for women and sixty-five for men. Machines do all the "perilous, fatiguing, unhealthy, dirty and disgusting jobs." All work stops at one o'clock in the afternoon, and the rest of the day is given over to educational activities or leisure.[23]

Icarian farms are just as rational, efficient, and scientific as the workshops. Large, mechanized family farms grow special crops assigned to them by the Assembly. The family keeps up-to-date with the latest scientific information published in the *Journal d'agriculture* and other works printed by the Republic. Carisdall describes a typical Icarian farm, run by "the good Mirol," as idyllic. Resembling the farm of Wolmar in Rousseau's *La nouvelle Héloïse,* Mirol's land is geometrically arranged on a model that sets aside acres for grains, livestock, and orchards. Cleanliness is everywhere. Carisdall exclaims that whereas on European farms "one ordinarily sees everywhere only disgusting filth, disorder and misery, I found everything clean, everything in order, everything as comfortable and elegant as I had noticed everywhere else." A veritable revolution in agronomy had ensued since 1782. Valmor informs Carisdall on their way back to the capital after visiting Mirol that cultivated acreage had doubled in size and that the products were "not only more abundant by number and volume but incomparably superior in quality." "In a word," Valmor concludes, production "according to national statistics" had increased "a dozen times" in fifty years.[24]

According to another model plan, distribution and consumption of the products of factory and farm are speedy, simple, and, of course, egalitarian. Workers and farmers earn no salaries; the Republic gives everyone what he or she needs. Committees of the Assembly, and their counterparts at the local level, see to it that an adequate supply of food and clothing go daily to each family, from great national warehouses, through an extensive system of state-run railroads, canals, and roads. Each person receives the same quality of goods and products as his or her neighbor. Only in the color of the clothing does the Republic allow individual choice; a harmless concession, Cabet writes, to female vanity since "certain colors go best with blondes, as you know, and certain others with brunettes." By this concession the Icarians are able to avoid "the caprices and ridiculous variations of fashion." All luxuries are proscribed.[25]

Work, either in the factories or farms, is a necessary function, sandwiched between the two more important activities of education and recreation. Of all the marvels of Icaria, none amazes Carisdall more than their system of education. It is indispensable. It gives the Icarians, Valmor says, "all the physical habits and morals [necessary] to man in society and above all to citizens gathered together."[26] It is a cradle-to-grave commitment open and free to people of all ages and both sexes. Dinaros tells Carisdall that the basis of the whole educational system is physical training. This begins with hygiene lessons for expectant mothers, and for those young women not pregnant, gymnastics. A sound body and a sound mind is the rule, and eugenics the objective. "Is it not true," Dinaros asks, "that our men combine suppleness with strength, whereas our women combine grace and health, and that must naturally bring forth generations of children always more robust and more beautiful than their fathers and mothers?"[27]

Academic training begins at age five and extends to seventeen for girls and eighteen for boys . They go to school at nine o'clock and return home at six. The curriculum is rigorous: science, literature, history, grammar, and mathematics. Drawing, painting, and music are also included. A sort of advanced education goes on in Icaria into young adulthood. Here, during a four-year period, the individual "specializes" and gains the "knowledge necessary to excel in their scientific or industrial pursuits." Some of this experience is on-the-job training in factories or farms. Teachers at all levels stress understanding of the "hows" and "whys," combine theory and practice, and avoid the deadening effects of rote memorization and recitation.

Moral indoctrination occurs at all stages of Icarian education. Parents instruct their children in filial devotion, fraternity, propriety, and gratitude. At school, teachers emphasize the importance of decency, honesty, and love of the community. Young Icarians between the ages of eighteen and twenty-one are given lessons in "civic conduct" that concentrate on "the constitution's real laws and the rights and duties of magistrates and citizens." As an adult, at the age of twenty-one, they apply their knowledge of right conduct and proper values in the everyday world of politics, work, and play.[28]

There is no doubt that the Icarians play more than they work. With all the extra time after the workshops close in early afternoon, the Republic has to provide amusements and diversions. In marked contrast to the dismal life of the French worker, Icarians spend their afternoons and evenings viewing public "spectacles" staged in large amphitheaters. Such extravaganzas are always patriotic. One such event celebrates Icarian Independence Day, an annual commemoration of the triumph of Icar over Lixdox and Cloramide. This pageant involves twenty thousand children between six and ten, thirty thousand boys and girls from ten to twenty years of age, eighty thousand adult dancers, a band of six hundred drummers, six hundred drums, and ten thousand instruments all combining to "delight the air with songs of victory and triumph." At nightfall the fireworks display begins. "A thousand fires which shoot up on all sides, which cross in all directions, which present a thousand colors and a thousand forms" culminate with a balloon ascension of "some 100 balloons, dispersed to 500 or 600 feet high over the city, discharging finally on it an immense shower of stars and fire."[29]

When not at the amphitheater Icarians go to dances, the theater, and concerts, or enjoy promenades and picnics. The dances are huge affairs held in stadiums or elegant public buildings. In one such building Carisdall and Eugène, seated in a balcony that surrounds a huge dance floor, observe a panoply of couples "dancing and waltzing" who are soon joined by children and the elderly. Finally, Carisdall describes how "the dance became general, intermingling all of the ages and all of the sexes and presented a most animated spectacle."

The same extravagant display is seen in the Icarian theater. They have fifteen thousand theaters and put on sixty productions simultaneously throughout the year. The Republic prints tickets for every family and distributes them by lot. Valmor tells Carisdall that "each family will have its notice like each single individual and each will know in advance the presentation to attend." If an Icarian does not like the assigned date of the ticket he or she just switches with another citizen through a "public tableaux of notices" of people who want to exchange their tickets. The productions are splendid.

Yet a sober motif permeates all this display. The plays have to convey a patriotic and moral message; they must educate as well as entertain. Cabet has maxims for Icarian pleasures just as he has for their political and economic life. All enjoyments have to be authorized by the people through the Assembly. "The pleasurable would be sought only after one has the necessary and the useful." One could "not allow any other pleasures than those which each Icarian is able to enjoy equally."[30]

The family, the basic unit of Icarian society, is a kin group of up to twenty related people living in one household. All adults are required to marry, and if one union does not work out, divorce is easy to get. Consequently, there can be no excuse for adultery—or for not remarrying as soon as possible. With the family intact, morality abounds. No prostitutes live in Icaria, and it allows no exhibition of nude paintings or statues, no pornography, and no graffiti. It prohibits saloons and gambling houses and, consequently, no drunks can be found in the streets. Tobacco, obtained in state pharmacies, is allowed only for medicinal purposes.

Valmor blithely states that crime has disappeared because, put simply, no motives for felonies survived the revolution. He explains this phenomenon to an astonished Carisdall with elementary logic. "What crimes could we have today?" he asks. "Can we know robbery of any kind when we do not have money, and when each possesses everything that he can desire?" "One would have to be crazy in order to be a thief!" "And how could we have murder, arson, poisoning since stealing is impossible?" he continued. "How can we even have suicides seeing that everybody is happy?"[31] Misdemeanors occur from time to time since, Cabet acknowledges, human nature will slip occasionally from the path of righteousness. But these transgressions are rare, and the only punishments are public ridicule (such as publishing the person's name in a newspaper or on a bulletin board) or prohibiting attendance at spectacles or the theater. So, in shocking contrast to France, Icaria has no police, courts of law, judges, lawyers, prisons, or exiles.

Icarian religion, like everything else, produces a personal code of conduct that buttresses the community. Cabet condemned organized religion as based upon superstition and ignorance, and considered it one of the pillars of political tyranny. Religion in his utopia is "only a system of morality and philosophy and has no other use than to bring men to love each other as brothers." Icarians practice a personal moral code of just three ethical rules: "Love your neighbor as yourself"; "Do not do to another the evil that you would not want him to do to you"; and "Do to others all of the good that you would desire for yourself." With no formal worship, every Icarian "admires, gives thanks to, prays to and adores the Divinity as he pleases in the interior of his home." They set aside special buildings for instruction in the history of religions, open to young adults seventeen or eighteen years of age (who, until that time, have been told of God and right conduct by their parents). There philosophers expose them "for a year to all of the religious systems and to all of the religious opinions without exception." Only then do Icarians adopt religious opinions that best suit their conscience. Cabet thought the effect of personal, rational choice in such matters would result in unity, not diversity, for the community. "Our Republic marches toward unity in matters of religion as in all other things because," Valmor says, "the influence of education, reason, discussion, all naturally lead to the most enlightened opinion which becomes universal opinion . . . we can speak of the universality of Icarians for the same religious belief."[32]

Icaria is, therefore, an organic society. Each part of the system leads to and reinforces the other parts. Its symmetrical and healthy physical environment provide the setting for a rational democracy of complete equality. The egalitarian economy, without private property or money, is based on a uniform operation of machine production, scientific agronomy, and mass distribution that assures every citizen the necessities of life. Democratic education stimulates the body and mind and prepares all Icarians for their political and economic responsibilities as adults. Leisure time is filled with uplifting amusements that evoke the highest feelings of patriotism and morality. Family life and mores stress commitment to the welfare of the Republic above self-interest and result in the elimination of serious crime. Finally, Icarian religion unifies all members of the community in a bond of brotherly love and public virtue and thus completes the circle of utopian felicity.

✳

Cabet wanted to portray an integrated community but he actually presented an eclectic, often undeveloped, and sometimes contradictory picture of utopia. For example, what happened to the unskilled laborer who was displaced by the machine? How did all the skilled artisans react to being turned into machine operators? What about the effects of monotony in standardized production? He was too optimistic about what would happen in an ever-expanding system of manufacturing made more efficient every year by mechanization. He assumed that ultimate benefits would accrue to everyone and that useless surpluses would never accumulate. He described happy and efficient workers contentedly toiling to bring about infinite productivity. Yet work in Icaria is only a necessary evil, a part of life to be made as short as possible. He was unconcerned with basic problems such as incentive, anxiety, and fulfillment in the job. Lastly, he avoided the nagging question of just how a society without any medium of exchange functioned in the day-to-day transactions of life.

Cabet never reconciled his conflicting ideas of gender equality with what he frequently called the "natural differences" between the sexes. Like Condocert, he asserted that the intellectual capabilities of women were the same as those of men. Young Icarian girls are educated the same as boys. Icaria's laws require "equality between spouses, with the husband's voice merely the preponderant one." Women have only light domestic chores, since the drudgery of house work is eliminated by furniture designed to eliminate dusting and by the services of national laundries. Icarian men "worship women" as the "masterpieces of civilization." But women cannot vote or hold office. Their liberal education leads only to jobs in the national workshops. In the assembly line, the women (unlike the men) have to maintain total silence during the morning hours. At ten o'clock, though, they are permitted to sing together in "glorious thanks to Icar" for creating a life of equality.[33]

In fact Cabet's ideas about gender relationships rested on a strict conservative code of separation and rectitude. In Icaria there are separate workshops for the sexes. Only women physicians tend female patients. Seduction is a criminal offense and means instant banishment. Young men are forbidden to flirt with or touch young women. Cabet condemned celibacy as "an act of ingratitude and a suspect state" and wrote that wedded bliss, "purified and perfected," reigns in Icaria.[34] Contemporaries, however, when they read the *Voyage en Icarie,* detected a twisted puritanical streak in Cabet. Marx and Engels, for instance, called him "a reactionary petit-bourgeois." And in 1856, Alfred Sude said that Cabet perpetuated "prudish prejudices" in the disguise of utopian communism. Sude thought it impossible to eliminate all institutions that preserved the family, such as private property and the dowry, and still preserve the patriarchal hierarchy of the domestic household.

Later investigators also faulted Cabet's ideas about sex and the family.

Henry Lux, in his 1894 book *Etienne Cabet und der ikarische Communis-mus,* claimed that Cabet never outgrew the French artisan code of morality. Despite his communism, Lux wrote, "he always remained merely the petit-bourgeois democrat." Paul Carée's 1902 dissertation pointed out that Cabet's communist system should have eliminated the family and marriage and he ought to have abolished both. Yet, Carée argued, Cabet needed to find a safe haven in his utopia for the traditional, subordinate role of women, even if it meant keeping "an institution which, one can clearly see, would be the seed of death for the community." Leslie Roberts, in a more recent article on Cabet, pointed to evidence of sexual conflict and repression. In discussing Cabet's "psyche and obsessions" she wrote that his "fear of or disgust at woman's reproductive functions and the various elements that go with it: menstruation, childbirth and menopause" reflected Cabet's guilt at the conflict between his puritanical views and living "with his mistress for many years and [fathering] her child out of wedlock."[35]

Whether Cabet was obsessed or not, his Icaria permits no deviation from its rules, on sexual conduct or anything else. For example, there is no real freedom of the press. One government newspaper operates in each province, and there is just one national journal. Icaria tolerates no play or book that criticizes the community. Long before Lord Carisdall arrived, the Republic had judged most books subversive and burned them. So the press in all its forms, Valmore says, is only permitted to be "the expression of our public opinion," or in other words, the will of the majority. And in Icaria only one official history of what had happened was ever published.

The *Voyage en Icarie* suffers from a number of literary and stylistic pitfalls. Cabet used the novel form, he said, to make his utopia attractive to a large audience. Yet he inundates the reader with tedious details of incidental aspects of Icarian life (for example, the operations of bakeries, or the intricacies of clockmaking). He knew nothing of character development. The main figures are two-dimensional mouthpieces for Cabet's ideas. Dinaros is Cabet lecturing. Eugène voices his diatribes against political conditions in France. Valmor allows Cabet to describe Icaria's physical surroundings and institutions. Cabet's attempt at plot, the flirtation between Carisdall and Dinaïse, remains unconvincing and verges on the burlesque. Although his writing is lyrical at times and his treatment of setting—gardens, promenades, sunrises, for example—can be moving, he has a penchant for hyperbole and vagueness in metaphors and similes.

Overall, Cabet created in the *Voyage en Icarie* an unresolved dualism, if not a paradox. On one hand, he sketched a delightful picture of complete democracy, harmony, and happiness. The government carries out the general will of an educated citizenry. Men and women are equal. The Republic satisfies all the basic necessities of economic, educational, and cultural life. Crime and vice disappear in a community of virtuous, selfless citizens. Icaria at its core is a dream of a society of perfect felicity and fraternity, freed of the restraints upon individual liberty that Cabet saw so rampant in France. Yet, on the other hand, he portrayed a community that crushes individual choice and initiative by a uniformity based upon majority will.

A contemporary, Alexis de Tocqueville, who studied democracy just before Cabet wrote the *Voyage en Icarie,* recognized the grave danger in any community where the "tyranny of the majority" holds sway. Unfortunately, Cabet never read *De la démocratie en Amérique,* or if he did, he never comprehended that the "unbounded confidence in the judgment of the public" easily leads to the imposition of the collective will upon the individual so as "to prohibit him from thinking at all." Nor did Cabet understand, as de Tocqueville did, that one way to combat the tendency of equality of condition to "harness and weary the mind" is to encourage free exercise of self-interest through voluntary associations.

Cabet did not realize that his Icaria substitutes one form of tyranny for another. Instead of the monarchy and police riding roughshod on individual expression, the general will of the community imposes conformity and censorship. Cabet might well have pondered the implications for his own utopia in Tocqueville's warning: "For myself when I feel the hand of power lie heavy on my brow, I care but little to know who oppresses me; and I am not the more deposed to pass beneath the yoke because it is held out to me by the arms of a million men."[36] The subsequent history of Icarianism, as it developed France in the 1840s and especially after it took shape in America, would bear out the dangers Tocqueville so eloquently addressed.

THREE

Icarianism in France

Cabet, oblivious to any errors of omission or commission in his utopian dream, intended to put it into practice as soon as he returned to France. Indeed, he conceived a well-organized plan of action. First he would revive and invigorate *Le Populaire.* Next, he would create "Icarian chapters" in the major cities and with them build a political party that would unite all elements of opposition to the July Monarchy. Lastly, he would replace Louis Philippe with a president modeled on "the good Icar," a benevolent dictator who would begin the transition to communism. During this transition, as in the book, the president would gradually abolish all property by attrition: as each proprietor died, his or her estate would revert to the government. At the same time the president would create national workshops, farms, and mines. By the end of the century, or thereabouts, France would be a propertyless, moneyless, and democratic Icaria.

First of all, he had to get his manuscript published. In April 1838 he sent it to Altroche, the editor of *Charisari,* telling him that a co-worker in the old *Le Populaire* named Louis-Antoine Pagnerre would soon be ready to publish it. Cabet asked Altroche "to advertise, or share, his ideas with the readers of the journal" even though, Cabet warned, the subject might be "too serious for a newspaper." When Pagnerre received the manuscript, however, he ignored it. He refused to be associated with any book advocating the abolition of property. Rebuffed by Pagnerre, Cabet then mailed a copy of the *Voyage en Icarie* to Nicod. His old mentor promptly criticized its radical ideas and broke off all further contact. Cabet then sent it to Marc-René Voyer d'Argenson, a French aristocrat and friend of Buonarotti. D'Argenson, in a brief letter praising the utopian dream, was the only republican to applaud the work. But he offered no assistance in getting it printed. Cabet, faced with no support at home, had to publish the manuscript at his own expense when he returned to Paris in late March 1839. How and where he raised the money for this venture remains a mystery.[1]

Cabet was obviously concerned about these rebuffs and very much worried about staying out of prison. Would the book, even as a novel, land him in jail for violating the press laws? Consequently, he crafted a preface in which he claimed that the book was just a paradigm intended to get people thinking, not a call for political action. Then, to be doubly sure that the authorities would not subpoena him, he tried a literary ruse. Instead of listing his name on the title page as the author, he called the book the *Voyage et aventures de Lord William Carisdall en Icarie,* translated from the English version of Francis Adams by Theodore Dufruit, master of languages.[2]

The subterfuges worked. Cabet survived the six months' probation given to any new publication without hearing from the police. Yet, while he was being overly cautious with the *Voyage en Icarie,* he wrote a small tract called "Note *à* X" in which he set forth a number of clearly seditious ideas. He called for the creation of a secret provisional government that would take power as soon as the monarchy was overthrown and legislate universal suffrage and tax relief. In late August 1839 he mailed a copy of the "Note" to Dupont and asked him to circulate it among his political friends. Dupont buried it.[3]

Cabet did not realize that the France of 1839 was not the France of 1834. The liberal republicans of the early 1830s, for example, had splintered into the moderates, led by Dupont, and the violent communists. To the Dupont group, utopian socialism was still respectable, but the moderates viewed communism, on the other hand, as a total rejection of capitalism and an abhorrent and dangerous ideology. Dupont thought communism crude, almost anti-intellectual, grounded in the emotional frustrations of an illiterate working class who were ready to throw off the "stupefaction" of the bourgeois system.

By 1839, fear of communism had begun to infect the country, and the months following Cabet's return saw a surge of hysteria over the spread of labor unrest. Workers struck in Lyons, Belleville, and Rouen, where they held "communist banquets," in reality noisy rallies, against deteriorating factory conditions, layoffs, and soaring bread prices. As the workers' misery increased so did their frustration with the government's refusal to do anything about it. The ministry, they charged, was preoccupied with an imminent war in Syria and perhaps one in Europe itself. So workers listened to the call of radical communist writers like Louis Blanc, Pierre-Joseph Proudhon, Jean-Jacques Pillot, and Théodore Dézamy, all of whom preached class revolution.[4] The proletariat, they said, must unite in its own interest, always historically separate from that of the middle class. Only militant action could eradicate the oppressors, the "possessing classes." Phrases like "march boldly," "stupid submission," and "break his chains" were common features of their rhetoric.

On October 15, 1840, rhetoric turned to terrorism, when a worker with connections to a radical Parisian society called *Les Communistes* tried to assassinate Louis Philippe. The following March the police raided a communist "banquet" in a Paris suburb and arrested its leaders on charges of subversion. They shut down all communist publications, in particular the newspaper *Le Travail* of Lyons. By the summer of 1841, 187 individuals had been arrested and brought to trial, and of this number 137 were found guilty of conspiracy to overthrow the government. The purge continued, especially in Paris, over the next three years.[5]

To Cabet's surprise, this explosive atmosphere helped his cause. Because of his earlier disavowal of violence and his appeal in the *Voyage en Icarie* for gradual, peaceful change, the book caught the attention of the skilled artisans, most of whom were faced with a dilemma. These French craftsmen viewed the idea of a violent revolution led by common laborers as anathema. Yet the masters and journeymen had never considered themselves linked with the bourgeoisie and their craving for law and order at the cost of civil liberties. They were, therefore, instinctively drawn to Cabet's Icaria with its benign "community of goods," its reasonable democracy, healthy environment, and glorification of marriage and family. At an alarming time of backlash against communism, then, Cabet rescued its essential message—a propertyless, classless society—and separated it from conflict and upheaval. He made it respectable.

As early as September 1841 Cabet hit the mark. In a pamphlet, *Ma ligne droite ou le vrai chemin du salut pour le peuple,* he again denounced violence in any form. Such action was "useless" for the popular cause because it gave the enemies of the people an excuse "to rant about uprisings, pillages, murders, to make searches, arrests, and seizures, to frighten the bourgeoisie, strangle the press, etc., etc." He told his readers to disarm, to disband all secret societies, and to condemn all violent protests. Instead, he said, workers must practice "civil courage," become fully aware of their legal rights and use these rights if arrested and interrogated. Only by knowing and insisting upon the fullest protection of the law, he argued, could the workers combat police harassment and governmental suppression. In the meantime, he concluded, the workers should be forbearing and try to persuade, not frighten, the public, because a revolution must take place in the minds of the people before a political revolution could begin.[6]

Earlier that year, according to plan, he resurrected *Le Populaire,* and its first issue of March 14 printed the endorsement of seven hundred signatures and boasted two thousand subscribers. Unlike the earlier run, the new journal was now "the newspaper of social and political reorganization."[7] "A government that wanted to use bastilles in 1833," he wrote, "can it have any other choice than bastilles in 1840?" The crises in foreign affairs (such as the troubles in Syria or the threat of war in Europe) were only subterfuges, excuses for repression of civil liberty. As a result France had degenerated into "egotism and political indifference . . . hostility . . . rivalry of others against the popular party." What to do? He called for a "devotion to the cause of the people" that would "brave all obstacles." "The mission of the people is excellent," he asserted, and "we count on their good sense, on their justice, on their proper devotion to the interests of humanity." "We have said and we repeat with the greatest conviction," he wrote, "that the community must and can establish itself only by the power of public opinion, by the will of the nation, and by the rule of law." "Communists and Reformists," he wrote, "unite for our common defense, let us be brothers in order to save ourselves; let us shun everyone who could alter our unity; let us discuss our doctrines and our principles, for . . . tolerance and moderation."[8]

Over the next five years *Le Populaire* became one of the largest-selling newspapers in France. The paper was always four pages long and printed in large type; its articles were short, the language simple, rousing, and peppered with hyperbole and exclamation points. Each issue contained two parts. In the first half Cabet focused upon domestic concerns and how problems could be solved with the ideas of "Communism" or "Socialism of the Community." By these terms he meant "unity," "fraternity," "democracy," "education," and "Christian morality." He cited anyone who in the remotest way endorsed a community without property and money: Plato, Plutarch, More, Mably, Locke, Montesquieu, Lamartine, Napoleon. All embraced the "community of goods" with its justice, liberty, equality, order, and happiness. Cabet devoted the second half of the paper to letters-to-the-editor, reports of Icarian activities throughout France, biographical sketches of heroes of the cause of humanity, and exposés on workers' miseries. Topics included police raids, mock trials, strikes, factory accidents, crimes caused by greed, suicides, sexual assaults, floods, and earthquakes. His message was always the same: all such evils could be avoided by the creation of the community. "None of this in Icaria!"[9]

In a series of essays, Cabet developed four repetitive themes that soon became an integral part of the Icarian canon. The motifs were nationalism, feminism, the "new feudalism," and communism-equals-Christianity. So effective were these essays that by the summer of 1844 the police called him "the head of the Communists."[10] His nationalism was pugnacious. He said that France should be fighting to preserve the democratic heritage of the Revolution against the combined assaults of the reactionary governments of Europe, just as the nation had done in 1793–94. He chastised the government for regressing economically. The core of the French nation, he said, was the common soldier, brave in battle but ignored by the corrupt monarchy.

Cabet claimed that French women were oppressed. Working women were degraded and brutalized and their innate beauty, kindness, patience, and sensitivity were all destroyed. Even middle class wives were not much better off, more often than not a species of male property. How to change all this? He reiterated the points of the *Voyage en Icarie*. Economic equality and the abolition of private property were the essential first steps. Next, there must be equal education for both sexes. Lastly, marriage had to be based on mutual love and respect, not on convenience or economic necessity. Such a union, and the family built upon it, he wrote, "conform more to the dignity, to the peace, to the happiness of the woman, than her isolation . . . in France."[11]

Cabet contended that a "new feudalism" controlled the country. Borrowing in part from Fourier's writings, he said that France was dominated by a league of wealthy "noble aristocrats" and "*grande bourgeoisie*." These "lords of wealth" had appeared under Louis Philippe and now controlled the Chamber of Deputies. Like the ancien régime, they passed laws to benefit only themselves, regardless of the impact on the nation. And, since everyone had to obey these laws, most citizens were little more than slaves. The results were everywhere apparent: monopolies, speculation in the stock exchange, outlawing of workers' associations, suppression of the free press. Consequently, the rich were getting richer at the expense of the people.

In *Le Populaire* more than in the *Voyage en Icarie* Cabet linked Icarianism with Christian morality. The community of goods and early Christianity were the same thing. Christ had been the "Great Communist" who condemned wealth as the paramount obstacle to salvation and encouraged his followers to surrender all their possessions and follow him. In article after article Cabet and his new friend, the Polish mystic Louis Krolikowski, explained how Christ had seen the Kingdom of God on earth as meaning the creation of the community without property or money. Jesus's messages, unfortunately, had been misunderstood over the centuries because Christ had spoken in parables and "enigmatic verse to avoid arrest by the Romans and wealthy Jews," both of whom rightly feared the Nazarene as a dangerous subversive. In a September 1842 essay Cabet focused on Jesus's revolutionary program. Christ, he claimed, wanted "the abolition of slavery, the equality and brotherhood of men, the freeing of women, the abolition of opulence and misery, the destruction of ecclesiastical power, and, finally, the creation of the community of goods"[12]

The strengths of Icarianism in the early 1840s also rested on Cabet's ability to articulate in emotional language the outrage many workers felt against the industrial revolution. They were being "squeezed like grapes," he said. The workplace was a "battlefield." The aristocracy of wealth "trampled upon honest workers and devoured them." All the while "the stock jobbers, dealers, the fat capitalists alone build colossal and scandalous fortunes." The worker was "swept away" by this "dissolution" and the "torrent" of "free competition." It was, simply put, a war of "the strong against the weak."[13] Again and again he reminded his readers of intolerable abuses: unemployment, low wages, long hours, and the condescension, indifference, and disdain of the wealthy and the government.

Cabet conjured up a nation disintegrating, moving rapidly toward economic chaos and political anarchy. The only force holding it together, in futile resistance to the impending disaster, was the power of an entrenched elite. Only by fundamental reforms could the calamity be averted and the honor and glory of France preserved. French men and women had to be awakened and public opinion organized into a political majority at the polls.

But his efforts to create a national political party were doomed by a fatal weakness in his thinking that was at first obscured by the wave of enthusiasm for the Icarian message. His message was both too simple and too complicated. From the beginning he reduced Icarianism to two grand doctrines: abolition of property, and fraternity. Then he tried to squeeze into these ideas almost every floating popular issue. Icarianism eventually became a facile creed and a political potpourri of issues. And after a while many of his followers became confused about what it was they were following or trying to do.

Cabet only added to the growing confusion. He began to equivocate and backtrack. For example, he initially crusaded for equality of the sexes. Yet in 1843 he said that women were morally suspect and their proper place was as obedient partners with their husbands.[14] Religion was another area of inconsistency. He preached Icarianism as a restatement of the Christian golden rule and "almost smacked his lips at the thought of the mass converts to be gained." Yet he was viciously anticlerical and saw the Catholic Church as the ally of Louis Philippe in the suppression of popular reform.[15] Nevertheless, despite conceptual weaknesses and logical contradictions, Cabet's message spread throughout urban France. By 1845, through the exhaustive work of loyal "correspondents," he had organized Icarian chapters in almost every major provincial city. He himself stayed anchored in Paris at the newspaper office at 18 rue de Jean-Jacques Rousseau.[16]

Lyons became the first citadel of Icarianism outside of the capital. There Cabet's correspondent, a factory foreman named Chapius, hawked *Le Populaire* and led discussions of Icarian doctrine. He reported regularly to Cabet, who visited Lyons in September 1842, and identified new lieutenants who could be counted on to build up a large network.[17] In the other cities Cabet relied heavily on the tireless evangelism of a Lyons salesman named Charles Chameroy. First converted to Icarianism in late 1841, he became a latter-day St. Paul of the Icarian gospel. Indeed, his motives were so evangelical that he referred to himself as the "advanced sentinel of the sacred battalion of Humanity." He preached that France had to replace a sagging Catholic faith with a belief in the "terrestial paradise" of Icarianism.[18] At Reims Chameroy converted a clerk, Louis Mauvais, who had contacts among skilled artisans. At Nantes he named a cobbler, Paul Guay, as correspondent. Another cobbler, Vincent Cöeffé, was appointed at Vienne, and Eugène Butot, a weaver, at Reims. At Toulouse the shoemaker Perpignan led the cause. The silkworker Rémond was the man in Grenoble. By late 1844, with an organization that reached out from Paris to the provinces like so many spokes on a wheel, Cabet felt confident enough to give his movement an official designation, "Icarian Communism," and to attach the label "Icarian" to all his writings.[19]

In all of this activity Cabet saw himself more and more as the personification of the "immortal Icar" and tolerated no challenges to his commands. He would not permit even his loyal lieutenants—let alone the average Icarian—to have a say in ideological or organizational matters. Anyone who questioned his ideas or plans was either ignored or expelled.[20]

Because of this rigid intolerance, he started to lose a number of key supporters. For example, Richard Lahautière, editor of the newspaper *La Fraternité,* became so fed up with the man's egotism that he started a campaign to discredit Cabet. When Théodore Dézamy, editor of *L'Humanitaire* and an early adherent to the ideas of the *Voyage en Icarie,* advocated the abolition of marriage, Cabet turned on him.[21] Dézamy, flabbergasted, in turn called Cabet a charlatan and a liar. The loyal Icarians from Lyons rushed to their leader's defense. They sent Dézamy vicious letters castigating him for having the audacity to attack a man whose "morality was irreproachable." They commanded him to apologize for "these deplorable errors." Dézamy refused.[22]

In spite of Cabet's dictatorial rule and fuzzy thinking, Icarianism showed some coherence during its first five years. The appearance of unity was due in large part to *Le Populaire.* A committee of about ten Parisians directed sales, kept Cabet informed on daily business matters, and managed the records. A second, smaller group composed of Krolikowski, the tailor Firman Favard, and cabintemaker Jean Pierre Beluze maintained contact with the provincial correspondents, the third part of the Icarian organization. The correspondents, on their part, received and distributed *Le Populaire,* collected funds from members and supporters, circulated petitions, and held public meetings.

By these means, as Christopher Johnson has amply documented, Cabet established the basis of a national organization of *communistes-Icariens.* He regularly received "addresses of adherence expressing the same Icarian convictions" from twelve major cities. And the editor of *Le Nouveau-Monde* commented that "the number of its partisans enlarges and the book of M. Cabet, *Voyage en Icarie,* circulates in the workshops." "During the middle forties," Johnson rightly concluded, "Icarian communism had come to France."[23] Indeed it had. By 1846 an estimated 100,000 men and women in 79 of the nation's 100 departments had become Icarians, and *Le Populaire* reached an all-time press run of 3,500 copies.[24]

✳

Who were these Icarians? What did they expect to accomplish as "Soldiers of Humanity?" The typical Icarian was a literate, married man between the ages of thirty and fifty with a predisposition for romantic altruism, reflective thinking, and Christian ethics. He abhorred violence, yet was convinced that the established political process would never overcome the myriad problems that pressed in upon France in the last years of the July Monarchy. As table 1 shows, the Icarians were mostly skilled, piece-work craftsmen who made their living without mechanization or standardization.[25]

The unskilled laborer, however, had little time for Cabet's utopia. For example, in the northern industrialized cities of Lille and Roubaix, almost no Icarians were found. In only three of the cities where Icarianism took root had industrialization advanced to the extent of mass production. In Rouen and Mulhouse, where cotton spinning predominated, and in Rive-de-Gier, where most workers were coal miners, there were few Icarians. Apparently Cabet's high-minded altruism and moral rectitude had little appeal to a proletariat who were "normally passive and without political consciousness during the initial phase of industrialization."[26]

Other sections of French society likewise saw nothing satisfying in the pages of the *Voyage en Icarie* or in *Le Populaire.* Almost no farmers were interested in Cabet's ideas, and he himself was never concerned about them until he realized that their skills were essential to his American colonization project. Icarianism never caught on with the followers of Fourier and Saint-Simon. Their main vehicle of propaganda, the public

Table 1. Icarian Occupations

Occupation	Percentage
Tailors	18
Shoemakers	17
Building Trades	8
Weavers	7
Cabinetmakers	5.5
Hatters	3
Mechanics	2.5
Locksmiths	2
Jewelers	2
Printers	1.5
Spinners	0.5
Miscellaneous Craftsmen	18
Professionals	4.5
Merchants and Bankers	4
Clerks and Shopkeepers	3.5
Foremen	2
Farmers	0.5

lecture, was attended primarily by the "respectable classes," and the police seldom disrupted or harassed these gatherings. Small property holders always shunned Icarianism (because they would have no status in such a utopia) even though Cabet had hoped that "they could be rationally convinced of the happiness for all to be found under communism."[27]

The skilled urban workers who embraced the Icarian dream lived in cities where commercialization had developed to the point that ready-made production threatened the craft industries. By the 1840s the earlier small workshops with a master and a couple of apprentices were being replaced rapidly by larger shops with up to twenty or more employees. Especially in the textile trades the older, specific-order production gave way to large operations called "confections" where employers reduced the variety of skills they needed and more strictly supervised daily routine. Tailors saw themselves becoming hired pieceworkers at the mercy of commissioned purchasing agents and contractors. One of them wrote in 1841 that "the shops selling ready-made clothing are destroying the existence of the signatories." The craftsmen found their social and economic status changed to the point where "the bourgeoisie merchant capitalist was emerging as the real employer."[28] The French artisans also faced grim economic circumstances. At best they were barely able to sustain wages of six francs a day. Others were not so lucky.

Shoemakers, for instance, in some towns found their daily wages reduced by half.[29]

In letters to *Le Populaire* these skilled workers complained about exploitation by "mercantile selfishness" and "violations of our rights" by the "egotistical bourgeoisie." To them, Cabet's utopia offered salvation. Jacques Rancière, in his imaginative analysis of the mind of the French worker, detected among the Icarians a poignant feeling of deliverance. Turgard, a maker of artificial flowers, said that in Cabet's writings he saw "paradise on earth, men living as brothers, each sharing with the other according to need and capability, equality, unity, community—in short, one for all and all for one." A Le Mans shoemaker, Emile Vallet, after reading the *Voyage en Icarie*, told Cabet that "the theory was beautiful." His entire family was "enthusiastic" about the idea of "establishing a society where reason and conscience would rule. . . . Without king or priest. No nobility but that of the heart. No poor, no rich. No tyranny, no oppression. A paradise on earth." Vallet was, like so many other Icarians, a man with a "sensitive heart," a "freethinker," and above all a "moral reformer."[30]

The Icarian temperament betrayed a persistent melancholy about what they saw to be, in Rancière's words, "the haunting reality of an intolerable world." To them France was a nation characterized by misery, prejudice, and irrationality, and their consciences could not accept such a country. An Icarian from Nantes, obsessed with such thoughts, wrote to Cabet that "death is preferable to life in the wretched society of today." A mirror salesman from Perigeux named Pepin told him that material success, if it ever came, held little satisfaction because material things were only "ornaments" and "illusory." Life, he said, was not worth living, but upon his discovery of Icaria, "our courage revives us and gives us certainty of a better future."[31]

The *Voyage en Icarie*, with its peaceful path to utopia, was particularly attractive to the wives of these skilled workers. One such woman confided to Cabet that Icarianism took her husband out of dangerous "secret societies" that siphoned all of their money and exposed him to the danger of arrest. Now that she and her spouse were out in the open as Icarians, everything had changed. "We no longer fear those dreadful searches, those terrible arrests, that ruined us in the past." And now, unlike before, the women could accompany the men to meetings where they "discuss things together." Women were also strongly attracted to Cabet's ideas about sexual equality, despite his emerging statements to the contrary. Many of his female correspondents saw this concept as the heart of Icaria and its key to the salvation of the world. One woman from Angoulême exclaimed, "What happy women are the women of Icaria."[32] Finally, a number of women—and men, too—were captivated by Cabet's moral message. They called him the "apostle of communism" and his ideas about Christianity "holy doctrine."

When Cabet changed from propagandist to messiah is difficult to determine. Certainly, up to 1843 he displayed no messianic tones in his writings. Quite the contrary, as late as August of that year he disclaimed any such role. Nevertheless, by that time he had become close friends with Krolikowski and was deeply affected by the man's religious mysticism. And by the spring of 1846 Cabet informed the readers of *Le Populaire* about his plan to write a book to prove beyond doubt that Christ's gospel was the essence of his community. Dézamy, already furious with Cabet, picked up on this evangelism and, in the January 1846 issue of *La Fraternité,* had derided him for trying to create a theocracy.[33]

In the summer of that year Cabet published his *Le vrai Christianisme* and dedicated it to Krolikowski, whose "numerous conferences" inspired the work. In this unimaginative, often dull combination of biblical history up to John the Baptist, a sketch of the life of Jesus and the Apostles, and a superficial account of the early Church fathers and famous popes up to Gregory the Great, Cabet as always was simple. "Communism is Christianity," he stated. Both were built upon brotherly love and pacifism. Christ's Kingdom of God on Earth was nothing other than an early version of Icaria. In both, "all men are brothers. . . . and only form one family." Both emphasize "liberty," "unity," and "the community" and substitute the "general, social, and common interest" for "individualism." "Yes," Cabet wrote, "it is an evident and manifest fact that *Christianity* for the Apostles, for the first Christians, for the Fathers of the Church, was *Communism*. . . . Yes, Jesus Christ was a Communist!"[34]

He spelled out five tenets of Icarian Christianity: equality, democracy, personal morality, absence of formal worship, and an earthly millennium. Equality meant Christian brotherhood. Christ had insisted that since all men were the same, they were equal "as a necessary consequence of brotherhood," whatever that meant. He cited the New Testament to show how Christ chastised and condemned the rich. He emphasized the parable of the workers in the vineyard to demonstrate Jesus's embracing of communism. In the early Christian enclaves Cabet found equality the practicing rule of conduct. Not only Jesus but also "the Apostles . . . were . . . Communists."[35] Equality led, without question, to Christian democracy. In God's Kingdom, Cabet quoted Jesus as saying, there were no princes or aristocrats. Citing Luke, he tried to prove that "he who governs is only the servant of his brothers"; consequently, "is this not radical and pure democracy?" In Christ's politics the highest standards of personal morality were just assumed. The Gospels, Cabet claimed, gave a code of conduct that demanded purity, modesty, moderation, and love of others.

Under such circumstances, he wrote, both in God's paradise and in Icaria there could be "no more sin, crimes, vices, or imperfections."

In Icaria Cabet saw a "new worship of Jesus" taking shape. In place of hollow liturgy he described a daily practice of the principles of brotherly love and the elimination "of sacrifices, temples, images, priests, ceremonies, and superstitious practices." He threw out the traditional Christian theology that saw the end of the world and a final judgment. Christ, he believed, did not refer in the statement "my Kingdom is not of this world" to a paradise in outer space. He meant "an earthly Kingdom of God." Cabet connected this Kingdom and his Icaria and fused *Le vrai Christianisme* with the *Voyage en Icarie.* "The Community," he concluded, "realizes this terrestrial paradise and [its] possible perfections, it is above all the Communist who ought to admire, love and invoke Jesus Christ and His Doctrine!"

Cabet's thinking had undergone a profound inversion. Earlier, in the *Voyage,* he had adopted Christian morality as a part of his secular utopia. Now he took the political and economic tenets of Icaria and meshed them into the framework of Christian eschatology. He was now more confident than ever that he could create the perfect society. In less than a year after the appearance of *Le vrai Christianisme* he called the Icarians to follow him in a quest for the earthly paradise, not in France but three thousand miles from Paris, at the edge of civilization, in the Trinity River Valley of Texas.[36]

FOUR

The Exodus

Cabet's decision to build his utopia in America had been germinating for some time. In a letter to the Democratic Society of London penned about March 1843 he mentioned a plan to create a "small community" on the "edge of a lake in America." He stipulated three requirements for success. First, it had to be a "small community" able to exist by itself, "a place where everyone could join hands." Next, it had to be composed of "elite men, of men superior by their *ability,* by their *character,* by their *devotion,*" who alone "have the chance to preserve harmony, concord, unity." He was quite specific as to the numbers involved: his community would contain "200–300 chosen persons, workers and others." The third ingredient was strong financial backing. He would need "all the *money necessary,*" he stated; "without that, nothing." A year later he wrote to Berrier-Fontaine, his London landlord, about this "great project" and promised to fill him in on details later.[1]

There the idea rested until the enthusiastic reaction in some Icarian chapters to *Le vrai Christianisme* convinced Cabet that he was a latter-day messiah who had to lead his flock to a New World paradise. Letters to *Le Populaire* pronounced him the "living martyr to the cause of human brotherhood," the "savior" of France. They praised him for his Christ-like qualities of dedication to equality, compassion for the oppressed, and exposure of hypocrisy. In August 1846 he responded by stating that "Communism can only say: I am the resurrection and the life." He would build a terrestrial utopia even if, like Christ, he came to disappointment and death. His writing lapsed into lofty metaphors like "appeasing the tempest" and "passing from the shadow to light, from the reign of Satan to the reign of God." Icarianism, to this man, no longer was a political theory or a social plan; it was a crusade.[2]

Perhaps Cabet's vision of paradise on earth and himself the savior of persecuted workers was in part a chimera of his evangelical imagination, but the problems the Icarians faced by 1846 were real enough for him to want to leave France. The nation was in the grip of a severe economic depression, caused by the failure of the 1846 wheat harvest, which pushed the retail price of bread to an unheard-of high. Unemployment increased as inflation severely reduced the buying capacity of French workers. Bread riots multiplied, and in some of these uprisings, such as the one at Tours in March 1847, Icarians were conspicuous participants.[3]

These hard times produced a serious fissure in Cabet's following. Men like Krolikowski and Favard, for example, complained that the riots threatened their emphasis on Christian brotherhood. And Icarians from the provinces sent letters that praised Cabet's commitment to moderation and told him to resist pressures that could lead to violence. Yet others, like Louis Desmoulins, a Tours physician, wanted action, now, to realize Icaria. These men feared that Cabet, with his growing mysticism, might prevent Icarians from becoming a force in French politics. Desmoulins, echoing this frustration, charged that Cabet was making a revolution only in his dreams and warned him of a growing dissatisfaction with his timidity and a plot to reduce, perhaps to eliminate, his influence. The cause of the insurrection, Desmoulins said, was simple: "You are the sole obstacle that prevents the Communist party" from becoming revolutionary.[4]

Then in February 1847 Cabet learned of the so-called Madeline Affair. At Luçon an Icarian weaver named Madeline had led a group of about twenty-five Icarians to nail up a communist poster in a public spot next to the town's cathedral. Madeline and his cohorts were arrested and brought to trial for sedition, but since the prosecution lacked sufficient evidence that Madeline had actually written the poster, he and the others were acquitted.[5] Cabet now felt he had to decide between the pacifists or militants, and if he chose one he was likely to lose the other.

By the spring of 1847, at the age of fifty-nine, Cabet once again feared arrest and exile or imprisonment. He learned that the prefect of the Paris police wanted increased surveillance of all editors who exaggerated the workers' miseries, and had ordered "the most active repression by the judicial authorities." And in March he found out that he had been targeted. Comte Tanneguy Duchâtel, the minister of the interior, had told the minister of justice that the next issue of *Le Populaire* was exceedingly dangerous. More than all the other radical newspapers, he said, it would arouse the "popular passions."[6]

In the meantime, more accounts of Icarian troubles reached Cabet. A priest in Champagne, he reported in *Le Populaire,* had instructed his parishioners to stop reading the paper. Another cleric had burned a copy of the *Voyage en Icarie.* An Icarian at Mirecourt had been fired from his job because of his devotion to Cabet. One of the leaders at Luçon had been arrested. A loyal disciple at Toulon had been dismissed from his position but then had used the free time to gain more converts to

Icarianism. An employer at Louviers had forbidden the circulation of Icarian literature, but this action, Cabet claimed, had only attracted more workers to the cause. At Nantes, Cabet said, even though the government tried to arrest Icarians for putting up posters, he was sure that such harassment "will only strengthen communism."[7]

On March 19 Cabet bragged to Berrier-Fontaine, "in confidence, if I want to go to found an Icarian colony in America more than a thousand workers of all sorts of professions, the elite of the people, would follow me there. . . . What do you think of the idea?" The doctor responded immediately. "Don't say anything more about colonies," he scolded. Cabet ignored the advice. On April 20 he told Berrier-Fontaine that his mind was made up and that he was going to publish the decision in *Le Populaire*. Cabet wrote that emigration was "the only means to avoid the persecution that is being prepared."

Berrier-Fontaine's last word on the subject was deeply pessimistic. It would not succeed, he predicted. And even if colonization worked for a while, being on such a small scale it would have no impact "on the vices of the current social order and on the preconceived notions of the larger society." It would be a waste of time. But Cabet, by then, was beyond reason. He believed in his own mission, the stories of oppression, and, more significantly, the threat of being arrested. On May 9 he announced his decision in *Le Populaire*: "Let's go to Icaria!"[8]

Cabet then had to determine where to go and how to get there. For help he turned to Robert Owen, whom he had met briefly while in exile and who, he hoped, might have information about a possible location in America. In July he met with T. W. Thornton, an English Owenite then living in Paris who had just published a French edition of Owen's *Book of the New World*. He told Cabet that he had already written to Owen about the emigration project and of the "zealous . . . head of the French Communists." Cabet asked Thornton to write Owen again about a location for Icaria. Cabet then contacted a young French Icarian residing in London named Charles Sully. This eager bookbinder was only too happy to mail Owen a package of Cabet's latest pamphlets and to convey Cabet's wish to meet as soon as possible. In late July, Thornton, then back in London, arranged for a conference between Sully and Owen.[9]

Sully was pleased at Owen's news. Owen told him that five months earlier a William Smalling Peters, agent for a Texas land company, had contacted him at Manchester with a proposition. Peters had described a golden opportunity, as he called it, for Owen to start another utopian community, this time in Texas along the Trinity River. There was, Peters had said, "no shadow of doubt" about the success of such an enterprise because of the "astonishing productivity . . . temperate, bountiful healthy climate . . . and grandiose magnificence of the place." But, Owen told Sully, since he personally was no longer interested in American colonization, he had been unresponsive. Sully conveyed the information to Cabet.

What Owen did not tell Sully was that in June Peters had written to his son, Robert Dale Owen. Peters detailed a plan in which 320 acres would be given to each married colonist and 160 acres to each single man. The settlement, Peters glowed, would blossom. "Nature here in the highest degree," he wrote, "had been elaborate in bestowing her best and richest gifts" in sugar cane and wheat crops. He ended the letter with an offer. He told Robert Dale that if he and his father would "partake" in this "great work" they would each "receive an equal share with me [of what Peters had already invested] or any portion you may see fit to engage in, which shall be made over by a legal transfer, with any additional conditions you may think necessary."[10] On July 9 he wrote directly to Robert to "still further interest you" in the scheme. Peters offered shares of stock "which is nearly the value of 10,000 [pounds]" to the senior philanthropist. He enclosed a *Prospectus* that gave all the details of the settlement as drawn up by the original trustees of the company.[11]

Cabet, totally unaware of any deals pending between Peters and Owen, arrived in London on September 9. The next morning he met with Owen and Peters, and during the following week they agreed upon a settlement plan. The Icarians would get three thousand acres of free land along the Trinity River. All they had to do was establish homesteads on the site by July 1, 1848. That being done, each family would get a warranty deed to 320 acres; a single male over seventeen would receive half that amount. Yet it was clear from the *Prospectus,* which Cabet saw at these meetings, and from the formal contract or "Concession" he signed in January 1848, that he could never build an Icaria in Texas. The land was surveyed so that the state of Texas retained possession of one-half of the tracts and the Peters Company reserved alternate half-sections of 320 acres to sell later on. The Icarians were getting a disjointed, checkerboard parcel of land where the self-sufficient community Cabet had in mind would be impossible to build.[12]

Nevertheless, he accepted the offer and returned to Paris. On November 14 he printed the news on page one of *Le Populaire:* "On to Texas!" He did not mention the noncontiguous survey. He only said that he was sending Sully to Texas to supervise the preparations while he remained in France to take care of all departures. He would appoint committees of admission in twelve cities to register and evaluate prospective emigrants. If they were found acceptable they would be registered for his final approval. He next announced contests for ideas on a uniform and anthem.

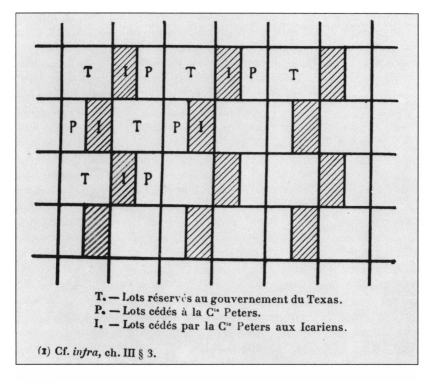

T. — Lots réservés au gouvernement du Texas.
P. — Lots cédés à la Cⁱᵉ Peters.
I. — Lots cédés par la Cⁱᵉ Peters aux Icariens.

(1) Cf. *infra*, ch. III § 3.

Diagram of the Icarian parcels acquired in the Peters Concession, showing the sections sold to Cabet (I), the sections reserved to the state of Texas (T), and the sections retained for later sale by the Peters Company (P). Prudhommeaux, *Icarie et son Fondateur*, 226.

He would immediately select the first Advance Guard to leave for Texas after the new year.[13]

Meanwhile in England, Berrier-Fontaine, who by now had resigned himself to colonization, helped Sully circulate a brochure that would "attract the attention of wealthy English philanthropists to your emigration project."[14] He published Cabet's *Prospectus. Grande émigration au Texas en Amérique pour réaliser la commanuaté d'Icarie*, a tract that misled everyone. The *Prospectus* stated that Cabet had contracted for a million acres and had already acquired three thousand of them in a "vast territory" along the Trinity River. The place was "salubrious, fertile, composed of woods and prairies, well-watered, whose climate resembles that of Italy." Icarians could easily get there by steamboat from New Orleans to Shreveport and then by "foot or in carts" over a "fifty league," ten-day trip on "the national road of Bonham."[15]

These fast-moving events fractured the Icarian chapters. For many loyal disciples who had stayed with Cabet while he changed Icarianism from a political movement into a religious crusade, the Texas scheme was too much. They agreed, at best, with Berrier-Fontaine's observation that to take Icarianism out of France would destroy it. Others were more caustic. They were convinced that Cabet had lost his mind. It was one thing to hold on to a lofty and uplifting, although perhaps unworkable, vision of Icarian brotherhood. But they were not willing to give up all they owned at the snap of Cabet's finger, leave their homes, culture, and *patrimony* to follow another Peter the Hermit into the wilderness.

Data on subscriptions to *Le Populaire* tell the story. By November 1847 they were 30 percent below those of the year before. Other evidence indicated widespread rejection of Cabet's call. Icarians at Tours protested the idea, and twenty-eight men from Nantes wrote that the cause of humanity had to be fought out in France. At Lyons a fight broke out between the *Cabetist* Icarians and the "ultras" or "revolutionary Communists." The latter group, apparently the majority of that chapter, felt that its doctrines were ready for application *in France.* They wanted no part of emigration. Cabet was called a coward, fleeing the "field of battle" before the fight even began. They did not want to leave France, like Cabet, as "fugitives." In Paris, poorer Icarians who might have shipped out to America complained that they had been excluded by the emigration fee of six hundred francs that Cabet required. He had flagrantly contradicted the Christian principle of brotherly love that he had formerly preached. The "doors of Icaria," one Parisian worker wrote, "were forever closed to them."[16]

Cabet tried to camouflage the upheaval and make readers of *Le Populaire* think there was universal excitement about going to Texas. He published whatever letters of support he got, always prefacing them as voices of the "majority" of his followers. He exaggerated claims of new endorsements at places like Toulon, Nancy, and Perigeux, where he falsely reported a six-fold increase in new members. He printed statements of approval from Reims but failed to disclose that only 99 of 443 Icarians signed the document. He exhorted his followers to be as "soldiers devoted to their posts, as soldiers of French democracy" for the "sacred cause of the People [and be] prepared to sweep away the despots." Cabet had a reason other than vanity to draw a distorted picture of enthusiasm for his decision to go to America. He needed money and, since he had agreed to have 3,125 Icarian homesteads along the Trinity River within eight months, he needed bodies.[17]

But Cabet only alienated potential supporters when on September 19, right after his return from the meetings with Peters and Owen, he published in *Le Populaire* his own rendition of what life in the American Icaria would be like. This statement, the *Contrat social,* described a dictatorship. He would be the *"Directeur-Gérant"* or managing director during the creation of the community. As *Directeur-Gérant* he would claim all power "that was indicated in the *Voyage en Icarie* and all that would be continually outlined in an Icarian program." He wanted full authority to supervise and regulate "all moral responsibility." He alone screened and approved new members. He was responsible for finances and received each member's "contribution" of six hundred francs as an unredeemable deposit. He made all purchases for the society and would direct its economic life. The only possible qualification of his absolutism was the promise of a vague sort of future democracy and elections.[18]

Icarians who were still with Cabet by September reacted to the *Contrat* with a curious silence; only a couple of letters in favor of it came to *Le Populaire.* Most Icarians agreed with Jean Baptiste Millère, "an Icarian sympathizer" as he called himself, who labeled this kind of Icaria "degenerate." Cabet, he said, had just put out a blueprint of a monarchy as absolute as that of Louis XIV. From Toulouse an "old patriot" named Chaudurie said he was dropping out of the emigration because of the *Contrat:* he wanted no part of despotism. Cabet responded to such rejections with a quick dismissal. He told Chaudurie, "We shall miss you."[19]

By December 1847 Cabet had most of the plans for the American departure in place. He had published the *Contrat social,* organized the departures at Le Havre through the committees of admission, and identified members of the First Advance Guard. Little was left to be done, Cabet thought, other than to close the deal he had arranged with Peters in September. So, on January 3, 1848, he went to London and picked up the concession document. That same day he returned to Paris.

The next morning at five o'clock he went to the office of *Le Populaire.* Two hours later the police arrived, took him into custody, and charged him with heading a secret society. They alleged that the emigration was a camouflage and that the Icarians really planned only to appear to leave Le Havre and land somewhere on the west coast of France to execute their "sinister designs." They released him on bail pending formal arraignment and trial. News of Cabet's arrest was reported in all anti-government Parisian newspapers. Letters of support poured into the *Le Populaire* and were promptly reprinted without editorial comment. Three weeks later he reported that the original charges had been dropped for lack of evidence. The government instead charged him with taking money for personal use from the funds he collected from prospective emigrants.[20]

By the end of January the First Advance Guard was ready to leave.

The sixty-nine men Cabet selected for this honor were those Icarians most eager to come up with the six hundred francs and to accept the *Contrat Social*. He named Adolphe Gouhenant, a forty-three-year-old Toulouse sign painter, as head of the expedition. On Saturday, January 29, just before midnight, Cabet led them to the *Gare du nord* and put them on the train for Le Havre. The following Monday he joined them.

On Wednesday evening, February 2 at the Château-Vert about a half-mile from the city, the entourage, with Cabet presiding, held a farewell banquet. At dessert one of the Guard, a physician named Leclerc, toasted their dedication to the happiness of humanity and pledged their devotion to Cabet's dream of Icaria. The next morning at the wharf the hand-picked troops, bedecked in uniforms of black velvet tunics and gray felt caps, huddled in the gray winter's cold. Relatives came to bid them goodbye. Hundreds of bystanders crowded together to observe the curious spectacle.

Cabet stepped before the Guard and, Napoleon-like, bellowed, "Are you loyal adherents without reservation to the *Social Contract?*" "Yes!" they yelled. "Are you sincerely devoted to the cause of Communism?" "Yes!" they hollered. "Are you willing to endure hardship for the benefit of humanity?" "Of course!" they screamed. Then, in silent procession, they boarded the ship *Rome*. Assembled on the stern deck they chanted the first couplet of their new Icarian anthem. As Cabet and their families gazed at the ship receding slowly from the dock they heard the steady but ever diminishing strains of the *Chant du Départ* sung to the tune of the *La Marseillaise*.

> Arise, workers stooped in the dust,
> The hour of awakening has sounded.
> To American shores the banner is going to wave,
> The banner of the holy community.
> No more vices, no more suffering,
> No more crimes, no more pain,
> The august Equality advances itself:
> Proletariat, dry your tears.
> Let us found our Icaria,
> Soldiers of Fraternity,
> Let us go to found in Icaria,
> The happiness of Humanity![21]

Back in Paris, Cabet made an about-face. Instead of focusing on the Texas utopia he turned instead to the political turmoil in France. On February 24 Louis Philippe was deposed and the Second Republic proclaimed. The next day Cabet printed the *Manifeste aux communistes icariens,* a hastily written tract in which he laid out an agenda for the new regime. Freedom of the press, abolition of taxes on "primary goods," and free education for all citizens were among the most important requirements. There must be no violence and no retribution, he urged, since "all Frenchmen are brothers." Astonishingly, he wrote that there must be no attack on personal property. Chameleon-like he had changed overnight from a mystical utopian communist into a pragmatic socialist. As to the great cause of humanity in America, he casually announced that he had changed his mind. He said that most of those who had intended to go to America had backed away. He would, therefore, dismantle the emigration.

The non-communist press welcomed Cabet back as a "sensible republican," and he reprinted their endorsements in *Le Populaire.* He instructed workers to avoid all demonstrations and, above all, to renounce violence. In mid-March he published *Bien et mal, danger et salut après la révolution de février 1848,* a history of what had happened in 1830 and a reminder not to go down that mistaken path another time. He discussed the need eventually to have freedom of the press, universal suffrage, and a strong foreign policy. Then he described what ought to be done right away. Bourgeois influence over the provisional government should be reduced, and the power of the people, meaning the workers, must be enhanced by enlisting all of them, armed, into the National Guard and electing them to its officer corps.[22]

The Guard issue became Cabet's temporary, yet futile, rallying point. He asked for demonstrations to delay the formation of the new Guard. He wanted a similar delay in the elections to form a permanent government. Both steps, he thought, would give him time to organize his somewhat fractured and, understandably by that time, confused following. On March 17, 1848, thousands of demonstrators gathered at City Hall in Paris to support these and other demands. Cabet was there, at the head of the throng. He presented the timetable: put off the election of the officers of the Guard indefinitely and postpone election of the permanent government until May 31.

The provisional government met this ultimatum halfway. They agreed to delay the Guard elections, but the national elections would have to take place as scheduled on April 23, Easter Sunday. These events made Cabet, at the age of sixty, a national hero for the first time in his life. But it was too late. He and Icarians by 1848 were stamped with the seal of communism and class warfare. Icarians were perceived by most Frenchmen as a subversive, secret society bent upon violent overthrow of the government and the destruction of private property.[23]

Another reaction against communism in April 1848 destroyed whatever chance Cabet had to gain public support. On the tenth of the month posters appeared all over the city addressed "To the People of Paris on their true enemies," the communists, "the most dangerous enemies of the Republic." The conservatives had launched their campaign for the Easter elections with the cry of "Down with the communists! Death to Cabet!" Such tactics were extremely effective and the conservatives, in coalition with some moderate republicans, took control of the National Assembly. No socialists or communists were elected, and the Icarians were crushed, branded as incendiaries and plunderers. Thornton, Cabet's erstwhile English supporter, observed that "though notoriously an advocate of peace and persuasion" the Icarians had been devastated by a backlash of "blind fury" against the communists. The impact, Thornton wrote, was to "drive numbers of them from their country." Escape, Thornton believed, was now the only alternative.[24]

On the evening of April 16 a mob surrounded Cabet's house, screaming for his arrest. Other Icarians, out in the streets of Paris that night, were threatened. For several days, one Icarian remembered, "Paris was prey to a veritable terror." Cabet went to his office at the *Le Populaire* but each night walked home with shouts of abuse ringing in his ears: He plotted to kill the leaders of the new government, to start another reign of terror! He was an enemy of the Republic! He planned, when in power, to hold all property—and all French women—in common![25]

Faced with this growing animosity, Cabet resurrected the emigration scheme. On April 25, at a small gathering of the Central Fraternal Society of Paris, he denounced and denied the outrageous charges that had been hurled at him. He added that under such "deplorable conditions . . . [we] are going . . . to resume the march of our emigration that we have slackened in order best to serve the country. . . . we will emigrate to the United States." "If we fail," he predicted, "it is because we allowed fatigue to conquer, . . . and humanity will benefit from our effort; it will know that our system is wrong." But, he added, "if we succeed, to the contrary, we will have shown the true course." One more time, though, on June 4, he stood for election to the Chamber of Deputies. He lost.[26]

Cabet reissued in *Le Populaire* another cry of "Let's go to Icaria," with little effect. The committees on admission sent him extremely discouraging reports. At Perigueux, where there had been hundreds of potential emigrés a year ago, only sixteen Icarians agreed to leave and only because their movement had been "completely crushed." At Nantes, a city where Icarian pilgrims also had been counted in the hundreds, just ten people were willing to emigrate. Many felt like the Parisian worker named Paquet who told Cabet that the Icarian dream was now out of reach. Some Icarians just wanted to fight for what was left of communism in France, and they joined in the violence of the June Days.[27]

The upheaval of the June Days was brought on by complex circumstances. The bourgeois triumphs in the national election, their continued control of the National Guard, the rhetorical excesses of the anticommunists, the failure of the new provisional government to develop policies that satisfied the workers' expectations—all played a role in the insurrection that broke out on June 23. By then Cabet had already left Paris for Marseilles to recruit new converts for the Texas colony.[28] The police, though, claimed that on June 22 he had returned to the capital and was in the streets the next day when violence erupted. That Cabet was actually involved in the insurrection is doubtful; he claimed he was not. He did, however, publish a pamphlet expressing his views of what had taken place.[29]

In the pamphlet Cabet said that class antagonism, hostility, and recrimination, not brotherly love, ruled in France, and this reality was the cause of the June Days. The epidemic of "hatred" and "vengeance" was, moreover, spreading. Who was responsible? He pointed directly to the bourgeoisie. They had an opportunity in the beginning to take advantage of the workers' pacifism, patience, and generosity to build a true classless democracy. But instead the bourgeoisie and the politicians they elected had ruined everything. The antidote for France was amnesty for the workers, the only alternative to open class war and anarchy. The remedy for himself and the Icarians: go to America.[30]

For the rest of the summer and fall Cabet vainly tried to resuscitate the emigration. But his opportunism had so alienated what was left of his following that its financial base was ruined. Indeed, most prospective emigrants now had to ask Cabet for money. As Beluze later recalled, "it was a horrible situation." Everything went wrong. Cabet was arrested for his alleged participation in the June 23 uprising. Fortunately, he convinced the court that he was still in Marseilles that day and was released.[31]

In *Le Populaire*, he told a fairy tale about what was going on in Texas. He praised the First Advance Guard for their "devotion" and "courage." He casually acknowledged some problems with "a new climate" but predicted that if they worked "more moderately" and took better care of themselves, things would come out all right.[32] He reiterated that the three thousand acres would serve as an ideal community site. Easy access to the Peters Concession was facilitated, he claimed, by a pleasant four-day trip by steamboat from New Orleans up the Mississippi and Red River to Shreveport, followed by a short walk or carriage ride to Icaria. His *Almanach icarien* of 1848 repeated this glowing account of the journey to Icaria and, to further attract interest, contained a map.[33] He reprinted optimistic letters from Gouhenant. He refused, however, to

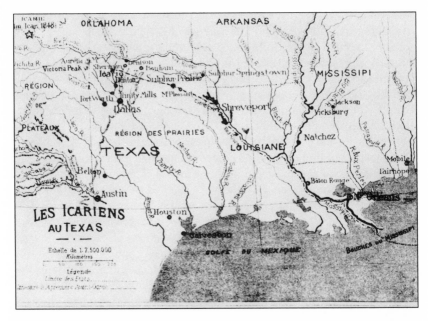

Map showing the route taken by the First Advance Guard from New Orleans
to the Texas Icaria at the Peters Concession, near the present city of Denton.
Prudhommeaux, *Icarie et son Fondateur,* 222.

release a letter he had received from Pierre J. Favard, the leader of the
Second Advance Guard, about a disaster in Texas. Instead he announced
that he himself would now leave France to join the Soldiers of Humanity.
Accordingly, he appointed Krolikowski managing editor of *Le Populaire*
and Beluze the business director of the "Paris Bureau," the central
recruiting office. Then, on December 3, 1848, he left the city, without
his wife and daughter, for Le Havre and, ultimately, for New Orleans and
the Trinity River.

✳

Within two years after Cabet left France, Icarianism in Europe, or what
was left of it, evaporated. It had started as a form of utopian socialism
and ended up as a confused messianic sect. But Icarianism was more
than just another phase of utopian socialism since there were significant
differences, in substance and in goals, between Fourier, Saint-Simon, and
Cabet. The socialists, for example, had always managed to keep a wage
system in their plans, albeit a fair one. Cabet was a communist who
insisted upon the abolition, not just the reordering, of traditional capitalism.

Workers must reject it entirely as the only viable response to the disloca-
tions and frustrations of the Industrial Revolution.[34]

More specifically, Fourier, a man of limited education, was hostile to
learning and mocked the failure of philosophers to understand and solve
the problems of mankind. Cabet was, if anything, an arrogant intellectual who insisted upon rigorous education as a pillar of communal life.
From the start Fourier sought a much different audience than Cabet, a
phalanx of recruits from all classes—engineers, artists, bankers, businessmen, workers—whose passions, properly channeled into "attractive labor,"
would guarantee prosperity. Cabet's pitch was essentially to the artisan.
Fourier dictated that a phalanx must be rural, in an agricultural setting
close to city markets. Cabet's Icaria was an urban utopia where farming
played only a supportive role to sustain city life.

Further contrasts appear when one compares Cabet to Saint-Simon.
Despite a mutual romantic Christianity, Saint-Simon only "uttered vague
but impressive prophecies about the coming new society." Readers of the
Voyage en Icarie saw precise descriptions of how the "community of
goods" functioned. Saint-Simon before his death in 1825 retreated from
utopianism and prodded his followers to try banking reform and transportation projects. Cabet moved, erratically, toward an insistence on a
commitment to create utopia, if not in France then in America.

Lastly, both Fourier and Saint-Simon were much different leaders
than Cabet. Fourier, when his followers started to promote his theories,
abandoned them as "bumbling friends who are assassinating me while
they think they are increasing my reputation" when they edited his
complex formula into a social science. Saint-Simon never really pushed
his ideas much beyond the confines of the *Ecole Polytechnique.* Cabet
led his Icarians in France and, afterwards, in the United States.[35]

In America the disciples of Fourier and Saint-Simon created small,
short-lived phalanxes that selectively applied the ideas of their creators,
while at the same time they made significant innovations to adapt to the
capitalist society of Jacksonian America. Here, the Icarians were led and
tightly organized by Cabet until his death in 1856 and, afterwards, by
the loyal Icarians who tried dogmatically to apply Cabet's utopian plans.
Cabet and his successors insisted all along, as the following chapters will
describe, that true Icarians must uncompromisingly adhere to and apply
the rules of life laid out in the pages of the *Voyage en Icarie.*

FIVE

The First American Icarias

Cabet arrived at New York City on December 31, 1848, in an uplifted mood, and his spirits were further buoyed at a reception given in his honor that evening by French socialists at the Shakespeare Hotel. At the dinner he predicted that America, thanks to the socialists, would assure that regeneration of which Fourier and Horace Greeley had been "the harbingers in the two worlds."[1] But the next morning his euphoria evaporated. He read in a New York newspaper a reprint of a scathing account of the Icarians at New Orleans written by a Bordeaux jeweler named Dubuisson and first published in that city's newspaper *l'Abeille*. The rest of the trip down the coast by boat to New Orleans, he later confessed, was "horrible." Despondent, he sent what he thought might be a "last letter" to Paris in which he placed his wife and daughter, "always sacrificed to [my] devotion to the people," in the care of Beluze.[2]

Cabet docked at New Orleans on January 19, 1849, and went straight to the two rented houses on St. Ferdinand Street where 480 Icarians awaited the appearance of their "Papa," as he now insisted upon being addressed. He found an insurrection on his hands. The dissidents, as he called them, 218 in number, wanted to wring his neck. Led by Dubuisson and a Spanish physician named Roveira, they wanted to liquidate the community fund of an estimated eighty-six thousand francs, have Cabet arrested for stealing, and lock him up in a Baton Rouge prison. Failing that, they told him they were returning to France to sue him for fraud. The others, temporarily organized under the leadership of a thirty-year-old jeweler from Charentonay, Jules Prudent, embraced him, their "venerated Messiah," with tears in their eyes. Cabet announced that he would convene a meeting of the "general assembly" in two days and then, together, they would decide what to do. In the meantime, Prudent told Cabet the details of a fiasco.[3]

Initially, Prudent said, everything had gone well. When the First Advance Guard landed in New Orleans last March 27 they were heartened to hear the dock cannon boom them a welcome. But on shore, to their consternation, they discovered that the celebration was not for them but for the news of the overthrow of Louis Philippe! Four of the Guard, led by the young architect Alfred Piquenard, wanted to turn around and return to assist the revolution. The others, though, had no second thoughts about fulfilling their assignment: to get ready, at the Concession, for the great migration they expected that summer.[4]

Soon after their arrival they heard from Sully, who had arrived the previous December to attend to preliminaries. He reported a grim situation. The trip to Icaria, he said, could not be made as they had thought. They could go by steamboat only as far as Shreveport, or about 350 miles, but then they would have to hike the rest of the way, over 300 miles, across unmapped prairie. Sully had some good news, though. He had been able to obtain four thousand dollars from a Titus County, Texas, businessman John Beckwell on a promissory note at 10 percent interest. With this money he had bought a farm at Sulphur Prairie, an outpost about halfway between Shreveport and the Concession, where the Guard, and later the immigrants themselves, could rest.

Undaunted, according to Prudent, the First Advance Guard had set off, with all their heavy luggage transferred to a steamboat, up the Mississippi River to Icaria. Just as expected they got only as far as Shreveport, where the Red River swung northward, away from their destination. When they arrived there they found out that Sully had already departed to get everything ready for them at the Sulphur Prairie rest stop. They were told by Americans that the only way to get to this outpost was to try to follow Sully over a footpath known as the Bonham trail.

What to do? Gouhenant said they had no choice but to persevere. Despite unpromising circumstances—no command of the English language, confusion over where to go and how they were going to get there—they made the necessary arrangements. They loaded two wagons and ox teams that Sully had purchased and divided themselves into two units. One group would leave right away to catch up with Sully. The other contingent would remain in Shreveport to construct temporary shelters for the expected thousands of Icarian immigrants.

On April 8, with one wagon loaded with food, twenty-five men headed west over the Bonham trail, calculating that it would take ten days to reach Sulphur Prairie. It took them thirteen. The journey was miserable. The wagon broke down. They waded through swamps and slept, without tents, on damp ground. The afternoon heat was scorching. Preparing for only ten days, they ran short of food. Meanwhile, back at Shreveport, the other party of fourteen men with the second wagon left to overtake the first group. Marching through "a country where one can travel ten to

fifteen leagues without coming across any dwelling," they met up with
them after eleven days, and the thirty-nine Soldiers of Humanity pushed
on to Sulphur Prairie. Then the second wagon broke down. They loaded
all supplies onto backpacks and continued in small clusters. On April 21,
at six o'clock in the evening, the first ragged cluster of Icarians reached
the rest stop.[5]

There, Sully, recuperating from dysentery, had told them that they
could never get title to the three thousand acres at the Concession
because it had to be cleared, worked, and houses constructed on it by
July, only two months away! After that deadline they would have to buy
it for one dollar an acre. By the best of Sully's calculations, with herculean
efforts, they might be able to start cultivating some of the half-sections
and build a few log cabins, but that was about it. Sully, therefore,
suggested that they remain at Sulphur Prairie and Shreveport until all of
the others arrived. Then they should reconsider what to do.[6]

Gouhenant, as leader of the First Advance Guard, rejected this sound
advice and decided instead to push on pell-mell to the Concession. So he
and twenty-six men left for Icaria, arrived there on June 2, and set to
work. By the July 1 deadline they had planted crops, erected some small
huts, and put up a fifteen-by-twenty-foot log refectory. Then the fever hit.
By August the Texas prairie became an inferno. Mosquitoes descended
on the Icarians in droves. Malaria swept through the campsite. Cholera
struck. By the end of the month everyone was sick. Four men died. Their
only physician went insane and deserted. One Icarian was hit by lightning.
On August 29, when Favard and a half-dozen men from the Second
Advance Guard (who had made their way to Shreveport and Sulphur
Prairie that summer) arrived, they could not believe their eyes. Favard
said they would have to leave as soon as their health would allow. He
then began to compose the letter that eventually would reach Cabet in
Paris in November.[7]

Favard urged Cabet to forget about the Concession, because neither
the women and children nor the necessities of life could be transported to
it over "these abominable roads." Wagons, at best, could travel only a
couple of miles a day. The region was forlorn. There were no towns and
only a few isolated farmsteads. Any Icarian family trying to come out
would have to sleep under the open sky in unimaginable torment from
the heat, insects, and rain. Illness, physical hardships, and a hostile
climate were only part of Favard's discouraging appraisal. He told Cabet
that they had incurred a debt of four thousand dollars just to cover the
costs of getting to Icaria and there was no way that amount of money
could be raised at the Texas site.

Favard blamed Gouhenant for the disaster and for sending Cabet enchanting and distorted pictures of Icaria that, if believed, promised a calamity for anyone who followed through with plans to come to the Peters Concession. Gouhenant, Favard charged, encouraged the Guard foolishly to push beyond Sulphur Prairie where, Favard believed, a community might have stood a chance of making it. "Everything might have been saved," he wrote. But Gouhenant, believing that he would be considered the founder of Icaria, moved on to the Concession and disaster. Moreover, Gouhenant was a traitor. They had searched his belongings and found papers that identified him as a secret agent of Louis Philippe! At that point, Favard related, Gouhenant "was shorn of his blond hair and curly beard, of which he was very proud, and kicked out of the community forever." The men then chose a twenty-eight-year-old lawyer named Rougier to lead them back to safety.[8] They broke up into small groups, divided the meager resources, and headed east toward Shreveport. The trek was a nightmare. Over the next few weeks this motley assortment of half-starved, vanquished utopians, shaking with fever, trickled into the river town. Some never returned. Four men had died at the tract and four others perished during the retreat. In October the survivors left Shreveport and came down the Mississippi to New Orleans.[9]

At New Orleans that fall, Prudent continued, the community began to disintegrate. Some wanted to go back to France right away. Others, like Piquenard, had already deserted and gone elsewhere to fend for themselves. Still others, like Favard, hoped that with Cabet's arrival things would pick up and that, in any case, it was now up to God. They set up a temporary government of sorts and dispatched two commissions to find another location where Icaria might begin again. One commission left to scout the Gulf of Mexico and another, under the German railroad engineer Jean Jacques Witzig, went north, up the Mississippi River.[10]

Cabet sat grim-faced listening to this tale of misery. Then he spoke. He denied any responsibility for what had happened. The Favard letter, he claimed, had arrived at the office of *Le Populaire* in November but he had read it just before he left in December. He said that all of his other information had been positive. Gouhenant's accounts, for example, had praised the "zeal" and "superhuman courage" of the First Advance Guard. Even so, he chided, the Advance Guard was the cause of the calamity on the Trinity River! They should have acted more prudently and not have pushed ahead so eagerly to the Concession in the face of mounting problems. They should have taken better care of their health, avoided working in the hot sun, and eaten a more balanced diet. They should have made sure that they had the appropriate medicine to treat fever and dysentery. If only these simple precautions had been observed, he concluded, then "all our hopes would have been realized."[11]

Cabet found additional scapegoats to blame for the Texas fiasco. The tumultuous events of the Revolution of 1848 had thrown all his plans off track. The February Revolution had disrupted the financial base of the emigration by preventing the regular, and successful until then, recruitment of the thousands of emigrants he had counted on for the American Icaria. He said that the Jesuits were at work in Europe and the United States to sabotage the Icarians' plans.[12]

But Cabet was feeding on his extraordinary capacity for self-deception. By the time he arrived in New Orleans the American Icaria as he had described it in *Le Populaire* was financially doomed, regardless of what had happened politically in France or what did not happen at the Concession.[13] In the fall of 1847 Cabet had unwittingly disclosed the terrible condition of its finances in *Le Populaire.* In an essay called *"Plan financier"* he revealed that the American utopia rested upon a grandiose assumption that it could count on five sources of money, of which only the first, the six-hundred-franc emigration fee, was at all realistic. The second source of money was to be the "subscriptions for Icaria" or donations given, over and above the six hundred francs, in money or in necessary materials, to the community. As an incentive, all donors would enjoy the honor of seeing their names published in *Le Populaire.* The third source of Icarian funds was to be huge loans taken out from capitalists. At reasonable interests, and secured by Icarian property in France, a totally fictitious collateral, these funds, according to Cabet, would augment in value ten, fifteen, a hundred times! The fourth base was to be credit advanced for important purchases as time and need required. The fifth and last financial pillar of the community was to be an American Icarian bank created by Cabet that would print money or "notes of circulation," he said, for "great enterprises that inspire sympathy and confidence."[14]

How much money was required in all of this? Cabet at one point talked of five million francs, or one hundred thousand dollars. Money had to be raised for transportation, food, clothing, lodging, furniture, machines, and tools. If it was not there, Cabet flatly stated, Icaria would fail. He quickly asserted, though, that all would turn out as he expected. Why? The plan, he preached, had at its service "the most powerful truth" that alone, in times of misery, could be capable of saving humanity itself. Icaria was based on "an army of elite workers, filled with enthusiasm, who in turn had the confidence, sympathy, and applause of universal public opinion." So his financial plan was a daydream. If it ever had the faintest chance of success it would have to rest, as Karl Marx cynically observed at the time, on an appeal to the heart and shielded purse of bourgeois philanthropy.[15]

On January 21, as promised, Cabet called a general meeting to order. He said that if a majority wanted to go home he would support the decision "in an instant." However, such a step would be ruinous for everybody. So, if an "immense majority" wished to continue he would hold on, devoted to their interests. Such noble self-sacrifice aside, Cabet felt that he had the Icarians in a bind. If they all went back to France they would never regain the time and money they had already invested. Anyway, by January 1849 they had only about eighty-six thousand francs (about fifteen thousand dollars) left in the treasury, not nearly enough to pay for everyone's passage to LeHavre. A bare majority of 280 decided to wait for the reports of the two commissions to see if there was any place in America where a second chance at Icaria could be found. But 200 Icarians voted to leave. Cabet refunded their fees and contributions, about fifteen thousand francs, or almost three thousand dollars. They returned to France, where many of them sued him for swindling.[16]

Why did some stay and others quit? The answer to this question reveals a crossfire motif of accusation and recrimination that reappears throughout the next fifty years of the search for Icaria in America. Those who remained, like the thirty-six-year-old notary clerk Alexis Armel Marchand, claimed that they were the true pioneers who gave up everything for the promise of a fraternal paradise. They were blindly devoted to Papa Cabet when he was alive and, after his death, to his ideas and goals. They drew inspiration from the hope of creating a sheltering community—where children were protected, women respected, and old folks taken care of—to replace the frustrations, uncertainties, and persecutions of their lives. They condemned the dissenters as apostates, egotists, and traitors to the cause of humanity. They denounced them for trying to locate Icaria in some fixed place when in truth it was a long-term journey: it was, as Cabet claimed, "in our hearts."[17]

Those who returned to France were, in the words of Jacques Rancière, "half-measure daredevils." They had followed Cabet to find a social position no longer attainable or sustainable at home and, like the tailor Aron, emigrated because "we cannot live here." But finding nothing of what they expected in America, they quit. Unlike the "Cabetists," these discouraged exiles still kept something: the carpenter Betrand, a family business; the crystal polisher Rousset, a job of ten francs a day. So even before Cabet arrived in New Orleans they hated him for trapping them with perverted images of paradise, an embellished Promised Land that was actually a desert of disease and disappointment. Chapron, a member of the First Advance Guard, expressed their frustration after he returned to Paris. "I did not abandon Icaria," he said, "Icaria abandoned me."[18]

For almost a month the 280 Cabetists huddled in the two brick buildings on St. Ferdinand Street, trying to decide their future. Most of them languished without work, uprooted in a land where only the French culture of the city offered solace. In late January they received a discouraging report from the commission sent to the Gulf of Mexico, specifically to look at possibilities in Galveston, Houston, and Austin. Time was running out. They had to pay rent and buy food, and by the end of February their treasury had been depleted by another ten thousand francs. If they tarried much longer they would not have enough money to get back to France. Health was another pressing concern. Some men from the Texas colony were barely recovered from the ordeal. And then they heard about a virulent cholera epidemic; many residents had already left for the countryside.[19] Some warned that they could never withstand another summer sweltering in the brutal heat and humidity of that crowded city. They waited, anxiously, for the report of Witzig's commission.[20]

Witzig and three other men had left New Orleans on December 31. In late January they arrived at Nauvoo, Illinois, after stopping briefly at a couple of other spots in their upriver trip by steamboat. They had heard of the forced expulsion of the Mormons from their Illinois Zion in 1846-47 by angry local mobs and vigilantes, and of the Mormons eagerness to unload their Nauvoo property at the best possible price. When they arrived they found a shell of a city that five years earlier had housed over 12,000 inhabitants. The Mormons had left behind brick homes, stores, workshops, and, close by, fertile, deserted farmsteads. The river itself promised limitless commercial opportunities. More important, it allowed easy access by steamboat for new emigrants still expected to arrive from Europe. Here, Witzig thought, was what Cabet had in mind when he decided to "go to America." Here, as Cabet realized when the commission reported to him on February 5, was the first ray of hope that his promises might still come true.[21]

On the morning of February 28, 1849, they voted to relocate to Nauvoo. That day the 142 men, 74 women, and 64 children boarded a steamship for the week-long trip up the Mississippi with their baggage, tools, and supplies. With less than sixty thousand francs to their name they headed north for another try at Icaria. Almost immediately their attitude and morale improved. Instead of abject despondency and fatigue, a cheerful enthusiasm spread among the pilgrims. Exhilaration replaced the ennui and malaise. Singing replaced grumbling and backbiting. The weather was brisk but "delightful." The enchanted Icarians absorbed the wide, panoramic river with its borders of forests flooded by surging spring channels. They passed the evenings together in serene comradery, chanting the "Song of Departure" under a clear, almost radiant, full moon.

Cabet must have felt himself recreating the imaginary voyage of his book in which the fictional Lord Carisdall, on board a steamboat, approached the mythical island-nation of Icaria. Carisdall had sat on "a long, broad, perfectly clean and level deck, trimmed with elegant chairs" and enjoyed "the magnificent spectacle of the sea while breathing its fresh air under a canopy."[22] Now, Cabet, gliding on the river toward his real Icaria, reflected that the Mississippi itself must have been "astonished to hear our Icarian songs."[23]

At St. Louis they transferred to a smaller boat for the second stage of the trip in the narrower channels and rapids above that city. All went as before: fine weather, fellowship, concerts, singing. On the last day they encountered ice near the rapids at Keokuk, Iowa, and for a while Cabet feared that the captain would ask them to get off and to transport their "immense luggage" by land over the remaining dozen miles to the Mormon town. But the next morning the river cleared and they proceeded, without incident, to Nauvoo.[24]

There, at nine in the morning of March 15, 1849, Cabet led the Icarians down the ship's bow-loading ramp to set foot on the soil of their utopia. After unloading their luggage the entourage walked the mile or so from the wharf to the northern bluffs, where the burnt remains of the Mormon Temple stood. There they found lodging that Witzig had arranged for them in homes and buildings adjacent to the Temple Square. And, as if to underscore the sense of relief at having arrived at last, safe and sound, in their New World utopia, Cabet reported that they were made to feel welcome indeed by their American neighbors. They "showed them a lot of sympathy" and appeared to want them to create a permanent Icaria in their town. Even the sad note of five deaths on the river trip because of cholera seemed not to dampen the new-found optimism. They were about to launch an experiment in social living, a model community, that could serve as an example to humanity itself.[25]

When he stepped ashore that morning, Cabet was sixty-one years old, a man of "ordinary" appearance, although some visitors to Nauvoo thought he looked haggard, if not worn out, bearing the "stigmas of his difficult intellectual labor, present difficulties, and anxieties on the way" to Icaria. His expression did, however, convey "intelligence and even a certain degree of kindness," a man who dealt with everyone without enthusiasm but "with courtesy."[26]

He met with David Le Baron and his wife Ester, agents for the three trustees the Mormons had left behind to settle matters at Nauvoo. For aesthetic reasons—the view of the river and the town—Cabet was interested only in the Temple Square. He had in the community fund about twelve thousand dollars, after deducting costs of the New Orleans trip, and he put down one-fourth of it for warranty deeds signed on

Map showing the location of the Icarian communities at Nauvoo, Illinois; Cheltenham, Missouri; and Corning, Iowa. Prudhommeaux, *Icarie et son Fondateur*, 664.

April 2, 1849. Cabet himself (not the Icarian community) received full title to three parcels in the "Wells Addition": all of the Temple Square, or block 20, all of block 81 just west of the Square on the bluffs, and lot four in block 82 (there were four lots per block). He then purchased horses, cows, food supplies, and tools. He contracted for two thousand acres of farmland, seven hundred of which were already under cultivation as four Mormon farms. And over the summer he rented on short-term leases several large houses close to the Square where the Icarians could live while the purchased properties were renovated and new timber structures put up.[27]

By late May Cabet sent a report to *Le Populaire* that they had started to build a refectory, workshops, bakery, butcher's shop, and infirmary. The Icarian men—joiners, carpenters, wheelwrights, blacksmiths, locksmiths, and mechanics—while waiting to get started in their assignments were making things to sell to the Americans. Cabet had future plans to share. "Soon," he wrote, "we will have our school." "Soon," he predicted, "we will have a newspaper (an American *Populaire*) in French, in English, and in German that will make known to America our doctrines, our system, our establishment, our Icarian community, and our progress."[28]

Icaria was completed, physically, almost overnight, but not without setbacks. Cabet planned to rebuild the Mormon Temple that, when finished, would serve as an assembly hall, school, and academy. Carpenters started to restore the interior wooden support walls that had been gutted in 1848 by a fire set by anti-Mormon vandals. They started to replace the wooden and slate roof, also destroyed by the fire. For a year progress was steady. Pierre Bourg, a Lyons Icarian who arrived at New Orleans in December and was later one of the officers of the Nauvoo colony, described the project in glowing terms. The Temple was of "magnificent limestone." Its architecture of sixty-foot-high walls, embellished with Mormon religious symbols of the sun and moon, produced a strange effect of seeing something both "simple and in good taste . . . altogether . . . grandiose."[29]

But on the afternoon of May 27, 1850, a tornado struck the Temple while eleven men were inside, destroying one wall and severely damaging the other three. Cabet realized that further work was too dangerous and ordered it stopped. He used what remained of the limestone to build, next to the demolished structure, a two-story Icarian school. Other troubles followed. A fire razed one of the stables, and another one ruined the windmill. Cholera, already a scourge in the spring, reappeared that summer with unrelenting virulence. During the first year twenty more Icarians were buried in the Nauvoo cemetery.[30]

But Cabet was intrepid. He pushed his followers to work, to organize; and work and organize they did. In remarkable sequence they completed

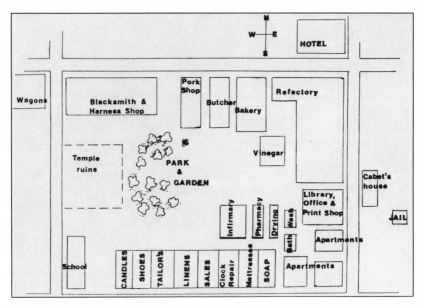

Diagram of the layout of the Nauvoo Icaria. Rogers, "Housing and Family Life, 42." Center for Icarian Studies, Western Illinois University.

the limestone school with separate living quarters for boys and girls. They put up two infirmaries and a pharmacy. They constructed a refectory that served as a dining hall, library, assembly room, theater, tailor shop, and living quarters. They transformed the stone Mormon arsenal into workshops. They erected a wash-house and laundry room. They built stables for horses, barns for cattle, and added a pig-sty. They explored the possibility of starting a coal mine.

Cabet cataloged and assigned all occupations, by sex. He gave men jobs in the workshops as tailors, masons, wheelwrights, shoemakers, mechanics, blacksmiths, carpenters, tanners, butchers, and so on. He had women serve as cooks, seamstresses, washwomen, and ironers. He opened a retail shop at St. Louis where Icarians sold products from their workshops as well as flour and whiskey. At harvest time they pulled extra manpower from the workshops to help the field hands. Within two years new emigrants doubled the size of the community to 365 Icarians.[31] All in all, in the beginning the Nauvoo Icaria seemed to Cabet to be a utopia in miniature, modeled on the *Voyage en Icarie*. For the aging French messiah it was the start of a dream come true.[32]

Cabet was as attentive to Icaria's political matters as he was to the details of its physical environment. When he disembarked at the Nauvoo dock he thought of himself as the temporary benevolent dictator stipulated in the *Contrat social.* And just after arriving at Nauvoo the men of Icaria reaffirmed his powers. But early in 1850 he relinquished absolute authority and instituted, a lot sooner than he had expected, "pure democracy."[33]

He abdicated power because he needed to get his communal scheme approved by a charter from the Illinois legislature, a body stung by the disruptions created by its awarding a home rule charter to the Mormons ten years before. These politicians wanted no more one-man-controlled communities in the Prairie State. So on February 21, 1850, the adult males of the community unanimously adopted an Icarian Constitution of 183 articles and four chapters; Cabet sent it to Springfield, where David L. Gregg, the secretary of state, signed the certification that made Icaria a legal corporation.[34]

The constitution called the community a "Democratic Republic." It would have a president, elected annually, who represented the community in all outside relations. The *Gérance,* or directors, chosen every six months, administered finances and food, lodging and clothing, education and health, industry and agriculture. There was a colony secretary in charge of the print shop. The General Assembly held all legislative power. Women had a "consultative voice" but no franchise except on certain questions "that particularly concerned them." The Assembly enacted the laws and could revise the constitution every two years. It exercised judicial authority as a sort of supreme court. Any disregard of personal rights, or injuries such as acts of nuisance, disorder, and violation of community principles and regulations, had to be brought before it. The Assembly could impose penalties such as censure, exclusion from the workshop, and expulsion.

It controlled who was admitted to Icaria and on what terms. An applicant, after turning over the six-hundred-franc fee, would be approved on a provisional basis for four months. At the end of the probation the *Gérance* would interrogate the candidate and then the Assembly would examine the person. A vote of three-fourths of the adult males was required to award the individual "definitive admission." One could easily withdraw from Icaria "without prejudice" by notifying the *Gérance* in writing. The Assembly would then fix the date of departure, a time not to exceed three months from the date of notification. Upon leaving, the ex-Icarian would receive any tools that he or she had brought into the community and one-half of the entrance fee payable in money and the remainder in IOUs, without interest.[35]

The ink was barely dry on the constitution when bickering started to surface. The first episode was over cow's milk. Since Cabet had spent just about all their money, they had been able to buy only three cows, and the women complained about not having enough milk for the children and no cream for their morning *café au lait*. Soon some men grumbled about the monotony of the meals, always of beef, broiled pork, corn bread, and cold tea. Others murmured that Cabet showed partiality in assigning work tasks and lodging. They griped about the "bureaucratic formalities" required in keeping track of daily work.

More ominous were charges that Cabet favored certain families over others and that he had started a secret spying operation. On April 1, 1850, twelve Icarian men and four women published a long protest. They listed, among other things, the "suppression of liberties," "intolerance of opinion," and the "censoring of private letters of domestic communications." They described a community dividing into two classes, "a majority that was satisfied" and "a minority that was oppressed." "Then you see," they concluded, "the spectacle . . . so eloquent in its naiveté of these unfortunate Icarians."[36] In February 1851 twenty Icarians (eleven men, eight women, and one child) left the community because, they said, of Cabet's encouragement of "inequality, servility, spying, and treachery."[37]

For a while Papa Cabet blithely ignored this ferment. He boasted instead about the prevailing "sentiment of duty towards the community" that he saw on his Nauvoo hilltop. He wrote about "the consummation of common enjoyment, following the needs of each according to the principle of Brotherhood and of Equality." He relished the sight in the Assembly of "democracy in practice, liberty in application, and the opening of the door to all peaceful reforms." "In Icaria," he stated flatly, "there [are] neither rich nor poor, domination nor dependence." There was only "the happiness of marriage and family for each one, education for boys as well as girls, and the benefits of education for everyone."[38]

Then without warning, in the summer of 1851 Cabet abruptly changed his mind and decided to relocate, to build a greater Icaria in the West. He announced that Nauvoo was only a staging area or a *"champ de manoeuvre"* for the ultimate objective of creating the definitive Icaria elsewhere. He believed the town exposed Icarians to the prejudices of "the older social organization," meaning the Americans, "against the community." He saw that his community constituted only 25 percent of Nauvoo's 1,131 inhabitants and feared that his flock would be contaminated by American individualism.[39] Then there were the Jesuits. Cabet believed that the order, through Gouhenant, had sabotaged the settlement at the Peters Concession. Although the local Catholic population was not large, he was convinced that there were enough of the "Papists" around to conceal another Jesuit plot.[40] Indeed, he attributed almost all troubles during those first years, especially the desertions, to "some maneuvers of the Jesuits," who were operating covertly and "contrary to the laws of the land and the laws of God."[41] Finally, he saw a real obstacle to any growth at Nauvoo in the high price of Illinois farmland. It was much too expensive, even if he had any money, for him to purchase the amount of acreage needed to sustain an Icaria that would soon, he expected, number in the thousands.

Others around Cabet shared his bizarre fantasies and supported the relocation. Alfred Piquenard, who had rejoined the community since his defection in New Orleans and was now a member of the *Gérance*, identified Nebraska as the target spot for the exodus from Nauvoo. And Jules Prudent, who was in charge of finances and food, pondered going (of all places) back to Texas! Nothing ever developed from either of these two suggestions. A third possibility, an Iowa Icaria, did materialize.

In the fall of 1851 Cabet dispatched the twenty-six-year-old jeweler Jules Renaud to investigate new federal lands just opened for sale in the southwest part of that state. When Renaud reported on the excellent fertility and the reasonable price of the land, Cabet petitioned for a charter from the Iowa legislature for a "banking and business corporation." The following summer he sent a First Advance Guard of ten men to begin erecting the buildings and, when the land was acquired, to break the prairie sod for planting.[42] And, so, in the bustle of constructing the Nauvoo Icaria, organizing its political structure, and planning the move farther west to a greater utopia, Cabet was able to ignore or dismiss any criticism of his presidency.

He was not able, however, to ignore the ex-Icarians in France who wanted him thrown in jail for his shenanigans. On the other side of the Atlantic, during the months after the breakup of the New Orleans group, his enemies organized their attack. Led by Thorel, a member of the First Advance Guard, they united with Icarians who had deserted before the emigration began. Together they brought charges of swindling against him in the Commercial Court of Paris.

How Cabet received this news is not known. The earliest sign that he knew of the charges was a letter he wrote to Louis Napoleon, dated September 10, 1849. Obviously asking for sympathy from the new head of the French government, he compared his situation with that earlier faced by Louis Napoleon himself. Had not the two of them, both exiled to London, been persecuted "to satisfy the passions and interests" of politicians? "Have you not been accused, condemned, imprisoned, sacrificed by politics?" Napoleon did not respond.

The complaint filed in the Commercial Court claimed that Cabet had used fraud and deception in advertising an Icaria that did not exist. He had built the enterprise on "imaginary credit." He had stolen donations and personal property. On September 29, 1849, the Court found him guilty in absentia. It sentenced him to two years in prison, a fine of fifty francs, and a five-year suspension of political rights. At the same time it had Krolikowski and Beluze arrested. Cabet's lawyer in Paris, Henri Ceilliez, appealed the decision, pleading that "it was absolutely impossible" for his client to defend himself. In December the Court only reaffirmed its earlier judgment.[43]

When Cabet heard of the ruling he told his lawyer to appeal to the Corrections Court of Paris. On May 6, 1850, he learned that this body, too, had condemned him. In late October he wrote to the president of this court to explain why he had been unable to come to France earlier. He listed the cholera epidemic at Nauvoo. Also, the "weakness" of his financial resources prevented him from raising the money to pay for the trip. He cited his responsibility as "President of Icaria to watch over the women and children" and to sacrifice his own "pressing interests for the good of the community." He ended by promising that if the judge would grant a continuance until the end of May 1851 he hoped that by then he could absent himself from Icaria "without any inconvenience." He pledged to appear before the court and to respond to his "blind accusers." Most of the Icarians at Nauvoo opposed his leaving, convinced as they were that the whole affair was a political matter designed to kill the community and that, anyhow, Cabet had been "infallibly condemned" in advance. He disagreed. He had to clear his name. Besides, it was his duty to sacrifice everything, to brave every danger, for the cause of humanity. And he thought—wrongly, it turned out—that Icaria was well enough organized and unified to survive his absence.[44]

On Sunday, May 11, 1851, he left Nauvoo for New York en route to France. After a stopover in London, where he tried but failed to meet Owen, he arrived in Paris on June 23.[45] He immediately turned himself over to the police in order to clear up a prison sentence that had been imposed on him just before he had left. (On November 30, 1848, he had been arrested and sentenced to a month in jail because some rifles had been found in the room of an employee of *Le Populaire*.) This small matter was quickly dropped, and finally on July 19 he stood before the court. Cabet was convinced that he would be found innocent after the judges heard all of the facts.[46]

For over three hours he held forth. He laid out his defense systematically. He developed his arguments cogently. If he had been as ambitious and as greedy as his detractors would have the court believe, Cabet said, then he could have had power, honor, and fortune just by staying in Paris in 1848 and linking up with the new government. He recited his accomplishments at Nauvoo. No other commitment was more moral, more pure, more stamped with the ideals of humanity, fraternity, equality, liberty, and justice, more permeated with disinterestedness. According to Cabet's account his peroration "brought tears to the eyes of the judges." Whether moved to tears or not, the judges set aside the "condemnation by default" of the Commercial Court.[47]

Vindicated, Cabet prepared to return to America. Before he left Paris, however, he made some changes. Dismayed to find out in June that his old ally Krolikowski had changed *Le Populaire* from an organ of Icarian doctrine into a newspaper of moderate republicanism, he stopped all publication. He tried to float another journal, *Le Républicain populaire et social,* but that effort failed. He now turned over full control of Icarian recruitment and fundraising to Beluze, as plenipotentiary head of the "Paris Bureau."

His reforms were cut short by French politics. On November 4, 1851, the bourgeois majority of the National Assembly arranged a coup d'état against the Second Republic, and Cabet feared that the new government might think him involved on the side of Louis Napoleon. He was correct. On January 26, 1852, the police arrested and detained him for interrogation in the Fort de Bicêtre. They released him after several days with the understanding that he would take the first train out of France. Finding himself in London, he toyed with the possibility of establishing another Icarian community there but gave up on the idea after a couple of months. Finally, in June, he left Liverpool on the steamer *Africa* for New York. He arrived at Nauvoo on July 20, 1852.[48]

SIX

The *Communauté de Biens* at Nauvoo

When Cabet returned to Icaria the dissension that would eventually tear the community apart was still not serious. Most visitors, the Icarians themselves, and Cabet described the Nauvoo Icaria as a sanctuary of brotherhood and fraternity. In many ways its layout resembled the fictional Icaria. Cabet, with professional advice from the architect Piquenard, symmetrically laid out the principal buildings on and near the Temple Square. And the General Assembly determined the size of every structure on the basis of a "general plan" adopted in July 1850 that stipulated the location and sizes of the refectory, living quarters, workshops, warehouses, streets, and gardens.[1]

The most important community structure was the ninety-nine-by-thirty-foot refectory, built in 1850 and located on the northeast corner of the square. The first floor was a vast room with a ceiling supported by five central posts and filled with tables and chairs for four hundred people. On the south end, with its solid wall without doors and windows, Cabet built a stage. The Icarians painted the walls with sixteen inscriptions that illustrated the central ideas of their credo. Blocked out in large, bold letters were words like *Fraternity, Equality, Truth, Patience, Economy,* and so forth; under them they sketched a few sentences that elaborated on how the idea was to be applied at Nauvoo.[2]

Meals were served in the refectory three times a day, buffet style, with all food conveyed up from the basement kitchen by a "sort of long railroad." By the mid-1850s the food had improved considerably from the simple fare of the first years. Breakfast was usually bread with soup, bean or potato, or meat left over from the previous day, served with *café au lait.* At dinner, always at one o'clock, they had fresh meat or "excellent fish" with potatoes, beans or corn, and fresh green vegetables. Beer, wine, or watered-down coffee and tea were the usual beverages. In the evening they almost always had a thick beef or onion stew with fresh water to drink.[3]

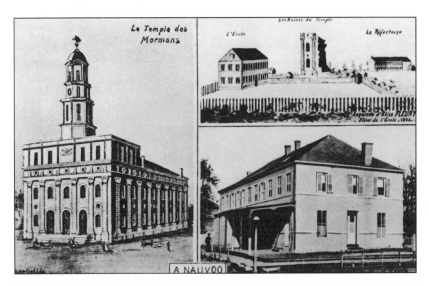

Icarian buildings at Nauvoo. The Mormon Temple before its destruction, the school and refectory, and the school about 1860. Prudhommeaux, *Icarie et son Fondateur,* 334.

Their living quarters in the beginning had consisted of rented Mormon homes and a leased forty-room hotel that served as a temporary apartment house. Every family was entitled to two rooms. A bachelor or unmarried woman was assigned a room in one of the smaller houses. More than one person, Icarians and visitors alike, complained that these accommodations were extremely uncomfortable, very cold in winter, and suffocating in mid-summer. The roofs leaked.[4] Their own frame apartments, simple two-story buildings erected by 1852, were not much better. The windows were poorly set and almost impossible to open for ventilation. Furnishings were standardized and spartan. Every family had a white pine bed, one wooden chair and table, a shelf, a small heating stove, a broom and bucket, and a chandelier. Their wardrobe, or clothes closet, was the trunk, or trunks, that the family carried across the Atlantic.[5] As for clothing, Cabet considered having a community uniform but gave up on the idea when he realized that it meant a sewing project for nearly five hundred people. So he reluctantly permitted them to wear what they had been accustomed to in France. Some Icarians had light jackets, others overcoats. Most adult men wore white shirts and blue slacks, and the women donned blue cotton dresses and blouses. The children were dressed in denim. For headgear they all relied on straw hats in summer and fur caps in winter.[6]

In addition to the refectory and apartments, the two other major community structures were the distillery and flour mill. Cabet recognized that selling whiskey might have been the way to "a rapid fortune," but he felt that such a venture was wrong in principle, that drinking was a "vicious habit." Yet the community, he knew full well even at this early stage, needed money. Consequently, he acquired on credit a distillery late in 1850 and within a year it made over one thousand barrels of bourbon. Then at the same location on the Mississippi River he purchased, also on credit, a flour mill and sawmill.[7]

Most Icarians walked to their jobs at the small workshops situated along the south and north sides of the Square. In theory Cabet believed that work must combine "mobility and variation," tempered with "steadfastness, continuity, order, direction, and discipline." And so he assigned each person a task he believed matched his or her talents and aptitudes. Each workshop had its director and assistant director charged with carrying out production orders of the *Gérance* and the General Assembly. Every director submitted a weekly written report to the appropriate officer of the *Gérance,* detailing the number of Icarians present, what had been accomplished, the kinds of accidents, and any infractions of rules and regulations. At the beginning of the month Cabet submitted to the Assembly a general summary of those weekly reports.[8]

Icarians rose in the morning to the call of a bugle at six o'clock in winter and five o'clock in summer. Then, after a shot of whiskey was distributed to each of the men, everyone went off to work. At eight o'clock they gathered for breakfast at the refectory, sitting in family groups. At nine o'clock, punctually, work resumed. At one o'clock they returned to the refectory for dinner and, promptly, at two o'clock every Icarian was busy again. Finally, at six o'clock the day ended with supper. Cabet reported that Icarians embraced this steady routine with eager devotion. He wrote to Beluze of their "scrupulous observance of the rules and laws."[9]

But Cabet's perception was superficial. Before long, certainly before he recognized it, a kind of malaise settled over the community. Despite his benign intentions, Cabet's workshop system failed to take into account either interests or feelings. Workers had no say in what they did. The shop foremen seldom if ever praised anyone for superior effort or performance. Instead, they harped on diligence and self-sacrifice. Cabet was forever switching people about from job to job so that no one stayed long enough at one task to become good at it. If they had artisan skills in one job they were shifted off into unfamiliar assignments. In just three months' time Cabet told one man to work in the dish-cleaning shops, be a gardener, report to the mill, clean the streets, lay bricks, clear the gutters, help plant corn, and pitch hay. This Icarian found such a regimen "exhausting, disgusting, and unproductive."[10]

The situation for farm hands was no better. Cabet eventually leased five farmsteads: one of 183 acres located nine miles from Nauvoo, a second one of 160 acres just outside the city, and three smaller farms five miles away, for a total of 663 acres, of which 543 were under cultivation. They harvested corn for livestock feed and for distilling whiskey, and a small amount of wheat, barley, oats, and hemp. They planted vegetables such as potatoes and legumes. By 1851 they owned 20 cows that daily produced 80 liters of milk. They kept 14 horses in the colony stable. They raised over 500 pigs for themselves and for sale in markets at Keokuk and St. Louis.[11]

But the farms were trouble spots from the start. First of all, only a couple of Icarians had experience in agriculture, and most men just did not want the back-breaking and, in summer, sizzling task of field work. Then, too, the location of four of the farms, miles from the community, isolated the men from the refectory meals. Cabet described these conditions as "serious inconveniences" and worried that his field hands were becoming too accustomed to an "individualistic lifestyle" that might make communal life difficult.[12]

Cabet identified certain tasks that were assigned predominantly to women. Their most important assignment was to prepare and serve the meals and, afterwards, to clean up. They had the responsibility for the laundry in a dozen or so washrooms and drying rooms located near the center of the square behind the apartment houses. Cabet told others to iron and sew, and he had young women under sixteen master all the skills of seamstresses. He expected every woman to take care of her family's living quarters. Mothers of children under three, however, were exempted from all community work and were permitted to devote their time to the care of their toddlers.[13]

Given the extreme variations of yearly temperature and the strenuous daily work schedule, it is no wonder that Icarians suffered ongoing health problems. A Toulon physician named Taxil, who joined the community in the winter of 1850, delivered babies and administered basic medicine in the infirmary and pharmacy, both of which were located on the south side near the center of the square, next to a park-and-garden open space. But Taxil left the colony a year later, and from that time on Icaria was without a physician; the women did the best they could by following the instructions in contemporary medical manuals.

Accident victims and people complaining of dysentery filled the infirmary. Women about to give birth or recovering from delivery stayed there, along with the elderly in poor health due to what they called "senility." And although Cabet complained that the number of infants (131 in 1855) and pregnant young women incapable of any work (35 that year) were a serious drain on the productivity and resources of the society, he took no steps either to discourage having children or to advise birth control.[14] The infirmary's monthly reports between 1853 and 1855 showed an enormous number of work days missed due to sickness, especially in autumn. The yearly average was 181 days a month, with about 16 people being hospitalized during a typical 30-day period. In other words, the infirmary was half-full all the time, and this loss to the community does not take into account those who just stayed in their living quarters when they were ill and whose numbers were never tabulated. The pharmacy records, though, reinforce a picture of Icarians who never felt well at all.

The barracks-like discipline, continuous supervision of the officers, the enervating climate, and disease all took their toll. By 1854 Cabet acknowledged the "misery against which we battle" but saw no way out of the suffering except to work harder. One visitor later recalled a growing languor. He remembered men and women as depressed and downtrodden, sitting apart from each other in silence, all in all just worn out from the work, the regimentation, and monotony. Or, as an American correspondent from the *New York Tribune* who came to Nauvoo in June 1853, put it, "all in a heap and nothing to eat but bread soup."[15]

Cabet was such a hard taskmaster because Icaria, financially speaking, was a sinking ship. He could not develop an economic program that allowed the community to pay its bills. In order to survive he had to rely upon admission fees from new arrivals and money sent from Paris, funds drawn from Cabet's royalties, and subscriptions to *Le Populaire*. Moreover, he had no talent as a businessman. A political agitator and propagandist, by temperament imprecise and volatile, impulsive rather than painstaking, he felt uncomfortable with figures. His flawed business talents had already surfaced in the earlier charges of swindling and fraud brought against him in Paris, not without some appearance on paper of being justified.

Cabet's fiscal reports always showed a debit balance, but his figures were misleading. Prudhommeaux, who personally interviewed a number of surviving Icarians for his 1907 work on Cabet, was rightfully suspicious. He concluded after carefully examining the reports that Cabet was in deep financial trouble as early as 1851 and that he concealed his plight from his followers on both sides of the Atlantic.[16] He continually overstated the productivity of his workshops and farms. He more or less put down presumed estimates, signed the balance sheets, and ordered the other officers to do so without questioning him.[17]

In order to attract a steady flow of new Icarians Cabet modified the rules of admission. In the beginning, an aspiring Icarian had to contribute 600 francs, possess a regular wardrobe, and have 220 francs to cover the cost of the trip from Le Havre to New Orleans. But in the spring of 1850 he promulgated a new law of admissions which the Assembly promptly approved. He reduced the entrance fee to 400 francs. Candidates for Icaria would endure a reduced testing period of only four months. Once admitted into full membership, anyone leaving Icaria would receive one-half of the admission fee. Then on June 12, 1854, Cabet put through the Assembly another revision, approved by a vote of 104 yeas, 15 nays, and 3 abstentions. The probation time of four months could be waived by a public question-and-answer session before the Assembly. At that time a vote would be taken on whether to approve the candidate. If approved, a second vote would be held to grant the person permanent status. This definitive admission required a majority of three-fourths of those present, including women. In case provisional members withdrew, they received back four-fifths of their contribution. If permanent members left they could claim a restitution of their wardrobe, tools, and one-half of the entrance fee, now reduced to 300 francs.

Despite shaky fiscal underpinnings, the Nauvoo community maintained a facade of solvency because of the regular arrival of emigrants, enticed by Cabet's glowing accounts of a life devoted to fraternity and humanity and by assurances of his own steadfast devotion to the responsibilities of leadership. In July 1852 the colony counted 365 members (176 men, 101 women, 88 children); in July 1854 it had 392 people (184 men, 101 women, 107 children); and in 1855 the Illinois census marshal listed 469 Icarians living in the town.[18]

Indeed, most contemporary accounts of Icaria in its heyday, roughly 1850 to 1854, pictured life there as genteel, even refined, with an artistic sophistication superior to anything found at the time in that part of the Mississippi Valley. Visitors, except for the few who saw through outward appearances to the growing internal tensions, and most Icarians themselves, described enjoyable pastimes in music and theater, bucolic excursions, and the intellectual give-and-take of the *Cours icarien* or Icarian Lessons.

The three main areas of recreation portrayed by Cabet in the *Voyage en Icarie*—music and dancing, the theater, and festivals—all were a part of daily life. Their orchestra of thirty-six musicians, under the direction of the Vesal flutist Claude Antoine Grubert, performed every Sunday afternoon. The concerts must have been more like municipal band performances than those of a symphony orchestra: the *Colonie Icarienne* on

September 27, 1854, listed four ophicleides (predecessors of the tuba), one clavichord, four trombones, six clarinets, five cornets, eight trumpets, one flute, one neocor (similar to a French horn), a bass drum and cymbal, two snare drums, and triangles. The orchestra played only popular tunes such as "Song of the Transporters," "Hymn of Harmony," "Second March of Two Days Work," "I Conserve It For My Wife," "Popular Invocation," and "No More Cries." And, from time to time, they reorganized slightly into a marching band and played military pieces.

The concerts became so popular with the Americans in and around Nauvoo that Cabet had to lay down restrictions on admitting them to these "musical *soirées*." In an 1854 pamphlet he conceded the beneficial results of "fraternal intercourse with all the citizens of Nauvoo" but stated that the refectory was not large enough to handle the crowds. Consequently, in six "rules for order" he limited the number of "visitors" to twenty persons, each of whom had to have a ticket obtained in advance at the print shop. Children could attend only if accompanied by parents. And, he wrote, "it is understood that admittance is allowed only under the condition that nobody will stand around the edge of the room or make any noise or occasion any disorder."[19]

The orchestra also accompanied the community's theatrical productions. Indeed, Jean-Marie Lacour, the worker from Vienne who visited Icaria in 1855, wrote that although they played pretty tunes their main activities were found "especially at the theater." His description of this aspect of Icarian culture is one of the best surviving accounts of theatrical life at Icaria.

> The stage is at the end of the dining hall. . . . Benches used for the meals are placed in such a way that everyone can see very well. There are some complimentary passes given to a few American families. Icarian actors are doing their best in order to render some comedies and vaudeville. I attended the performance of *The Salamander, The Hundred Stakes, The Miser's Daughter* and I myself was a member of the cast in *The Fisherman's Daughter*. It is the only recreation that we have here and it would have been very pleasant if everything had gone in a fraternal manner.[20]

Even though Lacour was in Nauvoo for less than four months he noted a production of one play each month, an impressive record.

The orchestra also supported song-and-dance excursions. Prudhommeaux believed that their delight in such activities sprang from their social background. "The Icarians," he wrote, "most of them of the working men and women of the big cities of France, liked very much to sing 'la gaugriole' or to hum melodies, so that [the community] was never embarrassed to set up a program."[21] These excursions, also called promenades, came nearest to duplicating on the banks of the Mississippi River the extravagant festivals depicted in Cabet's book. Lacour described two such outings along the river in a glen called the "Woods of the Young Ladies." On June 17, 1855, he recorded in his diary the "Promenade in Icaria":

> The sky this morning promised a beautiful day. Almost half of the members of the colony were part of this promenade. The band, composed of young men of the school, played several military marches. We descended along the river and arrived in a pretty little glen called the "Woods of the Young Ladies," where everyone gathered on the grass in groups of ten. A wagon arrived contained a dinner of ham, radishes, and beans. The more obliging went to fetch the drinks of muddy water of the Mississippi or soft water from a small brook a little distance away. The musicians organized themselves into a dance orchestra. Some of us took part in the dance. But when three o'clock arrived, the sun beat down in such a way that no one wanted to dance any longer; by then the tired musicians played only wrong notes on their instruments. For me, listening on the grass, all wet with sweat, I chatted about the sparse cheerfulness of the Icarian promenade.[22]

And Pierre Bourg, secretary of the colony before he died of cholera in 1850, portrayed this pastoral scene in his journal:

> We were nearly two hundred. . . . our venerable and venerated patriarch walked with a joyous air in the middle of us, our whole ensemble formed an appearance of a large and happy family. A magnificent sky, an air pure and fresh, the trees, the flowers, the fruits unknown to us, the prairie, the valleys, the forests, all of this luxury of light, of vegetation, of the vigorous American greenery doubled our feeling of holiday. . . . our promenade had, besides, a very attractive objective, especially for the women and children: to concentrate on the gathering of walnuts, an inexhaustible crop in this country. After having picked a grove of trees in the woods situated along the river, we went to have our dinner set out on the grass, in a glen, next to a brook, under a tent of foliage: and then, the repast finished . . . our orchestra played some quadrilles and waltzes in order to make us sing and pirouette like the mythological hosts of the ancient forest. . . . Finally, at sundown, very tired but happy, we returned to the communal building where at supper, promptly served, we were given a few chilly glances for having kept it waiting.[23]

Cabet located the Icarian library of over four thousand volumes, the largest in Illinois at the time, in the center of the square, convenient to the refectory, in the same building as his office and the print shop. Books could be used in a reading room, or, rare for the day, they could be loaned to individuals for an indeterminate period of time. The collection, mostly in French, included works on applied and theoretical science, history, biography, ethics, religion, and the arts.[24]

They shared thoughts gleaned from these books, or ideas stimulated by them, in the Sunday afternoon *Cours Icarien.* In the square, at picnic sites along the river, or, in bad weather, in the refectory, they gathered to discuss Icarian principles, to share ideas and, usually, to hear Cabet read from, or discourse on, his *Le vrai Christianisme.* Temporarily suspended in his absence, the *Cours* was reinstated on a regular schedule after his return because, he claimed, "it is one of the foremost necessities and one of the greatest advantages of the Icarian organization."[25]

Their system of education was the envy of everyone who visited Icaria. Cabet had made it clear in the *Voyage en Icarie* that equal education was the key to the success of the community. "Education," he wrote, "is considered among us as the base and foundation of society." At Nauvoo Icarians received free instruction from the age of four to adulthood. Everyone, he said, must be versed in knowledge and in the moral values of the community.[26] In the sturdy two-story limestone schoolhouse, children four and older studied, and even lived there during the week. On weekends they were allowed to visit in the apartments with their families. Girls were taught on one side of the building, boys on the other. Segregation, of course, prevailed in the sleeping quarters on the second floor.[27]

The youngest members of the school, the four-year-olds, were taught to read and write before beginning their formal curriculum at the age of five. From then until the age of fifteen they were taught reading, writing, grammar, arithmetic, geometry, history, geography, natural history, drawing, music, and English. They spent part of the day, though, out of the classroom. Boys, during the harvest, worked for a while in the fields, and the girls helped from time to time in the refectory or assisted in the sewing and weaving.[28]

Emile Vallet, who as a teenager lived at the Nauvoo utopia with his parents, remembered that a strict code of discipline prevailed in the school under male and female teachers, who had a "punishment room" for troublemakers. "Three of the older boys," Vallet recalled, "were taught separately from the others in a special room, by a special teacher, having shown an uncontrollable disposition and being considered a dangerous example." Vallet remembered that Cabet handled the moral side of their education and instructed them on "doing unto others as we wish

to be done by." He told them to "protect, live and work for the feeble, the
sick; to forgive; to hold the other cheek when smitten on the one; to be
kind, one to another; to love and respect their parents and everybody in
general."[29]

But the high tone of Icarian intellectual and cultural life could not
conceal for long the underlying stresses and dissatisfactions within the
community. Cabet only exacerbated the deteriorating morale. The harder
he pushed for order and morality, the more he became dictatorial,
impatient, and, finally, intolerable. For a while this darker side of his
nature was largely obscured by the euphoria that encompassed Icaria
after the terrible days in Texas and New Orleans. But as soon as Cabet
returned from Paris in July 1852 his meaner streak became more and
more the controlling side of his personality. "On arriving [from France],"
he wrote later to Beluze, "I found a great relaxation in the execution of
our rules and a great deal of small disorders resulting from allowances
and concessions that my absence had made almost inevitable." "It was
time to stop it," he said, "to reform the present [situation] and remedy the
evil."[30]

And stop it he did—with a moral purge. He would enforce, absolutely,
the Icarian principles of family morality and sexual purity. Marriage, he
stated, was indispensable to the community, the institution that both
"conforms to human dignity and provides Icaria with happiness and
stability." Therefore, it was a duty, and in his community "everyone must
be married" and "every precaution must be taken to assure the happiness
of the married couple." Of course, if life together were "insupportable to
one of them, divorce is permitted but everything is disposed to render
that remedy useless."[31] It followed, axiomatically, that he would tolerate
no philanderers in Icaria. This was not idle preaching.

In the spring of 1853 a young woman referred to as *"femme C.,"* who
was separated from her husband but whose parents were members of the
community, asked for admission. She was accepted and three months
later bore a child. In January 1855 she became pregnant again, this time
by a lover. She and her paramour were hauled before the Assembly,
which, despite a public repentance, found her guilty of "neglecting all of
her duties as a woman, bringing disorder and trouble into the community
and compromising its honor." It branded her lover, "E. G.," equally
culpable. It condemned their fornication as a "double infraction of the
most sacred laws of the community concerning marriage and public
morality." An example had to be made in order "to preserve the honor of
the colony." It excommunicated them with a paltry ten dollars as a
severance allowance.[32]

That same spring a *"femme G."* came to Icaria with her son and, without any money, requested provisional admission. She told Cabet that her husband was going to join them shortly, as soon as he could raise the required financial contribution. Nothing more was heard from him for two years. Then, in March 1855, the husband announced his impending arrival in a month or two, with the necessary admission fees in hand. At that time Cabet found out that *"femme G."* was already nine months pregnant and that her lover was one "H. C." "H. C." begged the Assembly for understanding. He confessed that the recent loss of his first wife, two children, and his brother had made him momentarily "misled," "foolish," and caused him "to forget everything, duty, respect." He pleaded guilty to "an act against our principles and our laws," but called attention to the fact that he still had a blind son "innocent of his father's faults" and asked for compassion. The Assembly expelled the two of them forthwith but for "reasons of humanity" allowed the boy to remain.[33]

A third episode involved a charge of blatant fornication. Early in 1853, that unfortunate year for Icarian virtue, two women, *"femme F."* and *"femme P.,"* said that they had seen a *"femme D."* flagrante delicto with a strapping nineteen-year-old named "G." Cabet investigated the charges and called the accused couple before the Assembly on February 15. It heard the allegations, namely that on January 20, about one o'clock, the two women F. and P. had gone to *femme* D.'s house for a social call. There, to their astonishment, they found *femme* D. and young G. in the very act! Young G., though, told the 182 members present (124 men and 58 women) that nothing of the sort had happened. He claimed that he was just visiting *femme* D. and while he was there she began "crying out" from an attack of "neuralgia." He tried to comfort her, he said.

The Assembly unanimously proclaimed the couple innocent and then turned on *femmes* F. and P. with a vengeance. They voted to evict them for vicious slander. Cabet, however, overruled the Assembly, thinking it best to let the matter rest with a lecture on the whole episode. He began by making it clear that whenever any fornication occurred in Icaria it was everyone's duty to let him know about it first. But, he said, calumny itself was also a serious offense that nothing could justify. He reiterated that the community was based on marriage and family and warned that Icaria's enemies always tried to spread the lie that it was a society of free love and promiscuous women. So they must vigorously protect marriage against all infractions; nothing must either trouble or compromise the reputation of the community.[34] As a precaution, Cabet instructed Beluze not to recruit any more single men and women, confirmed bachelors, or young married men without their wives.[35]

Another vital Icarian principle, as sacred as sexual morality but likewise as threatened, was equality. In the community, Cabet said, everything was to be for everyone. He insisted upon the surrender, upon provisional admission, of *all* property. Nothing was supposed to be retained, either in money or personal belongings. Nothing could be acquired by work or be received as a gift or legacy. Even before he left for France Cabet had tried as best he could to enforce such rules. Some Icarians arrived at Nauvoo with clocks in their baggage, but since it was impossible to provide everyone with a clock, no one could have one. All clocks were placed in the warehouse. Some women brought with them make-up and other toiletries, but because not every woman could have such items, no woman could have them. One woman came there with a silk dress, but Cabet told her to hand it over because no one else had a silk dress. He confiscated all jewelry, although some Icarian women hid theirs and, behind the closed doors of their two-room apartments, secretly bedecked themselves in clandestine jewelry parties.[36]

When he returned from Paris he was shocked at what he saw. Equality had given way to vanity and luxury. A grand inequality among the women now prevailed. Now jealousy threatened harmony itself. New arrivals were hoarding their clocks, toilet articles, and fancy clothes. Now the women wasted time primping. Cabet was fed up. He wrote to Beluze in July 1853: there would be no more "objects of luxury, nor of vanity, nor of silk, nor lace, nor embroidery." And, he told Beluze, "if one is an Icarian one will obey willingly: if one hesitates one is not an Icarian, and then it will be best if one does not come here."[37]

In the fall of 1853 Cabet decided on a complete overhaul. On October 4 he wrote to his wife that he "was going, after long explanations, to propose a reformation that, I hope, will be accepted and which will give me the greatest satisfaction." He had always condemned tobacco for health reasons and had asked everyone to give up the habit. All of the men obeyed. And while Cabet was present in Nauvoo, no one smoked. But as soon as he was gone the men started smoking their pipes and cigars. Then there was the alcohol problem. Cabet had permitted whiskey to the men as a morning dram before work. But now he heard of drinking in the workshops. Some men were drinking after each meal, and in enormous quantities. Some had pretended to be sick in order to drink. Some had hidden bottles under floor boards. Some were so aroused by bourbon that they became loud and abusive. A few men had gulped down sixteen liters of bourbon in less than a week. One Icarian was drunk all the time.[38]

On January 9, 1853, Cabet stood before an all-day session of the Assembly and announced the "great reform." Tobacco and whiskey were forbidden. He reminded them of their sacred doctrines and principles. He recalled the emigration and its hardships. He asked them to keep foremost in mind their ultimate mission to found an "Icaria in the desert" and to keep alive their devotion to the interests of Humanity. Then, on February 3, at the reelection of half of the *Gérance,* the Assembly accepted the new rules by a vote of 114 in favor and 3 abstentions. Cabet then undertook a full review of all laws. On November 21, by unanimous vote of the women and 104 to 17 vote of the men, it adopted his new Forty-Eight Articles.[39]

The Articles required that every initiate demonstrate full knowledge of Cabet's voluminous publications, accept without reservations the principles of Equality, Liberty, and Unity, renounce all individual property, surrender all belongings to the *Gérance,* and renounce tobacco and alcohol. Once in the community, Icarians had to execute "vigorously" all work assignments, because only by such diligence could the society prosper. Silence in the workshop was the new rule. They were to eat what was placed before them at mealtime without grumbling. They could show no signs of envy or jealousy. No swearing was allowed. No hunting or fishing for pleasure was tolerated. If a person was single, widowed, or divorced, he or she had to agree to get married or remarried as soon as possible. Lastly, everyone had to accept and obey all the laws and rules "without criticism and without muttering." He and his loyal *Gérance,* Cabet concluded, would see to it that the Forty-Eight Articles were faithfully and vigorously enforced.[40]

SEVEN

The Schism

The Forty-Eight Articles eventually caused a civil war in Icaria. The details of what occurred between the end of November 1853, when the Assembly accepted the articles, and August 1855, when a majority of the Icarians broke with Cabet, are found in Cabet's letters to Beluze, in pamphlets, and in the *Revue Icarienne*, the colony newspaper. The impetus for the insurrection was a system of surveillance that Cabet instituted just after he returned from Paris: he created a network of informants who met with him daily. The eavesdropping soon created so much distrust and suspicion that everybody thought someone was spying on them, and most likely they were right.[1]

Then in the fall of 1854 financial panic further poisoned the community. Two members of the *Gérance*, the carpenter Jean Baptiste Gérard, in charge of finances and food, and Alexis Armel Marchand, director of education and health, confronted Cabet. Icaria, they said, did not have enough money to feed, clothe, and house any more arrivals. Cabet would have to tell Beluze to stop sending recruits. Cabet was intractable.[2] The directors persisted. They told Cabet that he must not only limit admissions but he must expand operations of the distillery to bring in much-needed revenues. The two directors went on to challenge Cabet's recent crackdown. Whiskey, they argued, should be allowed in moderation. Nothing was wrong morally or physically with smoking. Hunting and fishing for pleasure were traditional French pastimes. Cabet's rigid discipline in the workshop was flawed. Silence was absurd and, moreover, each Icarian should be allowed to choose the job he or she was best qualified for, not the one arbitrarily assigned by Cabet. The meeting ended in a standoff.[3]

Gérard and Marchand's challenge, unfortunately, was only one symptom of serious trouble among the rank-and-file. By 1854 some Icarians began calling those who went along with Cabet's reforms "flatterers" and "sycophants." They started to attack Cabet personally, saying that he was an incompetent administrator and blind to the rising discontent. He was

Alexis Armel Marchand about 1857, leader of the Majority opposition along with Gérard, and his wife Marie and two sons, Armel (left) and Alexis (right). Center for Icarian Studies, Western Illinois University.

an aloof, haughty tyrant. Cabet's partisans responded: Papa, the founder of Icaria, was a self-sacrificing leader who had only the highest principles in mind. Then Cabet himself counterattacked. At a banquet held in the fall of 1855, he lectured on the topic of fraternity. But one of the opposition, mocking Cabet, read a newspaper while the president held forth. Some time after this affront Cabet suffered a minor stroke that left him partially paralyzed and, for a considerable time, bedridden.[4]

In December 1855, after his health returned, he told the Assembly that he was too necessary to Icaria for anyone to think the community could survive without his presence. Moreover, he was too devoted to them to leave. He had to finish his mission— defending "our women and children, our old folks and our sick, our widows and orphans"—if the majority would support him. Having secured this emotional support, he then laid down an ultimatum: seven conditions had to be met if he were to continue "to carry the flag of the community" and "to guarantee and consolidate the Icarian way." First, the "systematic opposition" must shut up or get out or be thrown out. Second, loyal Icarians must move against these culprits with energy and firmness to convince him that they were willing to do what was necessary to save Icaria. Third, women must promise to support him so that he could protect them and their children. Fourth, everyone must pledge anew to comply with the Forty-Eight Articles because he "did not want to waste his time discussing" the matter. Fifth, they must give him absolute financial control because only he knew the colony's needs. "Since it is true that I am alone responsible it is, strictly speaking, right that I have all the means to exercise that responsibility." So, Cabet dictated, "if you do not want to work to earn your food, I do not have the responsibility to feed you, to provide health care, etc." Sixth, he demanded the power to punish all infractions of the rules. "The public does not know as well as I do . . . all of the disorders and all of the vices that can exist in Icaria." "If you are not perfectly in accord with me in all of these principles" he warned, "if you do not have the necessary confidence, esteem, respect, and affection for me, . . . if you impede me instead of help me, then I do not want to be responsible for anyone or anything." Seventh, he had to be freed of all administrative details in day-to-day operation of the colony so that he could concentrate only on policy matters and his correspondence. "The divisions, the critiques, discussions, and quarrels in which I have had to intervene because I alone am in a position to calm things, have made me lose an enormous and infinite amount of precious time, have impeded and incapacitated me and caused incalculable injury to the society."[5]

At the end of this tirade he demanded a revision of the constitution in order to create a new, stronger presidency. The president should be chosen for a term of four years instead of annually and have full power over "high administration" and execution of the laws. He had to be able to choose and to dismiss "all the directors and administrators, all of the agents and commissions." He must have supreme control over education, industry, and lodging. He must have absolute prerogative in discipline and punishment.[6]

The Assembly reacted with stunned silence and adjourned. At their next meeting on December 15 Cabet asked for formal consideration and approval of his demands. On that Saturday afternoon he laid out a slightly modified version of his earlier ultimatum. He asked for a four-year presidency with sole authority over direction of Icaria and execution of its laws. The new president would have power to suspend any law for six months if he thought it "dangerous to the society," during which time it could be discussed and reenacted by the Assembly. The president would remake the *Gérance*, abolish the prerogatives of some offices, and appoint new officers. He would have absolute control over the Iowa venture. At the end of the four-year term the president would report to the Assembly on what he had accomplished. In the meantime the president was accountable only to God and his conscience.

When Cabet finished, Gérard got up and handed him a letter of resignation. As a designated leader of the "systematic opposition," he wanted no part of an ultimatum. The following day Marchand quit. On Friday, December 21, Gérard, Marchand, and three other men marched around the refectory singing the rousing words of the *La Marseillaise:* "the bloody flag of tyranny is raised against us." Cabet called the episode a "monstrosity." The next day the Assembly accepted Gérard's and Marchand's resignations by a vote of 93 to 52. At a special Sunday session, with almost all of the adult males present, Cabet's support visibly eroded. The Assembly elected as replacements for Gérard and Marchand, by a vote of 127 to 117, two supposedly neutral Icarians, Emile Baxter, who had just arrived, and Charles Mesnier, who was privately opposed to Cabet's ideas.[7]

Papa was in trouble. Icaria had split in half. The opposition saw him acting like the absolute monarch he had always condemned and a hypocrite of the highest order. Here was a man who violated his society's rules for constitutional revision. That document stipulated that a revision could take place only once every two years and that any changes had to have a three-fourths majority. Cabet should have waited until March 1857 to push any revisions, let alone advocate a fundamental restructuring of the society. But, they said, he obviously felt above the constitution, willing to do whatever was necessary to satisfy his vanity and lust for power.

The leaders of the opposition, now calling themselves the Majority, were the elite men of Icaria, present and past members of the *Gérance* and the workshop foremen. Behind them stood a large group of unskilled workers, the lowest social rung of the community, those given the least desirable living quarters and assigned the most menial tasks. Another part of the opposition was made up of men who were subservient to authority, willing to please and accommodate. Their wives, though, were domineering women, stingy on one hand yet driven by what one Icarian man called coquettishness. Never pleased, they were always critical of others and, moreover, bored. They hated Cabet by now because, by sheer business incompetency, he had almost ruined the community and, they said, all but destroyed their lives. The divergent elements of this opposition agreed on at least one thing: the only way to avoid disaster was to get rid of Cabet and his cronies and to try to salvage what they could of the community.

The Cabetists, as they labeled themselves, were Icaria's solid citizens, men and women satisfied with the community life in general and with their work assignments in particular. They valued security, law and order, and hard work. Most were skilled artisans—tailors, shoemakers, printers, carpenters—proud of their occupations and status. They were dedicated homebodies, glad that their work kept them close to their families. They felt appreciated. They followed the rules. Icaria had given a lot to them and they were determined, under Cabet's leadership, to keep it.[8]

Throughout January 1856 the battle ebbed and flowed. Neither side seemed to get the upper hand. The angry tone of the recriminations intensified. Cabet was a despot, the opposition said. The December "Marseillaise affair" was a childish display of temper, the Cabetists retorted. The dissidents yelled that Cabet ran the only newspaper, the *Revue Icarienne,* as a personal propaganda machine, always distorting the truth. He must share editorship with members of the Majority. Cabet reiterated that he alone could save the community and that obedience was the only alternative to individualism and egotism, to moral disintegration, economic collapse, and communal anarchy.

By the end of the month Cabet, sensing that he was losing support, offered another plan. He asked the Assembly to appoint a vice president to serve alongside him. He would allow the Assembly to propose new laws and to restrict the existing powers of the *Gérance,* but that was all. The opposition said that his proposal was just a rehash of the first one. Cabet still would be a dictator. He rebutted by calling attention to a poster he had just brought from the print shop. Entitled *"Coup d'état du Cabet,"* it listed his constitutional reforms and compared them with the laws that still governed France, Prussia, and the United States. A quick glance would demonstrate how democratic his new constitution actually was. But Cabet was only buying time, hoping to play on the emotions of communal loyalty that always surfaced on the upcoming anniversary of February 3, the date of the departure of the First Advance Guard, the birthday of Icaria.[9]

The February 3 celebration began as had all the earlier ones. Work stopped for the day. They decorated the refectory inside and out with French and American bunting and flags. As before, the festivities opened with a breakfast followed by the election, at eleven o'clock, of the president and new members of the *Gérance*. Cabet, Baxter, and a carpenter named François Martin (who replaced Mesnier, who withdrew after being nominated on December 23) were the candidates for the three offices. At once Cabet moved for a one-month adjournment in the hope, unfounded except in his own mind, that he could gather even more votes to get his reforms accepted and himself elected to a four-year presidency. Gérard objected. He cited some letters on the constitution written by Cabet in 1851 and published in the *Colonie Icarienne*, in which he defended elections only at specified times, one of which was the February 3 anniversary. He called for a vote. Only 64 men voted in favor of Cabet's motion, not a majority. The Assembly then adjourned and reconvened at four o'clock in the refectory for the banquet.[10]

The meal passed solemnly. Then the debates began. Cabet castigated his opponents as traitors. Gérard stated that he and his followers were the true Icarians, faithful to the constitution. They would not deviate from the law that fixed the election for February 3. They demanded, and got, the vote for the next year's president. Gérard won by 67 to 61 votes. Having disgraced Cabet, Gérard then tried to mollify him. On the ballots for selecting the *Gérance* he put up Cabet's name! Cabet retreated. He said nothing about serving on the *Gérance* but announced that he was withdrawing his motion to postpone the election for one month. Apparently the whole community bought this line, even Gérard. He resigned as president, embraced Cabet, and both sides shook hands. The women cried. Harmony now restored, the jubilant Icarians reelected Cabet to the presidency by unanimous acclamation, but only for one year.[11]

The weeks after the February showdown were only an interlude between the fighting. On February 17, fifty-seven Icarians, a majority of the provisional members admitted in November, left the community. But Gérard concluded that Cabet was never going to stop his machinations and would have to go. To be expelled by the Assembly, Cabet had to be found guilty of some wrongdoing, some overt offense against the constitution. In order to show that the man was guilty of misconduct, Gérard and Marchand decided to expose his handling of the colony's finances and show how his conduct had been an unmitigated, and concealed, disaster.[12]

He had the Assembly appoint an Investigating Committee on Accounts, made up of three titular members and two replacements. The Assembly chose Majority men: Gérard, Prudent, and a young wheelwright named Mathieu. The replacements, Marchand and Katz, were also from the opposition. On February 26, the committee changed its name to "Commission on the Surveillance and Verification of Accounts" and announced that it was looking at the activities of the Paris Bureau. Then it asked the Hancock County Court to issue Cabet a summons to turn over all the account books. At that point Cabet hedged. He released only the monthly cash records of the Paris Bureau between January 1852 and December 1855, saying that these were the only books he had in his possession and the only source of his own reports on Icaria's finances. The Committee conveyed this response to the April 12 session of the Assembly in a report written by Gérard. Even with the limited documentation furnished by Cabet, Gérard showed that an enormous discrepancy existed between the amount of money collected by the Bureau and the community's expenses during that three-year period: 115,576 francs had been collected for the colony, but expenses were listed only as 38,123 francs. Beluze, with Cabet's approval, had kept 7 of every 10 francs collected by the Bureau.[13] At the Assembly on April 22, Gérard moved to close the Paris Bureau and proposed that Icarians everywhere from now on correspond directly with the officers of the Nauvoo community. But Gérard was not finished. He had the Assembly create another commission of six men, chaired by Katz, with orders to take over publication of the *Revue Icarienne*.[14]

On May 3 Cabet printed his rebuttal, a pamphlet called *Toute la vérité*, a mixture of pathos, hyperbole, and blatant vanity. He portrayed himself as one whose whole life had been consecrated to disinterested devotion to humanity. He could have had a career of honor and authority in France. He was, he pointed out, in the spring of 1848 the editor of a newspaper that placed him as head of three hundred thousand Icarians or Democrats. He could have had it all—power, millions of francs. But he chose instead to come to America to build Icaria. Then there was his family, his suffering wife and daughter, who had to endure his exile in London, his persecution while editor of *Le Populaire,* and "all my court trials!" "All the attacks directed against me [were]," he said, "as so many assaults against their health." Now the charges by the opposition were "lances against me and condemned my family to live in alarm." But "if I sacrificed them I sacrificed myself in the devotion to the cause of [human] unhappiness that demands a liberator." After they were separated by the "immensity of the ocean" they "worried constantly about my health and well being." "What greater anguish," he lamented, "when saddled in a fight with a cruel" opposition? He had "no other solace but tears!" Since his wife and daughter were supported only by income from the Paris Bureau, closing it down would send the women to the poorhouse. Favard had suggested giving Cabet and his family a modest pension, but what good would that do? In a fit of petulance he condemned the offer out of hand. He and his family would perish from hunger or beg for charity before they would accept a farthing from men corrupted by "monstrous ingratitude." He ended by appealing to all faithful Icarians to stand behind him and predicted that "the Paris Bureau will not close."[15]

The final crisis came on the night of May 12, 1856. The session of the Assembly opened about seven-thirty in the evening under the gavel of Mathieu as acting president, with 118 men present. The agenda was the closing of the Paris Bureau. Cabet spoke first. He tried a gambit. He asked the Assembly to set aside the agenda and discuss all the insults uttered against him. Eugène Mourot, the *gérant* in charge of agriculture, jumped to his feet: Vote on Gérard's motion to close the Paris Bureau! Cabet turned on him. Stoop-shouldered, partially deaf, with a lilting Parisian accent, he packed all the charm of a small-town banker. Oozing with restrained fury, Cabet was at his pompous, mawkish best. "I want to save Icaria," he sneered, and "for that I will raise heaven and earth." "If I must," he threatened, "I will go to court [to get the community dissolved] and if they were open tomorrow then tomorrow I would have recourse there!" The opposition did not budge. "We want you out, right now!" Gérard barked. "You demand my resignation, do you?" Cabet whined, "So be it, but such antics will not accomplish anything." "If you want me removed," Cabet went on, "then you will have to do it by the rules. Put the request for removal in writing and bring it before the Assembly as the order of the day." "Then," Cabet growled, "I will show you what a man with guts can do when exposed to unworthy accusations."[16]

The rancor continued until two o'clock in the morning when Cabet, exhausted, moved for adjournment. He was voted down and the marathon continued. Katz went for the jugular. He looked Cabet straight in the eye and told him that he was a thief and a fraud. Here was a man posing as a saint, a savior of humanity, Katz snickered, "who kept for himself $1,600, found in his office, that he was supposed to send to New Orleans to pay the expenses of the overseas trip of the last contingent of new Icarians." His Commission had followed the money trail and had caught Papa red-handed! Cabet was dumbfounded. No one spoke. Prudent broke the tomb-like silence of the hall. He moved that a Committee of Inquiry of three men be appointed to draw up formal charges against Cabet. The motion passed 71 to 41.[17] After the vote one of Cabet's secretaries, the thirty-five-year-old lawyer Benjamin Mercadier, asked for the floor. He pointed out that the constitution required a three-fourths majority when a vote was taken on a matter of importance presented from the floor and not examined beforehand. Gérard, Mourot, and Prudent had had enough. "There is no more constitution!" they cried out in unison. Mathieu, as presiding officer, now supported Cabet and ruled that such procedure was in fact unconstitutional. The opposition ignored him. By secret ballot they elected Katz, Mourot, and the Italian professor of mathematics Ignacio Montaldo to the Committee of Inquiry. That done, at eight o'clock in the morning, the Assembly adjourned for two hours of rest. When they reconvened, they voted to close the Paris Bureau. There were 81 men in the opposition and only 54 who still stood behind Cabet. Later, when the men from the Iowa outpost returned to vote, the final tally was 91 against Cabet and 74 in his favor.[18]

From the morning of May 13 there were two separate communities in the Nauvoo Icaria. The refectory tables were divided and the Majority sat in one half of the hall, the Cabetists in the other half. Neither side spoke at meals or any other time, except when the necessities of daily work required it. A strong, icy, French politeness descended, like a cold river fog, on the utopia. The Majority claimed as their territory, for gatherings and recreation, the central garden area of the square just west of the refectory. The Cabetists took possession of the smaller field adjacent to the Temple site. Observers saw both groups trying desperately to enjoy themselves and sometimes their outdoor activities were noisy, boisterous, even rowdy occasions. Often they were just dreary, quiet, mournful pastimes.[19]

This charade lasted for two months. Cabet printed address after address to imaginary Icarian allies in France. He asked them to help him fight opponents who, with their "insults and outrages" wanted "to destroy the Icarian system." He proclaimed his self-sacrifice to Icaria and his persecution, now as before, by hateful, self-serving enemies of humanity. As the martyr to equality and fraternity he had to protect himself against assassination by thugs. So he created a bodyguard of seven hardy Cabetists to stay by him day and night.

The Majority ridiculed him as a blockhead. Each evening they posted on the refectory door all of the charges that had appeared that day from Cabet's printshop, and each allegation was greeted with bursts of laughter. Worse yet, in sarcastic tolerance, they just ignored their venerable lame-duck president. Perhaps they hoped that some of the Cabetists would come over to their side now that their leader's fate was sealed. After all, before the schism many had been close friends and co-workers. But this farce could not go on indefinitely, and the constitution, the focus of the

May confrontation, brought on the irreparable split and the expulsion of Cabet and his followers from Icaria.[20]

Article 138 of that document stipulated that on September 9 three members of the *Gérance*, elected a year ago on that date, had to be reelected or replaced. The problem lay in the makeup of the sitting *Gérance*. It had three Cabetists plus Cabet as president and only two opposition men. Given the reality of political power in the colony after the May 23 session, Gérard and the Majority were not about to sit by and let their enemies, by control of the *Gérance*, make matters worse. So in July the Majority announced that the September election would be moved ahead to August 4. The shoe was on the other foot. "Illegal!" Cabet cried out. It was unconstitutional for the Assembly to reduce the term of office of a *gérant* from twelve to eleven months! He introduced a motion to that effect in the Assembly, but it was rejected. On August 4 the Majority, now a consistent 82 to 62 majority over the Cabetists, moved against Cabet. They elected three of their own men to the *Gérance*, (Gérard, Lafaix, and Mourot), and empowered it to take control of all administrative decisions. Cabet, though still president, was powerless. Understandably, he condemned the whole procedure as a criminal usurpation and pledged to respond accordingly.[21]

For a few weeks, though, he did nothing, and a fragile calm enveloped the Temple Square, a time of suspended animation. Nothing was done, literally. All activity stopped. The Cabetists increased the guard around their leader's apartment and at his office, located in the printshop adjacent to the refectory. Loyal women stood next to the men as palace guards, prepared for an imminent assault by Majority's goons. The new *Gérance* ordered everyone back to work immediately and reaffirmed the regulation that anyone not working would be denied entrance to the refectory. Then they added further proscriptions. Those who disobeyed the work order were to be refused communal clothing and housing. Cabet, driven to the wall, called his people to action. Storm the refectory! Show the Majority who was really in charge of Icaria! On August 6 the Cabetists broke into the refectory. On August 7, they assaulted Gérard and almost strangled him to death while Cabet, surrounded by his bodyguards, looked on with a haughty sneer on his face. Gérard, fortunately, survived without permanent injury.

Cabet moved out of his apartment to another house about ten minutes' walk from the square. He called the place "little Icaria" and started to publish another newspaper, the *Nouvelle Revue Icarienne*, in French and English. At the same time he made plans to leave Nauvoo. He sent Theophile Heggi, a Swiss carriage driver and former *gérant* in charge of clothing and lodging, to St. Louis to find a new location for the Cabetists.

He dispatched Vogel, a forty-year-old hatmaker, to the Hancock County seat at Carthage to file for legal dissolution of the society.

On August 19 the new *Gérance* took over the school and replaced the Cabetist women with their own teachers. Cabet would not stand for such a purge. He sent Madame Raynaud to the square in a horse-drawn wagon shrieking "Help! Rise up!" The school children, scared to death, screamed. Icarians from both sides rushed to the schoolhouse fearing that somebody was killing the youngsters. The Majority, realizing what had happened, burned Cabet in effigy.[22]

That was it. The good American citizens of Nauvoo had their fill of their French neighbors. They called the sheriff. He quickly restored order in the schoolyard and then reported the incident to the town mayor. The mayor called on Cabet and told him to leave. By that time the Cabetists had little choice. Gérard and the Majority had locked them out of the refectory and the supply warehouse. The only way the Cabetists were able to get money to purchase daily supplies was to sell bottles of whiskey, which they had apparently taken the precaution to horde, to Americans on the streets of the town.[23]

The inevitable happened. On September 27 the Majority formally expelled Cabet and his supporters. On that afternoon, sitting as an Assembly, eighty-four men and forty-nine women adopted and then signed the *Fourth Address of the Faithful Icarians of Nauvoo to Icarians of All Nations.* In this document they laid out the charges against their founder. Among other things, they stated that Cabet, by lies and "incessant maneuvers," had tried to destroy the community since December 15, 1855. He had brought financial ruin and had wiped out the colony's credit. He had absolutely refused to comply with the decisions of the Assembly. Since August 4 he had forbidden his followers to return to the workshops and fields. He had preached civil war. He had taken up residence in exile, from which he had used "all the resources of trickery, hypocrisy, and lies to achieve his goal: the annihilation of the community."[24]

Cabet had his answer. On October 8 he printed the *Grounds for which the Minority Demands the Dissolution of the Icarian Community.* He claimed that he had first asked the Majority for a peaceful dissolving of the society, by "mutual consent," but they had refused. They had proposed instead a list of intolerable demands. They had insisted that he and his adherents forfeit one-half of the reimbursements they would be entitled to, under their constitution, upon leaving the society. The other half of their entitlement was to be paid out to each person in a miserly twenty-dollar lump sum and the rest by a five-year note, without interest. Obviously, since an amicable separation was out of the question, he had no option left but to request the Hancock County Court to dissolve the society.

On October 13 he put out a second statement, this one directed at his supporters. He announced that Heggi had found lodging in St. Louis "in order there to realize completely the separation and there to begin anew the community under the name of Icaria." He considered the society already annulled and dissolved since last May 12 because of the illegal actions of his opponents. He asserted his right to claim all of their belongings but said that he would not insist upon it but rather he would leave such matters up to an American judge to decide. He would, however, in departing with the Cabetists to St. Louis, take along the "necessities of life."[25]

Cabet produced a third document that October, an agreement signed by all of his supporters that put forth the rules of a new community. Dated October 13, the *Declaration of Rights of the Icarians* specified thirteen conditions that he demanded as the price for continued leadership. It left no doubt about who was in control. The first one stipulated that Cabet, as "the representative of all," be president for a four-year term with absolute power. He could name all of the officers and committees, "with or without the confirmation of the General Assembly." He could call and suspend this body at will. He could promulgate all rules and regulations. He could manage all finances and, of course, he alone would receive all funds sent over from the Paris Bureau. Admission to the society was made easier, however. There were to be no more required cash contributions since they were "abnormal" and "the cause of dissension." If one left the community, he or she would receive a severance pay according to the "disposable resources" available at that time. However, everyone had to promise not to leave Icaria until after February 3, 1859. While in the society, though, all Icarians would toe the line and "practice religiously" all of the "Icarian principles." Specifically he insisted on "good manners, temperance, solicitude, order, economy, organization, discipline, and solidarity." There would be no whiskey and no tobacco. Cabet would run the newspaper, supervise education of the children, conduct the *Cours icarien,* assign the work, and take care of all correspondence.

Seventy-one men and forty-four women (excluding Heggi and his wife and two other Cabetists who were with him at St. Louis) signed a statement agreeing with all of Cabet's demands. "We adopt them completely and sincerely," they pledged, in order "to defend the community and make it prosper." "Citizen," they told Cabet, "you are always for us the *Founder of Icaria.* " They praised him for "never deviating from his democratic and Icarian principles." He inspired in them "confidence without limits." They considered him "the representative of all of the minority," and reiterated their ultimate goal "to continue the true Icaria."[26]

By mid-October the first group of the Cabetists was ready to leave. On the morning of the fifteenth a somber procession of thirty-four men, women, and children wound their way down from the high Nauvoo bluffs on which, seven years before, they had established their utopia. After crossing the broad river plateau past rows of still deserted Mormon homes and shops, they arrived at the wharf and boarded a steamboat for St. Louis. On October 22 a second departure of ninety-five people (thirty-five men, forty-five women, fifteen children) traveled the same melancholy path to the riverside. Finally, Cabet himself left Nauvoo on October 30 with twenty-two men, fourteen women, and twenty-two children. Only an unnamed man, appointed by Cabet, remained behind to "represent us" and "defend our rights and interests."[27]

Cabet penned his valedictory in an address dated October 20, 1856. "It is done," he said. His "oppressors" had won, tyranny had worked. He spoke of the recent events at Nauvoo as a "civil war" in which "violent oppression" had been inflicted upon his followers. He told of the "inhuman barbarity" in denying them all the necessities of life, such as food, clothing, and medicine. They were literally "condemned to die from hunger and the cold" while their opponents lived in "abundance and profusion, in drunkenness and vice." He identified the perpetrators of those "incredible infamies" about his character: Gérard, Katz, Mourot, Marchand, and Prudent. "Abominable ingrates," he called them. More than that, the experience convinced Cabet that "demagogy is next to democracy, there is revolutionary spirit and the spirit of party next to the spirit of the reformer, that sensualism and materialism are next to the spirit of order and economy, finally that the spirit of egotism is next to the spirit of Devotion and Fraternity." "At the end of my career," he said, he was still "attached indissolubly" to the cause of the people. He disavowed any vengeance. He promised that he would start another recruitment drive in France and exhorted his readers to support it "with devotion." "Get ready," he said, "prepare yourselves to come and join us by next February." "Hope, therefore," he concluded, for "trust and fraternal dedication."[28]

The Majority of 219 Icarians, however, had the last word. On October 25 they adopted a formal explanation for their action entitled *A Resolution of the General Assembly of the Icarian Community for the Expulsion of Cabet.* It indicted Cabet with violating Icaria's constitution and laws. He had incited "violent demonstrations of the men of his party." He had "with all his might endeavored to bring forth a financial crisis in the community." He had disrupted "to a great extent the peace of the City of Nauvoo, trying to oppose our annual election of the 4th of August last."

He had "authorized and favored the stealing by his partisans of tools, books, musical instruments, drugs, account books, registers . . . belonging to the Icarian Community." He had "induced the men of his party to refuse to perform their daily labor" or to fulfill "any of their duties as members of the Community." Cabet, in simple terms, had "either by his speeches and incendiary hand bills nearly succeeded in stirring up a kind of civil war in the Community." It concluded that "Etienne Cabet member and President of the Icarian Community is hereby expelled from the said Community."[29]

By Friday, November 6, 1856, Cabet and 179 followers—78 men, 46 women, 7 teenagers, and 47 children—gathered at St. Louis in the three buildings that Heggi had rented for them at New Bremen in the German section of the city. Cabet seemed relieved, almost cheerful. The next morning after an early breakfast he returned to his apartment. There, a little past eight o'clock, he suffered another stroke. One of the young girls found him on the floor and called for help. Mercadier, still his secretary, and three other men quickly arrived and carried the old man to his bed. He seemed to recover somewhat, his speech improved, and he spoke about details of what to do to get the next Icaria underway.

But later that afternoon his condition worsened. Mercadier summoned a French physician named Pollac, apparently a friend of Cabet's, and another doctor, an American named Martin, who arrived at his bedside by early evening. Cabet had developed a fever and respiratory complications. The physicians tried the accepted procedures: they applied mustard plasters on his back and chest to relieve the congestion and put cold compresses on his forehead to bring down the fever. They tried to raise his head a little to help him breathe. Nothing worked. At about five o'clock the next morning he died. Cabet was sixty-eight years old.[30]

For a week his corpse, dressed in velvet suit and slippers, lay in a simple metal casket in one of the Icarian rooms. On the afternoon of November 14, a Sunday, the Cabetists placed in the casket twenty-eight volumes of his published works and a bottle in which they sealed a list of his loyal supporters. Then they closed the lid. Mercadier led a cortege of ten men, some of them wearing *sabots,* to the Old Picker Cemetery in south St. Louis, where they interred Cabet with the rites of the Free Mason. "Brothers!" Beluze announced in Paris on December 2: "It is necessary to add one more martyr on the long list of those who have died in the service of the People and of Humanity. . . . Citizen Cabet, the venerable Founder of Icaria, is no longer."[31]

✳

The disruption of the Nauvoo Icaria and Cabet's death marked the end of the most vital phase of Icarian communitarianism. The Nauvoo utopia before the schism was a miniature version of the mythical "community of goods," the closest the Icarians would ever come to creating the ideal society Cabet portrayed in his book. The Illinois community, like Cabet's Republic, supplied every member with shelter, food, and recreation. On the Temple Square they created an integrated society with a refectory, living quarters, workshops, gardens, a pharmacy, library, and a school. Their concerts, theatrical productions, and promenades along the Mississippi River replicated the cultural life described in the book. Even though a spreading malaise eventually enervated, and acrimony destroyed, the communal ambiance, for a time its compelling spirit was seen everywhere on the Square in the words of Bourg, as "the work, study, and practices of brotherly love."[32]

Such ideals meant that the risks and pains of community life were shared by everyone. And, for a while, they were. Professor Montaldo washed dishes and headed the school. Shoemaker Jacques Pierre Vallet was a cook and gardener. Another shoemaker, Louis Tabuteau, even after he had one arm amputated when he caught it in a threshing machine in 1850, cheerfully accepted the job of a plowman walking behind the horses. Martin Hippolyte Mahay, a lithographer in France, toiled in the kitchen, then went to the infirmary and finally to the joiner's shop. As the young clerk named Pech who was assigned to the laundry put it, "we all work with tireless zeal." Since "we are doing everything for the love of humanity," he said, "rather than love of money, there is no limit to our desire to work."[33] The carpenter Stanislas Pierre Savariau, foreman of the joiner's shop, wrote in the late summer of 1849 that "the laborious jobs are shared by all." "I take my turn as the others do," he observed, "because the task is a duty bringing us only the esteem of our brothers." "Jobs normally preferred by outcasts," he reflected, "are presently the lot of a goodly number of us, people of the most remarkable intelligence, moral value, and cultivated minds."[34]

At its best the Nauvoo Icaria was a solicitous, family utopia and Cabet served as its venerated father. The twenty-five-year-old machinist Eugène Camus wrote to his parents and friends in France that they would find here "love for you, for your wives and children." It was "the most tender affection that can derive from a doctrine as beautiful as ours."[35] The frequent outings reinforced the feeling of a sheltering community that protected and comforted. Bourg's letters glorified these pastoral jaunts with descriptions such as "egalitarian," "decently," "without jealousy or care." "Each helping or being helped on the upward or downward slopes of our excursion," he recalled, "chats, friendly calls, and jokes springing up and being exchanged among all indiscriminately." New arrivals, he predicted, would find a carefree community and a peaceful refuge.

The Icarians at Nauvoo turned to Cabet with cult-like devotion. And Papa demanded disciplined, proper behavior, and above all obedience. In some ways he dealt with the Icarians in the same high-handed manner that his predecessor at Nauvoo, Joseph Smith, treated the Mormons. Both were self-proclaimed prophets whose decisions had to be accepted on pain of expulsion. Cabet, like Smith, alternated between paternalism and egotistical bombast and tolerated no insubordination. His personality was shaped by contradictory impulses: humanitarianism, gentleness, and rationality warred with vindictiveness, meanness, and violent outbursts of temper.

Perhaps the Nauvoo Icaria can be understood by comparing it to the Fourierist societies at Brook Farm, Red Bank, and the Wisconsin Phalanx. Both the Icarians and the Fourierists hoped to create a New World utopia on doctrines that originated in the Old World. As pioneers they initially shared an unbridled optimism, confidence in material success, and faith in their perfectionist plans. They promoted their enterprises with a bloated propaganda that concealed the harsh realities of communal life. They were hit with crippling debts. Neither Icaria nor the phalanxes attracted farmers, but drew their membership from city dwellers. For example, only 10 percent of the men at the Fourierist colonies were of farm backgrounds even though the colonies were essentially agricultural operations.

Most of the men at Icaria and the phalanxes shared the same ambivalent attitudes toward women. They preached female emancipation and equality, but in the community itself emancipation meant freedom to work at domestic chores and child rearing. As Carl J. Guarneri's recent study has found, the Fourierists, rather "than constantly questioning paternalistic notions of women's spheres, . . . simply envisioned a broader field for feminine influence than the isolated household, namely, the communal home." "The community was the household writ large," Guarneri observed, "where the mothers and daughters infused social relations with cheerfulness and love." "Phalanx women's role and expectations," he concluded, "were shaped by domesticity even as they enlarged its frame."[36] Much the same can be said of Icaria, where women were assigned traditional domestic jobs. Women were important participants in the elaborate community festivals such as Icaria's February 3 Anniversary, or Brook Farm's April 7 commemoration of Fourier's birthday. But they were the cooks, waiters, and dishwashers. Women were politically second-class citizens in both the Fourierist and Icarian communities. Brook Farm, much like Icaria, allowed women only participatory discussion rights, not the franchise, in communal meetings.

It would be a distortion to emphasize the similarities of the "Associations," as Guarneri has called them, and Icaria. They had markedly different utopian creeds. The Fourierists predicted an immediate millennium through the application of social science. They were not ready for setbacks and quickly abandoned communal life in the face of difficulties. The Fourierists, Guarneri wrote, "did not inspire a faith strong enough to overcome its own internal contradictions."[37] Icaria was a state of mind and they hoped confidently for the attainment of Cabet's "earthly paradise" some day in the future.

The Icarians more than the Associationists met the criteria that Rosabeth Kanter found as the key to the success of the Mount Lebanon Shakers and the Oneida Community. She discovered that they endured because of the "commitment mechanisms" that held them together as a group and set them apart from outsiders. Such mechanisms as the requirement for a simple, austere life, willing subordination of individual will to an authoritarian leader, denial of property rights, and carefully controlled child rearing were indispensable.[38] The Fourierists, diametrically opposed to the Icarians in regard to such mechanisms, glorified personal freedom and promised individual wealth. Their communal structure was never an end in itself but a halfway house to the remaking of America. The Icarians, though, like the first Puritans in Massachusetts Bay, wanted to be a beacon light to the world, a model moral community for others to emulate.

There were other, less important, contrasts between life at the phalanxes and at Nauvoo. They held to different standards of admission. The Associationists admitted virtually anyone of "good moral character." Even the Wisconsin Phalanx, where applicants were screened, took in over two-thirds of all newcomers. Such laxity meant that Phalanx members were "strangers to each other." To become an Icarian required money, a knowledge of Cabet's works, and an ideological commitment. The Associationists wanted to make work attractive by rotating tasks, providing a fair compensation, and keeping the work day to under ten hours. The Icarians were expected to work themselves to the bone for nothing. The Phalanxes allowed in large number of unmarried adults, and Brook Farm, in particular, "was predominantly a singles community" of men and women in their mid-twenties. And one member of the Wisconsin Phalanx joined because she saw it as "an ideal place for bringing up fatherless boys."[39] Icaria was a paragon of rectitude.

The Fourierist communities, unlike the Icarians, were leaderless. Brisbane, who could not stay in one place for any length of time, would not join a phalanx, much less offer to direct one. At Red Bank Charles Sears, the "leading mind" of the community, abdicated after a couple of years when, in 1855, an exodus of thirty members was followed by a fire that destroyed its main buildings. He then shifted his commitment from utopianism to railroad promotion, to a job as a railroad land agent, and finally ended up as an active campaigner for the Greenback Party.[40] Cabet, although ultimately rejected by most Icarians, never entertained the thought of deserting the cause of humanity.

But the Icarians at St. Louis, without Cabet, followed a path that would lead them, unwittingly, to a communal life closely resembling that of the Fourierist phalanxes. And the Majority, after they relocated from Illinois to Iowa, also abandoned the Icarian lifestyle they had known at Nauvoo and transformed themselves into a small, isolated, and, some said, a culturally impoverished agricultural commune.

EIGHT

Cheltenham:
The Urban Icaria

After Cabet's funeral, back at New Bremen, Mercadier reminded the downtrodden Icarians that they must renew their devotion to the beloved founder and to his ideal of creating the "community of goods" in America. All agreed. To that end, on Tuesday afternoon, November 10, they chose a provisional *Gérance* that would hold their positions until February 3, 1857, when, with both men and women voting, they would elect a permanent president, a board of directors, and adopt a constitution. But things did not go exactly as planned. The problems that had to be tackled immediately—finding adequate shelter and work, taking care of and educating the children—prevented the drafting of a constitution by the February deadline. They did, however, elect Mercadier as president and a four-member *Gérance.* Meanwhile, unexpected news from Paris bolstered their morale. In January, Beluze informed them, erroneously, it turned out, that he had already raised a subscription of ten thousand dollars that they could draw upon.[1]

Mercadier, in his first report in February 1857, described how they were crammed into three rented buildings located about a mile apart from each other. Such facilities could never support communal life. To make matters worse, the Icarians had no coal or wood for heat. They had no furniture, not even tables and chairs, nor any dishes or utensils. "We arrived in St. Louis," he wrote, "without tools, belongings, with little money, with our old people, our nursing infants and numerous children." They had some "who were sick, others infirm, all were exposed to the many inconveniences of a large city [that] they knew nothing about and whose language was foreign to them." Their clothes, he stated, were adequate, "generally in better shape than our spirits."[2]

They made the best use of what they had. They designated the largest of the three buildings as a refectory; once they got chairs, it was capable of seating about 150 people, nearly everyone. By the end of November they had purchased dinner plates, knives, forks, and spoons. By February, when Mercadier wrote his first account of the community, their larder was stocked. Yet they never replicated the communal meals they had known at Nauvoo; instead they improvised a pecking order in the refectory. The female cooks first served Icarians who went into the city to look for jobs; then they fed the rest of the community. The best Mercadier could say was that, all things considered, they were eating well.[3]

Calling themselves "a Philosophical People," they started to make changes in communal life that pointed them toward the routine of a Fourierist phalanx. They allowed Icarians to take on permanent wage jobs in St. Louis. In order to eat, the men—tailors, shoemakers, carpenters —and the women with experience as dressmakers had to find employment immediately. Fortunately, the city of 78,000 people in 1856 was a bustling river port with a high demand for such skills. By February an "army" of Icarians, as Mercadier described them, went by trolley each morning into town. By early spring, though, they had started a couple of small workshops at New Bremen. Fourteen woodworkers made furniture for communal use and, of course, for sale in the city. Six or seven coopers plied their craft in a room in one of the houses. Mercadier congratulated everyone for their enthusiasm and dignified devotion to the challenge. Their survival, he said, would have been "very difficult in the circumstances in which they had found themselves if each member of the Society had not assumed the burden handed to him."[4]

After establishing the economic foundations of the community they discussed how to educate their children. They had had no choice but to send their children to the public schools, a change Mercadier considered "an enormous inconvenience." At first nothing satisfied them as a replacement. But by December 1856 they located a school, not far from the main house, that passed inspection. So, Mercadier wrote, "without dismissing all the advantages of an Icarian education we have not hesitated, in the position in which we find ourselves, to send our children to this school where, besides, they have the advantage of quickly learning the English language."[5]

At nine o'clock each morning they sent their twelve boys and fourteen girls to the nearby public school. The curriculum was solid, even by Icarian standards, with lessons in reading, writing, grammar, arithmetic, history, and geography, and only lacked their emphasis upon hygiene and music. Just to be sure their children were not corrupted by this outside exposure, however, the Assembly appointed two adults, Boulanger for the boys and Rose Chicard for the girls, to give "Icarian instruction" in the evenings. And on Sunday afternoons they taught them "Icarian principles" in the *Cours icarien,* using Cabet's *Le vrai Christianisme* as a text.[6]

Although some parts of the Nauvoo Icaria had to be sacrificed in St. Louis, the Icarians were unwilling to give up other aspects of their earlier life, whatever the obstacles. For example, they would have a newspaper. Fortunately, Cabet, after moving to his new home outside the square, had bought a set of type and a wooden press. Now with Etienne Ravat, a printer from Grenoble, they started the weekly *Nouvelle Revue Icarienne* to advertise the skills and services of Icarian workers and the items made for sale in the community. Ravat also published an *Almanach icarien*, reports from the community workshops, and Mercadier's speeches. On January 1, 1857, in commemoration of Cabet's birth, their music director, fifty-five-year-old Charles A. Mesnier, put on a concert "to the great satisfaction and to the applause of everyone." On the February 3 celebration of the departure of the First Advance Guard, he gave a second performance. That same day they put on a small skit, an improvised reenactment of the scene at the Le Havre wharf.[7]

A favorite pastime was the *soirée,* when they gathered in the dining hall to talk about the day's events or news from Paris. They collected in the same room all of the St. Louis newspapers, American and German, and deposited them on racks for casual reading. On Sunday nights they played games that "amused and instructed." They planned spring picnics, promenades and "other merry-making" that they had enjoyed so much at Nauvoo.[8]

Good health aided their buoyancy. In this regard they were lucky. They did not have a physician, so they took special care that areas surrounding the buildings were kept exceedingly clean. With a chest of medicines hauled from Nauvoo they set up a "small pharmacy" that soon contained medicines purchased in town. In these first months, despite occasional concern about another cholera or typhoid epidemic and "small indispositions," they proved to be a robust lot.[9]

But their financial situation was not at all salubrious. Mercadier said as much in his first report. It showed that Cabet had salvaged the paltry sum of $526.33. By March 1857 they were able to earn just $2,453.95 from wages and the sale of furniture and barrels in the city, and had received $1,600 from Beluze, for a total income of $4,580.28. But their expenses came to $4,348.83, with $200 still owed to the creditors. Moreover, Mercadier predicted that living costs would increase because of rising food prices. He tried to paint a rosy picture by pointing out that work was steady. He knew, though, that the St. Louis Icaria, just like the one at Nauvoo, could not survive without substantial help from Paris.[10]

So the Assembly, at its January 18 session, tried to solidify the connection with the Paris Bureau. It denounced all charges levied by the Nauvoo

Majority against Beluze. It resolved to redouble their mutual efforts, their "ultimate accord," in the creation of Cabet's Icaria. His loyal disciples had a duty to fulfill the obligation which the Majority had renounced, the support of Madame Cabet and her daughter. The two women had been put in a "cruel position" of being cut off from their financial support and "losing a husband and father." The resolution promised Madame Cabet and her daughter a lifetime salary based on what the office brought in the previous year, "with the power to increase it if need be." Mercadier was designated as the sole authority in any dealings with Beluze.[11]

By the summer of 1857 the Icarians felt optimistic. "We have won out," Mercadier wrote, "thanks to [our] activity and good organization, escaping the misery [of] the retreat from Nauvoo and the sudden death of [our] leader." He predicted a rapid advance into a "state of well-being," of "new enterprises in the general interest of the Icarian cause."[12] They abandoned the building farthest away from the refectory and replaced it with one close by. Expecting new arrivals from France, they set aside space for bachelors and unmarried women in one of the structures. They stored firewood and water for the coming winter. They outfitted a kitchen with a modern stove. Their food was wholesome and varied. Their tailors and seamstresses replaced their outworn Nauvoo clothes "almost immediately." They even planned to adopt an official Icarian uniform. A blacksmith worked in the yard. Silence, originally required by Cabet in the workshops, was abandoned. Tobacco was permitted. They lifted the interdiction on whiskey. Cultural and recreational activities increased. At a banquet on May 12 they celebrated the anniversary of that memorable session in the Nauvoo Assembly the year before with a small theatrical production. On July 4 they enjoyed a band concert. Each Sunday evening in the backyard of the main building everyone visited as "members of a large family."[13]

Mercadier added to the rising euphoria in September when he announced that they were going to find a better place to live. He had become convinced that the New Bremen facilities, without real workshops or farms, could never sustain communal life. If he could have had it his way he would have replanted Icaria as far away from St. Louis as possible, as Cabet envisioned, on the western frontier. He realized, though, that this plan would be impossible because the Icarians were skilled artisans, used to the routine of urban life. So he struck a compromise: he chose a suburban location, a place called Cheltenham.[14]

Cheltenham at one time was a thousand-acre farm, originally called Sulphur Spring, owned by a fur trapper named William Sublett. In 1834 Sublett had built a large stone house and four cabins, probably slave quarters, as a retirement estate. When he died in 1848 his heirs sold the property to St. Louis financier Thomas Allen, who saw in it unlimited commercial opportunities. He named it Cheltenham. But Allen's profits from the investment never matched his expectations, and he put the property on the real estate market. He was more than eager to unload the heart of Cheltenham, the buildings and thirty-nine acres, on Mercadier.[15]

On February 5, 1858, Mercadier wrote to Beluze. He told the Parisian that he had recently purchased a new property for Icaria. Situated six miles west of St. Louis along the route of the Pacific Railroad, it was a "charming" tract of prairie and woods, of white and green buildings, traversed by a small river. All in all, he assured Beluze, it presented a pleasant, natural appearance that gladdened the heart.[16] Mercadier also confided to Beluze the unbelievable cost of the purchase. He had agreed to pay $25,000 with only $500 down and the rest due in ten annual installments at 6 percent interest. Allen, whose instincts told him that this venture was not a secure one, had added a stipulation. He attached to the mortgage a Deed of Trust stating that in the event of a default of one annual payment he could sell the property without any court action to stop him. After giving Allen the $500 downpayment, Mercadier had $59 in the communal treasury.

Beluze must have been speechless. He had already cautioned financial prudence as far as expecting any large cash flows from Paris, in light of his difficulties in securing the $10,000 loan. But Mercadier was worse than Cabet in such matters. With the community accounts showing a 1857 loss of $16.97 ($4,810.33 in expenses and just $4,793.36 in income), with receipts from Beluze that year of just $616.19, the decision to buy Cheltenham was insane. But Mercadier rationalized that since the rent on the New Bremen buildings was already high, $1,250 a year, the Icarians were in the long run better off at Cheltenham.[17]

Within a few months after the purchase of Cheltenham Mercadier began to realize what he was up against. He wrote in his semiannual report called *Inauguration du cours icarien* that in order to meet expenses they would have to come up with $1,350—fast. He admitted that "we must not count on" money from Beluze since he needed funds "to cover the expenses of the administration of the Bureau." By the end of 1858 the Icarians' debt was $35,000 plus interest. Cheerfully, Mercadier announced that this figure was offset by his estimate of the value of the colony's assets: $33,544, including the improvements the Icarians had made on the property since they took full possession on May 8.[18]

Forever optimistic, the Icarians who marched out behind Mercadier on the road to Cheltenham that balmy May morning saw what they wanted to see. They saw, in the words of one young man, a community of their dreams. "What we possess today," he wrote, "is only an insignificant part of the great land we will have." "See our city, our lands, our public buildings, our gardens and walks." "How everything has changed," he went on, "what progress! What improvements! . . . What innovations with industry, agriculture! . . . What a striking demonstration of the practicality of the Icarian system. . . . Everybody breathes happiness." "The Icarians alone," he stated confidently, "have solved the social problem."[19]

Typically Icarian, the first thing they did when they got settled in Cheltenham was revise the constitution. Some members of the community, led by the volatile cap maker from Colmar named Vogel, insisted that the Assembly abolish the powerful president and *Gérance* and substitute a weak executive and even weaker board of directors. He brought the plan to the Assembly in November 1858 and was defeated. Mercadier, of course, opposed any tampering with the status quo. He tried to deflect some of Vogel's criticisms by promising not to stand for reelection on February 3.

But Vogel and the dissidents would not accept compromise. The debates of the December 1858 and January 1859 sessions of the Assembly were stormy, with accusations going both ways. Vogel defended his motives and his plan of reform. He denied Mercadier's accusation that he had insulted Cabet's memory by insisting on a "parliamentary government." Mercadier sarcastically told Vogel that it was "imprudent" for him to advise anyone on what to do. Vogel's ally, the tailor Dieuaide, a bachelor who had joined the Nauvoo Icaria in January 1855, argued that the present constitution was not a democracy at all but an aristocracy. He said that Cabet's solidification of presidential power had been only a temporary remedy to save Icaria from disintegration, "an exception." Now, he said, "some people would like to make the exception the rule." Another Vogel man, Titus Uttenveiler, a forty-year-old German from Dittenhausen, likewise condemned the "single direction." "The president will lay down the laws and he will carry them out," he claimed. Clearly, he had "too much responsibility."[20]

Then Uttenveiler, perhaps unknowingly, hit on the central issue. It might have been acceptable, he said, for Icarians to agree to a temporary, all-powerful presidency if the president were Cabet, but Mercadier was no Cabet. "Since the death of citizen Cabet," he stated, "I have more confidence in the Society than in individuals." Mercadier then introduced letters he had just received from Beluze in which thirty French Icarians condemned any move to change the existing structure of the presidency as an attack upon the memory of Cabet. Other members of Cheltenham thought the whole discussion academic. Salarnier, an Icarian who had been a part of the first outpost in Iowa, said that "whether there are one or several directors, Liberty and Democracy have nothing to do with the question"; since "the People lay down the law, they alone [have] the executive power to enforce it."[21]

On February 17 the majority of the Assembly, backing Mercadier, decided to show who was boss. They "reenacted" what they called the Engagement of October 13, 1856, the strict moral pledges that Cabet had demanded before they left Nauvoo. There would be no more smoking and no more whiskey. A week later Vogel called his supporters together in a secret meeting in the woods two miles from Cheltenham. He might be able, for the sake of the community, to swallow the Mercadier presidency, but to be told that he could not smoke his pipe or have a bourbon and water was intolerable. He and five others sent the *Gérance* their written intention to withdraw.[22]

At the March 19 Assembly, Mercadier read the text of his *Addresse aux Icariens de France,* in which he briefly summarized events up to that time. He noted the resignation of the six men. "All those who have not accepted the Engagement, the basis and social contract of our society," he declared, "are considered as no longer a part of it." Mercadier then told them to get out, "without delay." Forty-four Icarians, led by Vogel, packed up and left for St. Louis. Mercadier was glad to be rid of these "transient Icarians," newcomers who came only to enjoy Icaria, not to try to build it. These "non-Icarians," he said, knew nothing about Cabet's ideals.[23]

The impact of the rupture was immediate and damaging. Vogel and his supporters took with them $188 in cash, $588 in IOUs, and $1,800 worth of clothing and tools. They had performed important functions at all levels, and Cheltenham never recovered the loss from an economic point of view. Those who stayed behind could not come to grips with the event. They tried to comprehend and explain it as an outgrowth of a "revolutionary spirit" that lingered in the Icarian temperament, an urge to constantly misrepresent, to fight, to overthrow. What Mercadier and his followers did not comprehend, and never understood, was that without toleration, a willingness to admit error, and a spirit of compromise, no community, no family for that matter, could stay together for long.[24]

But the Cheltenham Icarians, before the division of March 1859, enjoyed a semblance of communal life reminiscent, on a much diminished scale, of the Nauvoo Icaria. In three workshops, tailors, coopers, and shoemakers plied their crafts. Other craftsmen (carpenters, shinglemakers, cartwrights, blacksmiths) were employed outside the colony. Most women were seamstresses, although some found jobs as domestic servants.[25] They cleared cellars beneath the frame houses, one of which served as the infirmary. They built stables, bought a cow and several pigs, but were short of enough horses and mules to plant crops.

Icarians who did not live in Sublett's stone house, which served as an apartment building and refectory, lived in three frame houses with their children. The food taken together in the refectory had changed little from the New Bremen diet. Candle lighting, rationed for a time at New Bremen, was replaced by lard oil lamps. And even in the middle of winter Mercadier boasted that "heating is about all that we could wish for" because of a large, nearby supply of "mineral coal." Their clothing, though, was as meager as before.[26]

Education was still a problem. Without a community school they kept their children in two public schools near Cheltenham. The American teachers, Mercadier confessed, did an acceptable job. They "appear to us to put their hearts and souls into the exercise of their functions," he said, and Icarians helped out by donating "essential books" such as French grammars. The curriculum was pretty much the same as in the city: arithmetic, grammar, geography, and music. The Cabetists had hauled over a thousand volumes from the Nauvoo library, and they kept them in the refectory. Mercadier complained about the lack of medical texts in the collection, as well as the absence of "good works of all kinds, above all instructional books for all ages, and above all for the use of children." And theft was a problem. Many books came back irregularly, and some not at all.[27]

On February 3, as always, they celebrated in gala fashion a banquet in honor of the departure of the First Advance Guard and the birthday of the "Icarian Nation." They decorated the dining hall the night before with garlands and artificial flowers. At one end of the room they hung a portrait of Cabet inscribed with the words "Honor to Cabet, Founder of Icaria." At the other end they placed a framed inscription that read, "To the Icarian Engagement of February 1848." Festivities began at four o'clock with everyone singing, to the accompaniment of the band made up of adults and young Icarians, the "Song of Departure," followed by some testimonials by Mercadier and the *Gérance*. The menu included roast beef, macaroni and cheese, mashed potatoes, and coffee. During the meal musicians played Icarian hymns and songs. At about half past six they returned to their living quarters to freshen up for the evening's events. That evening the band played *"La Marseillaise,"* or "Andante" by Gustave, and selections from *The Barber of Seville*. Another group put on a one-act play called *La Reine de Raineaux* (The Queen of Raineaux), which dramatized the rewards of orderly conduct and diligence.[28]

On Sunday afternoons the band often put on concerts. Once a month some Icarians performed plays such as *Jacquart* or *La Fille de l'Avare* (The Miser's Daughter). In the winter of 1859 they organized, in the words of Jean-Louis Brière, a bricklayer from Lorraine and member of the Iowa detachment, "three balls in which people danced quadrilles, waltzes, polkas, and the schottische." And everyone, having been given dancing lessons, was "animated." "*Citoyennes* and *citoyens*, children, everybody contributed," Brière wrote. "Games, choruses, singing, comic songs, declarations, music, everything was pressed into service." "These . . . parties are the gathering of all the members of the big family."[29]

On Sundays they revived and invigorated the *Cours icarien*. As Mercadier described it in a pamphlet entitled *Inauguration du cours icarien*, everyone had to take part, and not just intellectually. They had to "participate with . . . heart and mind." He tolerated no tardiness or lethargy. He insisted upon enthusiastic orthodoxy. The *Cours*, he said, assured a steady reinforcement of the love of community. Icaria "will be . . . saved by our perfections and lost by our imperfections," he predicted. He harped on the same message every time. Icarians must be fraternal and sociable, be sober and temperate, engage "according to one's strength" in useful work, and stay healthy. Lecturing "principally to women" he told them to avoid "those resources that are particular to the facial care and coquetry that the community cannot satisfy." At the *Cours* the adults either read aloud or discussed whatever seemed appropriate to communal fraternity. After this period of "sharing" each person who had not read or spoken commented on sections of Cabet's *Le vrai Christianisme* as they passed the book from hand to hand. Then the children recited moral stories they had learned from their parents. At the end of the afternoon, the band played more hymns "to make the *Cours* enjoyable." Then, in closing, Mercadier said that "all the advice which we could give comes down to the simple words: We have only to continue in the path which we follow and the Icarian Cause will realize all the benefits which we expect of it."[30]

The Icarians indeed were in need of good advice. By the spring of 1859 they were sick, both physically and financially. Despite improved conditions at Cheltenham, better heat and lighting, for example, the list of those ill and unable to work increased alarmingly. Between October 23, 1858, and February 3, 1859, they lost about 1,500 workdays. They did not have an infirmary, even though they had planned to get one in operation, so "it was necessary to tend all the sick at home." The most often heard complaint was dysentery and fever, "veritable epidemics" Mercadier called them, that hit almost every family. And the unrecognized source of the infections was the nearby River des Pères, an open sewer whose foul water and swamps were a breeding ground for flies and mosquitoes.[31]

Icaria's financial health by that time was just as precarious. Mercadier's February 1859 report summarized income from their work and sales and published a comparative inventory of assets. Receipts averaged $143.50 a week, a decline of $8.50 over the 1857 figure, for a total annual income of just $7,514. But he never kept regular accounts and, just as Cabet had done, used only estimates, albeit more precise ones. His 1859 inventory listed total net assets of $16,764.74, up from $10,699.00 the year before. But he did not indicate what the society still owed: $4,540 for machines and instruments, $274 for new furniture, and $334 for livestock.[32]

The Cheltenham Icaria, like the Nauvoo utopia, had no bookkeeping, and Mercadier confessed as much. He stated that "no one disputes the advantages" that would come in knowing "of the gains and losses of the Community, for the order, the management, and the knowledge of what happens." In auditor's terms, no one knew what the net assets were or if the president's figures were reliable. In fact, if he had carefully included every liability, his 1859 report would have shown a debt of about $7,000 and income of $7,500, giving Cheltenham a $500 balance to cover the next year's expenses, costs that would run over $1,500.[33]

Their financial straits became acute after the exit of Vogel and his followers. Mercadier's fall reports were discouraging indeed. Even with the admission of twelve new members, raising the number of Icarians to 127, only 93 were listed as able-bodied workers. In August, high absenteeism because of sickness had almost depleted their ranks. Prices for their goods in St. Louis had fallen, and so had wages, because of the impact of the Panic of 1857.[34]

The *Gérance* advised Mercadier that if the community wanted to survive he would have to make fundamental changes. They told him the newspaper would have to be shut down because it had made barely $60 that year, even though it theoretically had 480 subscribers. The Paris Bureau was a siphon, absorbing in its alleged operating costs over a third of anything it was supposed to have taken in by way of subscriptions and donations. The *Gérance* insisted that Cheltenham sever all ties with the Bureau. Mercadier agreed. Like Gérard before him, he concluded that he had to take control of all the European recruitment and fundraising. However, he waited until the spring of 1860 to tell Beluze the bad news.[35]

Before that, the tempest hit. Mercadier, frantically trying to save Icaria, did the unthinkable. He attempted to turn it into a phalanx run on the Fourierist model. He said that Icarians must become capitalists and learn to sell their products at bigger profits. They must "study commerce," learn "how to make contracts, learn to buy at the lowest price and sell at the highest." The workshops must "manufacture on a large scale, work quickly, not waste a single moment." "Commerce," he said, must be understood as "the exchange of products," and "up to now [it] has been neglected too much in the community." "That," he said, "has been a big mistake." Now "we must be familiar with the commodities and raw materials provided by the markets of New York, England, France, Paris, Rio de Janeiro, Buenos Aires, etc."[36]

In a letter to Beluze on January 3, 1860, Mercadier explained the depth of their predicament. "We have put off our creditors as long as possible," he lamented, and "now they are presenting all their bills." The wolf was at the door and the coming year was "going to be grave for us." Their landlord at New Bremen had just sent a notice that unless they paid $1,300 in back rent he would take them to court. Banks that had loaned them money with their Cheltenham property as collateral now refused further credit. Allen, his Agreement of Trust in hand, pressed for the mortgage payment of $1,500 due in February and for assurances that the next six annual installments of $3,000 each would be forthcoming. To cover these demands, Mercadier had only $300 in cash and $235 worth of unused credit. Cheltenham was on its last leg.[37]

But the Icarians went right on spending and living as though nothing was wrong. They dug irrigation ditches in the valley to drain a swampy area around the river. They planted fruit trees. They installed a pump to supply fresh well water to the refectory.[38] Then, in April 1861, the Civil War began. Although they totally ignored both its coming and its causes, their sympathies, in a pro-Southern state, were with the North. They started to organize for the defense of Cheltenham in the event that Confederate troops appeared at their gate. When Lincoln called for volunteers five Icarians signed up. The next month, a company of Union troops was billeted at Cheltenham and created an enormous drain on their food supplies. In June, Mercadier marched off with twenty young Icarians for a three-month hitch in the Northern army.

Under these circumstances, panic gripped the community. All work ceased. Allen became irritable and then intractable about the payments. When Mercadier returned that fall he found the pantry empty and all the cash gone. Then, in November, nineteen more young men enlisted in the Union army, a move encouraged by Mercadier because it would cut down on the number of mouths to feed. Besides, each volunteer received a guarantee of a $414 annual pension, clothes, and 160 acres of tillable land in the west by virtue of the Homestead Bill, then pending in Congress. The Civil War killed Cheltenham. As Mercadier himself admitted in December 1862, "the American war hit like a low blow." There was another sudden exodus. Four men said they were leaving, with their families, because no one appreciated them. Another man walked off

Jean Pierre Beluze, head of the Paris
Bureau. Prudhommeaux, *Icarie et son
Fondateur*, 461.

because he had not found the sympathy and happiness he had expected.
Another one departed without giving a reason.[39]

Cheltenham by the fall of 1862 had become an Icaria of twenty-one
men, twenty-nine women, and thirty-two children hounded by creditors,
trying to maintain community life—common meals, evening soirées, the
Sunday *Cours Icarien.* But the next year it hemorrhaged. Each week
there were more desertions. Beluze announced that he, too, was finished
with the colony, that "discord" between himself and Mercadier had
made any future collaboration impossible. The Cheltenham president, he
said, corrupted by the "pernicious influences" of St. Louis, had moved
Icaria toward Fourierism. More disturbing, Beluze charged that Mercadier
and his friends had distorted the democratic nature of Icaria in their
"efforts to sustain [this] enterprise [and] seemed to be reduced to knowingly
abetting fraud." "Cabet," he concluded, "would be very sad if he could
see the state of the society that he had wanted to found to regenerate the
world." He himself was no longer interested, other than by a "sympathy
made up of souvenirs and regrets," in the destiny of "dear Icaria."[40] After
Beluze's defection, Mercadier resigned and moved into a rented house in
St. Louis, where he opened a store that sold novelties and "fancy goods,"
probably a gift shop.

In January 1864 the handful of people—eight men, seven women,
and a few children—chose Arsène Sauva, a thirty-four-year-old tailor
from Tallard, as the next president. On a bleak winter afternoon he

gathered the group together in a General Assembly. He asked for advice on what to do. Heads bowed, tears in their eyes, they had nothing to say. Several days later they were ready to leave. Sauva, the last to depart, locked the gate and went into the city to turn the keys over to Thomas Allen. Afterwards, like Mercadier, some Cheltenham Icarians went to live, and die, in St. Louis. Others, like Sauva, moved north to Iowa to join what was left, by then, of the Nauvoo Majority that had relocated to Cabet's outpost on the rich prairie lands of southwest Iowa, near the town of Corning.[41]

NINE

Corning: The Commune

After the exodus of the Cabetists from Nauvoo, the Majority was decidedly more comfortable than its beleaguered counterpart in New Bremen. They had the buildings, workshops, and farms; and the fall harvest was stored in the barns. In fact, the 221 Nauvoo Icarians were better off than before because they had shelter and supplies that were intended for over 500 people. And they were elated at having won the battle, convinced more than ever that they would prove Icaria a success.[1] But Gérard knew that they must assess where they were and what they wanted to do. To expedite these crucial decisions he asked the *Gérance* to prepare a series of reports on Icaria's current strengths and weaknesses. Accordingly, in January 1857 Marchand, as secretary, submitted a general inventory. He listed 81 male workers and specified the various tasks they could perform. The women, he said, could still maintain the kitchen, infirmary, and laundry room. He saw some trouble spots, however. The school had been neglected and needed repair. The Cabetists had damaged some of the crops before they left and had stolen some clothing and library books. Charles Ferrandon, the carpenter in charge of the shops, said that although the workers had all basic operations running, some of the buildings, like the school, were dilapidated. The distillery had just one person to run it. The German artist J. C. Schroeder, in charge of finance, told them that receipts were $24,122, of which about $17,000 came from the sale of whiskey, flour, pork, and beef to Americans. Expenses totaled $22,433 and included outlays of $11,000 for equipment, $7,000 for food and clothing, and $1,200 sent to creditors.[2] But, he emphasized, they would have no more money from Paris. Also, the community would face high legal fees in fighting Cabet's motion to dissolve the charter. Finally, he cautioned that hard times were spreading up the Mississippi River valley because of the Panic of 1857, and creditors were going to insist upon larger payments.[3]

At the April session of the Assembly, after they had had time to discuss these reports, the men voted to follow Cabet's original plan, liquidate all Illinois assets, and relocate to Corning, Iowa. In preparation for the evacuation they adopted a twenty-six article "Law to Organize the Icarian Colony of Iowa," basically a restatement of their 1851 constitution. They elected Marchand as president and conferred on Gérard and Prudent authority as trustees to dispose of their property and satisfy the creditors. In January 1858 the first group crossed the frozen Mississippi and headed west to Adams County, Iowa, over the "Mormon Trail" in canvas-covered wagons.[4]

Gérard and Prudent gazed at the vacant Temple Square. They knew that in the nadir of the economic depression they would be lucky if they realized anything near the value of the community assets which, according to the last inventory, amounted to an estimated $60,000. They advertised twenty-five "*emplacements*" for sale, seventeen of which were in the Square: eight apartments of more than a hundred rooms, a refectory, sewing shops, various workshops, a forge, stables, and a school. After all the sales had been completed, Thomas Gregg, editor of the Hamilton *Representative,* reported that "the Temple block, with the four frame buildings . . . and the mill and appendages" brought an aggregate of over $21,000. The trustees had received only one-third of what they had expected.[5]

Since their total debts by that time amounted to over $32,000, the trustees were left with an $11,800 obligation. To cover this liability they took out a loan for that amount at 10 percent interest from William Shepherd, an English-born railroad investor and banker from the town of Jerseyville. They put up the 3,100 acres in Iowa, valued at $1.25 an acre, as security. On September 8, 1860, the last step in the relocation of the Nauvoo Icaria was taken when the Iowa community received an official charter of incorporation from that state designating it as an "agricultural society."[6]

The early days of the Corning colony had been grim. It had no roads, let alone rail and river transportation, and its closest supply center was seventy miles away at St. Joseph, Missouri. The first reports to Nauvoo complained that they had to live like Indians and trappers. As one man put it in a letter sent back in the winter of 1853, this was no place for the faint of heart. Just to get to the place, he lamented, he had to hike sixteen days over crude footpaths. He had to sleep under the stars, just like the unfortunate Advance Guards in Texas, and cook meals over campfires. At the colony they lived in log huts with dirt floors covered by straw. And to get essential provisions such as salt and sugar, two men had to make a month-long trip in ox carts to St. Joseph. Emile Fugier, who came there at the age of fifteen with his mother, later remembered that to survive under such conditions "it was necessary to have amazing endurance." No children were born in those years because, Fugier said, couples were just "too poor to dream about repopulating."[7]

By the summer of 1853 a band of fourteen men and four women had set up a permanent camp on the south bank of the East Nodaway River about a mile south of Queen City, a new settlement of American families who, like the Icarians, lived in log cabins. Laboring under a sweltering sun and suffering bouts of fever, they cleared fifty-six acres and brought in a small harvest of eighty tons of hay. By September, with the help of work crews from Nauvoo, they had started working on a log kitchen-dining hall, a fruit cellar, and smoke house. They built a kiln and made bricks with materials from a nearby limestone pit. The only farmer among them, a man named Krisinger, saw to it that they erected a stable and a chicken coop. By the end of the year twenty-six Icarians were living at the outpost utopia.

Daily life was hard and monotonous. Meals were always the same: cheese and corn mush for breakfast, boiled potatoes for lunch, and meat and cornbread at dinner. On the Nodaway River they built a "basin" where, one of the men reported, "our *citoyennes* go and wash the laundry."[8] By the spring of 1854 they had finished ten more buildings, two-room cabins with dirt floors and fireplaces, designated as family huts. Their furniture, of black walnut, was rudimentary: a table, a few chairs, a bed, and wall pegs for clothing. They used glass, carted from St. Joseph, for the small windows, which the women decorated with muslin curtains. That fall they began the construction of a saw and grist mill on a channel of the Nodaway.[9]

In April 1855 another twelve men, seven women, and six children came out from Nauvoo. Now they had a shoemaker, Joseph Mignot; a harness maker, Michel Brumme; a baker, Pierre Caillé; and a blacksmith, Jacques Cotteron. An anonymous traveler who came through their village in April 1857 described "a population of about sixty persons [in a] neat and compact" community with four hundred acres under cultivation. He said that the Icarians were a "frugal and industrious, moral and temperate people." He praised "their industry and enterprise, to say nothing of their liberality in dealing with travelers." This characteristic, he remarked, was "in strange contrast with the apparent instinctive disposition to swindle emigrants that are dominant traits of their American neighbors."[10]

The 1860 census and their own inventory, dated December 31 of that year, showed that they owned 366 acres of cultivated land and 2,759 acres of timber and prairie grass worth $31,000, and farm machinery valued at $1,258. Their livestock included horses (19), dairy cattle (35), "other cattle" (37), oxen (29), sheep (130), and pigs (300), all together valued at $4,100. Other items in the inventory, more specific than the census, were 400 books of the Nauvoo library and a steam engine that did not work. They had produced about 2,495 bushels of corn, 500 bushels of oats, 300 pounds of wool, 250 pounds of butter, 30 tons of hay, and some sorghum molasses. They had slaughtered a few cattle that brought in about $32. Their financial situation, though, was shaky. There was no one to whom they might sell any of the products. By 1862 their debts had soared to an estimated figure of between $15,500 and $17,561.[11]

Ironically, the Civil War, the calamity that destroyed Cheltenham, saved the Iowa Icaria. Only two of their young men volunteered to serve in the Union army; the rest stayed and worked. Beginning in 1863, Union troops moving between the Des Moines and Missouri rivers regularly stopped there for supplies. It was the only place short of St. Joseph to purchase food for themselves and grains for their horses and mules. Federal purchasing agents at St. Joseph started to pay premium prices for their wool. The income was a godsend. Their "Statement of Revenue . . . Since 1860" showed that by the beginning of 1865 they had enough cash to pay off their creditors. By July 1867 they owned "1,729 acres of land, all paid for except for about $800, . . . which they planned to pay off by the first of the year.[12] By then outside visitors, curious about the village of wooden-shoed, French-speaking farmers, began to come to the colony and write down their impressions and observations. These accounts, a reminiscence of Marie Marchand Ross, the first child born in that Icaria, and surviving Adams County records tell a good deal about what life was like in this frontier farming community.[13]

Icaria had changed considerably by 1870. It was prosperous. In 1861, for instance, the Icarians had paid only $135.38 in taxes; in 1870 the county collected $629.82. They now had 700 acres in crops (corn and wheat mainly) and 400 in pasture and timber. Their livestock had increased to 40 horses, 140 head of cattle, and 600 sheep. The C.B.& Q. railroad now ran through the northern part of their land and connected them with Omaha.[14] Just like Nauvoo, they had a general assembly, a president, and a *Gérance* in charge of industry, agriculture, lodging, and clothing. But these Icarians wanted no reappearance of the authoritarian rule of Cabet's utopia. Instead, they empowered their president only to represent the community to the outside world, not to rule it. And the *Gérance* could do only what the Assembly, at its annual meeting, specifically authorized it to do. Or, as Sauva, now relocated at Corning from Cheltenham, commented, "our system is pure democracy and we experience no difficulty in its application." "Our officers," he stated, "are elected to execute the decisions of the General Assembly and have no other power."[15]

Marie Marchand Ross at the age of
sixteen. Center for Icarian Studies,
Western Illinois University.

Marchand, the President for all but three years until 1876, was an
even-tempered administrator. Albert Shaw, who visited the community
in the 1870s to gather information for his doctoral dissertation, interviewed
the man a number of times. He found him well educated, "serene and
kindly in manner, lofty in his standards of right and duty, almost a mystic
in his devotion to communism and the welfare of mankind . . . a true type
of altruist." The women, however, were as restricted in their power as
they had been at Nauvoo. In the Assembly, they had only the right to
participate in discussions and could vote on just three special questions:
admission-rejection matters, constitutional changes, and selection of the
gérant in charge of housing and clothing, who could be a woman.[16]
    The Corning Icarians, however, looked the same as they had at Nauvoo.
The women wore dresses made out of calico and dark blue Amana cloth,
purchased from that religious community located about a hundred miles
to the east. The men wore farmer's denim overalls. Their diet had
improved over the bland fare of the log cabin days. Breakfast, taken in
their homes without the bugle call and whiskey for the men, was bread
and butter and *café au lait*. At noon in the refectory they ate the day's
main course of meat, fresh vegetables, and milk or water. They announced
this meal with a dinner bell. At supper they sat down again in the
refectory, as they wished, to a serving of stew.[17]
    The Corning utopia looked different from Nauvoo or Cheltenham

because families lived in private homes. They put up a row of frame houses, surrounded by flowers and shrubs, on the east and north sides of the community. The average home was a one-and-a-half-story structure about twenty-two feet by fourteen feet, with an attic and a basement. The refectory functioned as a kitchen, winter storage space, and dining hall—with nine round tables, eight to ten people at each. On the walls of this main room Schroeder and his sons painted landscapes topped by rows of women's heads with curling locks, joined by garlands of vines and flowers running along the ceiling edge as a border. Over the door they sketched in huge letters "Equality." At the other end above a fireplace they placed the word "Liberty." The second story of the refectory, reached by a circular stairway, was used as a recreation hall for the men and had a billiard table. In the other half of this room they placed the library with ceiling-to-floor shelves. Icaria also had a bakery, a pharmacy, run by Marchand, a laundry, shoe shop, blacksmith forge, corn barn, and slaughterhouse.[18]

In these simple structures the Icarians carried on the daily routines of communal work. Women were the seamstresses, cooks, and laundresses. Teenage girls hand-stitched the clothes under the direction of an embroiderer named Mourot, whose husband, Eugène, was the *gérant* of industry. They marked each piece, including socks, with a family emblem for identification at wash time. Ignacio Montaldo's wife, a professional milliner in France, made dress hats. Madame Marchand wove their work hats from straw with the help of the girls; enough of them were made to sell to nearby farmers. In the main floor of the refectory two women set and cleared the tables. In the basement, two other women cleaned the dishes and, with the help of a couple of men, washed the dirty linen and clothes. After the laundry was cleaned they sorted the folded and ironed clothes into family bundles and put them into baskets for delivery to the homes. Whatever their assigned task, the women knew that they would rotate jobs every Sunday.[19]

Some of the men were craftsmen. Joseph Mignot and Jean Meindre, both in their late fifties, made the sabots or outdoor wooden workshoes. Michel Brumme stitched the high-topped boots and other items such as belts, straps, and harnesses. Jacques Cotteron was the blacksmith, and Pierre Caillé the baker. Marchand, in addition to his duties as president and pharmacist, made the soap, turpentine, wax for candles, and shoe polish. Most men, though, worked in agriculture, boys alongside their fathers. But the Icarians were not efficient farmers, and one visitor, A. Massoulard, a French Shaker, thought their methods "barbarous." For example, instead of using manure for fertilizer they dumped it into the Nodaway River or just let it sit in piles indefinitely. They knew nothing of

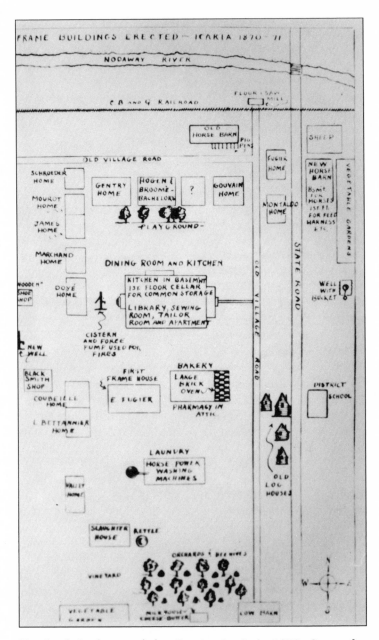

Sketch of the layout of the Corning Icaria in 1870. Center for Icarian Studies, Western Illinois University.

crop rotation and planted corn and wheat in the same fields season after season. The only thing they did well, in Massoulard's opinion, was breed livestock. He was impressed with the number of fine horses, pigs, cattle, and sheep. Abandoning the proscription against tobacco, the men smoked, but the community did not purchase tobacco as part of its supplies: smokers were "reduced to cultivate [it] in their spare time." Four men ran a combined flour and saw mill. All in all, the community was based predominantly upon agriculture, reluctant to enlarge the profitable milling operation, and unenthusiastic about hard work in general. Trouble lay ahead.[20]

While the men and women worked at their tasks and the toddlers played at home with their mothers, the rest of the children went to school. Their first school, a crude log cabin, was replaced in 1870 by a county schoolhouse within walking distance just east of the colony.[21] Each morning the seventeen-year-old Hortense Montaldo, and later William Moore, a former Shaker who joined Icaria in 1875, led the children in physical exercises. Then came singing lessons, followed by instruction in reading, spelling, and arithmetic for the younger Icarians and, for the older ones, chemistry, natural philosophy, physiology and hygiene, and geography. After regular hours Schroeder gave all the children drawing lessons.[22]

By the early 1870s the Iowa Icarians were for the most part enjoying themselves. Their simple and wholesome life in many ways resembled that of their Amana neighbors. Both communities insisted on the surrender of all property. They both were agricultural villages aiming to produce "enough food for the society's population and, in addition, raw materials for various business enterprises." And both societies augmented food production with raising of livestock, mainly sheep.[23]

Of course, the two societies had fundamental differences in values and goals. For example, the Icarians never embraced celibacy; far from it, they extolled married life. Icarian education was the antithesis of the Amana system since it was preeminently intellectual, artistic, and moral, while the Amana school was geared only "To guide and train Amana youth in the 'so important ways of God,'" as Bertha Shambaugh wrote in her history of that colony. It "requires unflagging energy; and so the Amana school has no vacation." It was, consequently, devoted to prayer, psalm singing, and vocational training.[24]

Certainly Amana had nothing like the cultural and recreational diversions of the Icarians. For example, every other Saturday the Icarians tried to produce an operetta. That day they cleared the refectory tables and used the west end of the hall as a stage. Although the performance was always in French, which they still spoke in the community, they invited

Americans from Corning or neighboring farms to join them. On other Saturday evenings they held dances, with a small band of trumpets, French horns, flutes, and clarinets providing the music.

On Sunday afternoon Sauva started the *Cours icarien* in imitation of the one he had known at Cheltenham and the older Icarians remembered from Nauvoo. Sauva's *Cours icarien* was predictable. He always read from Cabet's writings. Next came songs and recitations of poems. Now and then adults gave lectures on Icarian principles or recalled past events in New Orleans, Texas, Nauvoo, and Cheltenham. Marie Marchand Ross wrote that in these "inspirational" meetings she "enjoyed learning new songs and poems and listening to talks on all subjects." Oneidan William Hinds, who lived for a while at the colony, confided to the editor of the *American Socialist* that entering the refectory on a Sunday afternoon he heard "selections from the writings of their great apostle, Etienne Cabet, recitals by the young, or songs, perchance, which would stir your Socialite enthusiasm." He was particularly struck by the recital of fifteen-year-old Henriette Vallet who, he said, "put great expression into the words:

> It is indeed time that hatreds were forgotten;
> That all people rallied under a single flag;
> The way to salvation for us is smooth.
> The great liberty of which humanity dreams,
> Like a new radiant sun, rises
> On the horizon before us.[25]

On summer days they went on picnics where "nearly all the colony folks would go in several big wagons." Just as on the promenades in the woods near the Mississippi of the Nauvoo years, they packed a lunch and headed for a cool spot near the Nodaway River, where women spread blankets and men cast for spring trout. They put up rope swings for the children. A typical picnic included French-fried potatoes, flapjacks—a crude imitation of crepes made with rough flour and eggs—pies and cakes, and lemonade or coffee. Fish, fried over an open fire, along with the flapjacks was the main course. After lunch the children and young people played games like hide-and-seek or climbed trees or picked flowers. Some just swung back and forth on the swings. "When it began to get late," Marie Marchand Ross wrote, "the horn was blown again to warn everyone that it was time to go home, and all who had wandered away came to the camp as fast as they could." On the return trip "the way was made lively by songs and laughter and all planned to have another such fine outing again soon."[26]

July 4 was a festive mixture of Franco-American patriotism. It began the evening before at the mill, where they raised an American flag to a volley of rifle fire while the band played the "Star Spangled Banner." Sauva had the children cut out letters from red and blue paper and paste them on the refectory walls to spell out "Equality," "Fraternity," or quotations from Cabet's writings such as "All for each and each for all." On the morning of the Fourth everyone mounted ox wagons, decorated with red, white, and blue bunting, for a three-mile trip to Corning to watch a parade. One wagon carried all of the young girls, decked out in white dresses with red and blue sashes. Once in town, Marie Marchand Ross remembered, "they saw lemonade and ice cream stands, dancing platforms, speakers' stands, and the like, but in all this the Icarians took no part." "They remained grouped together, spread their lunch on the grass and just took in the sights." After the parade and fireworks display, late in the afternoon, they returned to the community and held a banquet for themselves and any American friends who wished to join them. When the meal was finished and the tables cleared and moved to the sides of the room, the music began and a dance, again open to all, lasted into the night.[27]

The other major holiday, this one exclusively Icarian, was the February 3 commemoration of the departure of the First Advance Guard. It was a vital reassurance of their legitimacy and their continuity with the original goals of Cabet's Icaria, "the greatest day . . . of the year." It reminded them to recommit themselves to the principles upon which Icaria had been built: unity, brotherhood, democracy, equality. Plans were always made well in advance, starting just after Christmas, by selecting French plays and songs for the occasion.[28] Marie Marchand Ross recalled one such event. It started at noon with a huge banquet in the refectory, "the best the community could afford," topped off with wine and black coffee sweetened with sugar instead of sorghum. After a dessert of pies and cakes they sang Icarian songs such as *"Le chant du départ"* (The Song of Departure) or *"Partons pour Icarie"* (Let's Go to Icaria). Then came toasts and speeches. A. A. Marchand, the only one left who had been at the Peters Concession, vividly recounted the hopes, hardships, and horrors of that odyssey. Others told of Cabet's life, his exile in London, and the reasons for leaving France. This solemn interlude finished, they placed benches in front of a makeshift stage and, with a fire blazing in the hearth and the room mellowed by the glow of candles, they sat down to watch four-year-old Marie recite the fable *La lumière sous le boisseau* (The Light under the Bushel) and enjoy a play selected for that evening. After the performance the adults and young people danced to the music of their orchestra until bedtime.[29]

At the Corning Icaria cooperation was the rule. Gone were the regimented job assignments Cabet deemed so essential at Nauvoo. Marchand, a genial patriarch, saw no need for the uniformity and obedience that Cabet had almost instinctively expected. Gone too were the internal divisions. The blaring brass bugle that had sounded reveille at Nauvoo had been replaced with "a real cow's horn with a mouthpiece."30

The women, although as disfranchised as before and still doing the same domestic chores, showed none of their earlier quarrelsomeness. Marie Marchand Ross described a daily routine of chatting, sometimes singing, taking turns doing the dishes, sewing and washing clothes, making cheese, and picking strawberries. She detailed how they often left Icaria to visit with their American friends. "Going outside among strangers in this way," she wrote, "the women of the colony found it necessary to follow some of the styles of the world." Still many women remained more or less like Madame Deffauday, who although an "invalid . . . not able to work, and suffering most of the time," nevertheless was "really a genius, all love and spirit."31

Young Icarians continuously interacted with Americans. Throughout *Child of Icaria* Marie Marchand Ross described how these outsiders were regularly invited to their dances and vice versa. "The young people," she wrote, "were naturally eager for amusements of all kinds . . . and they contrived to arrange for dances, picnics, games, etc., but there were so few young people in the colony that they began associating more and more with the outside world." "Indeed," she confessed, "there was as much visiting back and forth and even staying with friends over weekends without troubling to ask the Assembly's permission." President Marchand had no objection whatever that his daughter and her friends wanted to be with Americans. And when Will Ross asked if he could take Marie alone "to a dance at Pete Humbert's the next night," Marchand "said it was all right." He said, "I thought that if a young man was honest enough to ask me like that, he must be all right and I had no fear of entrusting my daughter to him." Americans "from neighboring farms who came to the colony dances," Marie remembered, "often came to visit on Sundays." And on "weekend evenings together at the common dining hall they sang, played games, or danced."32

The Icarians tolerated a lot of coming and going of entire families. The Montaldos left and returned. Gérard and his family stayed at Icaria until 1863, when he decided to buy a farm for himself in Adams County. Yet he often came to the community and remained close to his compatriots until his death. The Gauvain family joined the colony and "later left to go back to the outside world" but often returned for long visits. George Rouser arrived with the Gauvains and departed, only to return a few years later. The American John Dye, a printer wounded in the Civil War, after living with the Shakers, the Oneida Community, and the Amana colonies, became an Icarian in 1876 and started the colony newspaper *La revue icarienne*. He left two years later, without any formalities, to live in an Old Soldier's home in Norfolk, Virginia.[33]

The community had to hire six American men on a permanent basis to do field work, because most of the young Icarian males left the colony rather than spending their adult lives harvesting corn and slopping hogs. "They had not been bred to the farm," Marie Marchand Ross wrote, "and they aspired to making their way in the outside world in some professional career." "It was a great loss to the community," she lamented, "for they had brought new life there." In addition to the American workers the Icarians welcomed a constant stream of visitors. These notetakers, she said, "were of all kinds, cranks, students of French or students of economics, members of other communities, reporters from neighboring towns or cities, and even persons from abroad."[34]

By the mid 1870s, however, some visitors detected beneath the Icarian cooperation and congeniality a growing friction between two groups, each with different opinions of what the community should be. On one side were the older Icarians, led by Marchand, who wanted little change in their pleasant pastoral life. On the other side were younger men, calling themselves "Progressives," and their families who had arrived at Icaria after 1870, or, in a few instances, the sons and daughters of the older Icarians, who demanded fundamental alterations in community rules and attitudes. They were enthusiastic "Internationalists," communists fired up by the Paris Commune uprising of 1871. They wanted Icaria to continue the fight for the rights of workers everywhere, just as Cabet had done when he led the original emigrants to America. To accomplish this goal they felt they had to revitalize an Icaria that had gone to seed, a utopia that had lost its fervor and commitment to the salvation of humanity.[35]

Among the most vocal of the new arrivals were Emile Péron, Simon Dereure, and Alexis Tanguy. Péron, the youngest, had been active in Paris in the communist movement and in workingmen's clubs. He arrived at Icaria with Dereure, a thirty-eight-year-old shoemaker and musician who had served in the Commune. And Tanguy, a forty-two-year-old artist, had fled Paris for his life because of his part in the insurrection.[36] Once at Corning they immediately set about to instill an active intellectual life in what they saw as a stagnating community of stolid corn farmers. Specifically, they wanted to change the *Cours icarien* to focus on social problems and how Icarians might solve them. They wanted debate, not amusement; discussion, not bland recitation. The Assembly, controlled by the older Icarians, refused to discuss the matter.[37]

Detail of a painting of the Corning Icaria about 1875 by the German artist
J. C. Schroeder, showing the refectory, shops, private homes, and orchard.
Center for Icarian Studies, Western Illinois University.

In 1876 another fight broke out over the admission of socialist Jules Leroux and his wife. They had arrived that year to be near their two sons, Paul and Pierre, then provisional members. The senior Leroux made no secret of his disdain for the flaccid Icarian idealism. He sarcastically described Marchand and his colony as living an "existence of small farmers, lively more or less, associates in growing pigs, sheep, legumes, vines and cereal," uniting for the lofty goal of "mutual assistance in self-confidence and in shearing." What a shocking contrast to his dream of a "Humanity-city" where everyone enjoyed "the fruits of the earth, the products of industry, the factory and its machines, where art and science equally belong to everyone . . . a society where there is an end to monopoly, inequality, oppression, and misery." To top it off he brought along a printing press and started to publish these ideas in his own paper called *L'Étoile du Kansas et de l'Iowa.*[38]

Marchand and the older Icarians did not know what Leroux was talking about, and whatever it was, they wanted none of it. First things first, Marchand said. The crops had to be planted and harvested, the mill kept running, animals taken care of, bills paid. Jules, pressured by his sons, petitioned for admission. The Assembly turned him down. It next refused to grant Pierre Leroux full membership. Paul, though, had already passed the six-month probation period and was a member in full standing. The Progressives were furious.[39]

Right after the controversy over Leroux's admission, the Progressives broached another bone of contention, the "petite gardens." These gardens, they claimed, were not gardens at all but large plots of land, some about a half acre, that contradicted Icaria's renunciation of private property. Although started innocently enough in the 1860s as a means to plant seed vines and vegetables they had become, Fugier said, a conspicuous scandal. Péron insisted that in the upcoming harvest all such gardens should be stripped. It was the principle of the thing, he said.[40]

Next, the Progressives criticized "retrogressive acts of the majority" who, in defiance of democracy, had no "regard for the rights and opinions of women." The women must vote. If the Assembly would not enfranchise every adult regardless of sex, Péron said, the older Icarians should consider "an amicable separation." Marchand and the "Conservatives" (the name the older group now adopted) flatly refused to take up the request. That being the case, Péron said, the Progressives wanted out, one way or another.

On September 26, 1877, Péron lectured the Assembly. He said that they were withdrawing and explained why: the discriminatory admissions policy, the disgraceful petite gardens, and the outrageous franchise. Sauva, supporting Marchand, offered the Assembly a statement that

listed the Progressives by name and disputed their allegations. He identified as "separatists" Péron, Dereure, Tanguy, Paul Leroux, and seven
others, including Marchand's son Alexis. The Assembly adopted Sauva's
statement by a vote of nineteen to thirteen. Tanguy, speaking for the
Progressives, said that because the majority refused to accept the idea of
a peaceful separation, he had no doubt about their real intention. Rather
than compromise, they would destroy Icaria, start a revolution by forceful
division. So be it. The Progressives, he warned, would no longer take care
of the livestock, do farm work, or participate in communal life. The two
groups left the dining hall in silence.[41]

During the first week of October 1877 the Progressives wrote their
Social Program and *Reciprocal Engagement* and asked for signatures.
The first document asserted that a true Icarian must dedicate "his
knowledge, energy, and existence to the general interest and the cause of
the people and not to the interest of some individual or to a mediocre
community." The Progressives demanded that women be given equal
rights with men. Icarian rules should be based upon scientific demonstration, experience, discussion, truth, and reason, not on blind faith in
Cabet's writings. They wanted an end to the rigorous admissions requirements. Anyone of good moral character should be allowed in. They
wanted a wider distribution of propaganda to the cities of America and
Europe so that Icaria could be a beacon to "the suffering and oppressed."
They wanted the colony to stop concentrating on agriculture and begin
craft industries to sell products in Corning, because only by diversifica-
tion could it be "great and prosperous." They wanted to replace individual family homes, the "source of inequality, selfishness, and individualism,"
with communal buildings. The *Reciprocal Engagement,* much shorter
than the *Social Program,* stated that they would continue the real Icaria,
after the existing "pseudo-community" had been dissolved.[42]

At the October 6 meeting of the Assembly, the Progressives formally
moved to dissolve Icaria into two "autonomous branches," each living in
separate locations. At this point the Conservatives capitulated. Since the
Progressives would not work to sustain the community it faced imminent
destruction anyway. Besides, Marchand believed that their *Social Program,*
if implemented, would wreck the Icaria that many of them had taken
twenty years to build. So the two sides selected a commission of three
men from each camp to choose the separate sites.[43]

During the winter and spring of 1878 some of the Progressives, feeling
that they had been ostracized, just packed up and left. Tanguy went off to
make a living as a house painter. Dereure departed and opened a shoe
repair shop in Corning. Others found work as farm hands. The Conservatives retaliated. They refused to turn over to the remaining Progressives

any food or supplies, the old Nauvoo trick. The Progressives then hired lawyers and filed suit in the Circuit Court of Adams County. They claimed that Icaria was a corporation and the law gave them a legal right to community goods "proportional to their needs." The Conservatives retained their own lawyers. They charged that the Progressives were ruining the corporation. The Conservatives set up guards at the work-shops and temporarily locked the warehouses. In the meantime, before the court could rule on the petitions, Icaria operated like a poorly rehearsed morality play. Each party took turns using the refectory for meals. Every morning each group harnessed the horses to work its appropriated parts of the fields. Each side gathered its share of meat, fruit, and vegetables from the now unlocked warehouse. Each group took wine from the kitchen.[44]

In an atmosphere of continuous acrimony the six-man commission started to meet. But its efforts collapsed. The three Conservatives on the commission were intransigent. They would never accept the Progressives' claim that the older Icarians were the ones who had to leave. Such a suggestion, Charles Levy said, was preposterous, "an insult" effecting "supreme disdain." "You young fellows," he shouted, are the ones who must move out! "You have your youth, enthusiasm, capabilities." "You have the work habits to clear the fields." With all these advantages, "you want to sit still, here on what we have created?"[45]

On November 24 the Progressives brought their own relocation plan before the Assembly. Péron, their spokesman, suggested a division of the property in two equal portions. The Conservatives went wild. "The young fellows want their part! Their part!" they screamed. "But what is their part? What have they done for Icaria?" "What value is there in a stay of two years for Paul Leroux, of eighteen months for Laforgue and Péron. . . . during their presence in Icaria, have they been able to add to its patrimony?" The Progressives stopped trying to reason with them. They resolved instead to rely only on legal remedies. All further discussion, Péron said, must be in front of a judge who would, he predicted, end everything by ordering a dissolving of the corporation and a liquidation of all communal assets.[46]

The final battle started on January 14, 1878, when the Conservatives, nineteen of them, appeared before the Circuit Court of Adams County and presented to the judge a written statement. It offered cooperation with the "separatists" to restore to Icaria its "good disposition" and "to repair the material and moral damage" that they had done. But if the "separatists" were resolved to continue their present course of action, then the "elders" of the community were prepared to give each of them a departure gift of $100. They argued that when this gift was added to the

Alexis Armel Marchand about 1880.
Center for Icarian Studies, Western
Illinois University.

refunds the Progressives would be entitled to under the constitution, the
Progressives would receive over $8,000. The Conservatives, of course,
would stay in possession of the communal property. The judge gave the
Progressives until February 10 to respond.[47]

They refused to respond. Instead, on February 21 they published an
article in the *Corning Union* that declared they were ready to submit all
matters to a jury trial. Sauva, who by that time was acting as the leader of
the Conservatives in the face of Marchand's unwillingness to get further
involved in the fight, convened a meeting at the refectory on March 2.
They rejected a jury trial as too time-consuming and expensive. Besides,
they suspected that American juries lacked knowledge of Icarian principles.
They suggested instead that the court appoint a board of arbitrators
made up of former Icarians. The Progressives said yes, but no. The idea
of arbitration was acceptable but they wanted the board made up of
Americans. It was a standoff. During the spring and summer, while
awaiting the court's ruling, both sides claimed, in print, to be the true
heirs of Cabet. Sauva put forth the Conservatives' view in *La crise
icarienne.* The Progressives printed their version of the story in a newspaper called *La Jeune Icarie.*[48]

The judge rejected arbitration and ordered a jury trial. In August both
parties were present at that session of the Circuit Court. A lawyer named

Davis represented the Conservatives, and A. M. Mac Dill was the lawyer for the Progressives. On August 9 Davis argued against dissolving the community. He claimed that the separatists were dishonest propagandists who wanted to use Icaria to circulate world-wide communist propaganda, an emotional point before an Iowa jury. He said that they planned to open stores in Corning in violation of the intent of the charter, a sensitive point for local businessmen, who did not welcome competition from an organized community. In sum, the separatists were troublemakers who were trying to take Icaria "far beyond that which was outlined in its charter of incorporation." The Conservatives, Davis concluded, by a perfectly legal procedure in conformity to their own constitution, have employed the means to end this "menace," namely expulsion.[49]

MacDill, for the Progressives, pointed out that the older Icarians needed a two-thirds majority of the voting members of the Assembly to expel anyone, and their number, nineteen, was not two-thirds of the thirty-two adult males in the colony. Moreover, under Iowa statutes, the Icarian community had no right to exist at all because it had in fact violated the law. It had operated a sawmill for profit in defiance of its charter that had created only an agricultural corporation. It also had allowed private property in the form of the petite gardens. So the charter must be voided and the assets distributed equally among all members of the community.

On August 16, the jury deliberated from eleven in the morning until six that evening. It decided that the community had violated state corporation laws by (1) operating an industry in the saw mill and raising sheep for selling wool; (2) allowing two Icarians, Schroeder and Tanguy, to sell their services as painters to Corning families who wanted their homes decorated; and (3) failing to charge some members the stipulated subscription mentioned in the charter. On Saturday the judge declared the charter abrogated and named three American trustees to distribute all community property. The court also named two Icarians, a Progressive and a Conservative, to represent the interests of their respective parties.[50]

The trustees, in addition to dividing the colony's assets, implemented an "understanding" that each side would reorganize physically into separate communities. The older group would remain on the original site and claim the western half of the land. The Progressives would put up another Icaria on the eastern half of the property and would locate their buildings a mile away from the Conservatives. The mill could be used by everyone. The legacy of the split was bitter. As one observer of the events put it, "one of the saddest phases of the Icarian strife is that it has made enemies of the same household, setting wife against husband and children against parents, and widely sundered ties that should have grown stronger with each succeeding year."[51]

TEN

The Final Icarias:
Young, Speranza, and New

There can be little doubt that the split of the Corning colony in 1878 marked a turning point in the history of Icarianism. Over the next twenty years, the dream of the "community of goods" faded. Three times, in small groups, they tried to keep Icaria alive as they thought Cabet would have wanted, and each time they ended up in a community farther removed from what Cabet had wanted or, at best, what they had known at Nauvoo. Nevertheless, in August 1878, when the court rendered its verdict, both sides confidently believed that they would succeed in the creation of a utopia.[1]

Much remained to be done that year, however. The most important matter was to determine how much property the Progressives could claim. The trustees determined that distribution would be based on the length of residence and the amount each person had donated upon admission. Both sides, anxious to get things settled, told the trustees to proceed. They gave the Progressives over one-half of the land, about 1,204 acres, designated as the "East," along with joint use of the saw and flour mill; the Conservatives were allocated the "West," including the village itself and cultivated fields and orchards.[2]

The older Icarians rejected the trustees' ruling that, since their half contained most of the community's assets, minus the mills, they should assume all the debts. While the Conservatives were happy to stay in their homes and shops, with only nineteen adult males they could not handle a debt of $7,888. The Progressives, led by Fugier, then offered the Conservatives $1,500 if they would switch parcels. On February 3, 1879, Marchand agreed. Within a month the trustees worked out the details. The Old Guard consented to move within two-and-a-half years to the vacant prairie land allocated to them. Six months after the removal, the Progressives would pay them a $1,500 displacement indemnity. The trustees then divided equally the $7,108 worth of personal property.

Final documents of the separation were signed quickly and the court gave its approval on March 11, 1879.[3]

On April 1, 1879, the Progressives filed the "Articles of Incorporation" with the Adams County Recorder. This document shows the pains these Icarians took to avoid the mistakes of the first Iowa colony. They were careful to stipulate a comprehensive purpose of incorporation: to provide mutual support, to provide for the comfort of the old, sick, and decrepit, to transact business of "all kinds," to build schools, and to develop the fine arts. The charter required that compensation upon leaving be $100 times whatever longevity formula the corporation might later decide upon.[4]

In October, after some considerable discussion, they adopted a constitution drafted by Péron that created "Young Icaria." His elaborate, disjointed, philosophical preamble laid out the historical and theoretical basis of the community. Péron condemned exploitation, theocracies, ignorance, autocracy, and usurpations. He praised the "inevitable triumph" of the family, individual equality, and the sentiment of liberty, all of them implied in the formula "to each according to his needs; from each according to his abilities." He ended the preamble with an appeal for renewed dedication in the fight against the enemies of mankind and continued commitment to work for perfection, peace, and happiness.

Péron wrote that their Icaria was based upon the highest concepts of equality, liberty, fraternity, unity, and the rule of law. Celibacy was "considered as a transgression against the law of nature." There was to be no personal property; each member was a "co-proprietor of everything." They abolished the presidency and the board of directors. Only the General Assembly, in which both men and women voted, was sovereign. The Assembly annually elected four "delegates" as an executive branch to look after "the administering of details" and to spread the "principles which tend to the political, philosophical, and economic emancipation of mankind."[5]

On December 8 the Assembly decided the rules on admission and withdrawal. The regulations, also drafted by Péron, cautioned newcomers not to be seduced by "inordinate enthusiasm for the beauty of the Icarian system." Beware of illusions. Be very much aware of the "inconveniences" of living in a communal society. Do not be swept away by Cabet's writings, because, Péron wrote, "it is a long distance from the desire to the realization, from the principle to the fact, from the theory to the practical embodiment." Everyone admitted to Icaria had to surrender all property to the "social fund without power of recall." No fixed monetary deposits or contributions were required. After a six-month probationary period an individual became an Icarian by majority approval of the Assembly. One could leave at any time by giving a written statement to that effect one month in advance of the departure. A provisional Icarian would get back $100, but a full member received $100 plus what the Assembly decided to allow "under the title of gift, such sum of money or such property as the financial condition and interest of the community . . . shall at the time permit it to give."[6]

For a brief time the reorganized utopia seemed to flourish. Five new families joined as "provisional members," including two barbers, the eighteen-year-old Alix Gillet, and Armand Dehay, a thirty-two-year-old socialist and son-in-law of Jules Leroux. By the end of 1880 seventy-two names were listed as living in Young Icaria. Péron edited their newspaper, *La Jeune Icarie.*[7]

That fall they harvested a bountiful crop of corn and wheat and an ample supply of fruit from the orchards and vineyards. At Corning they went ahead with plans to start a retail outlet for straw hats and brooms and to operate a blacksmith's shop and a shoe repair shop. They reduced the debt of $7,888 to $4,000. Péron taught the children in the schoolhouse across the road to the east. They improved and expanded the refectory. They planted ninety acres of new ground, purchased two horses, and bought more machinery. Their standard of living and their cultural life increased with a variety of activities that went on almost continually. They held dances, performed comedies, and gave musical concerts by the river. At the Corning gazebo the band played summer concerts that brought in altogether about fifty dollars.[8]

But Young Icaria proved to be too divergent, attracting people of incompatible backgrounds, experiences, and expectations. As the historian Albert Shaw, who interviewed these Icarians, put it, "There were too many clever men, and no one with a gift of leadership sufficient to assimilate and unify the group. . . . there was no real 'solidarity.' "[9] Moreover, while most of the men were willing to work in skilled crafts and commercial activities, they abhorred the hot and dirty routine of planting, weeding, and harvesting. When it became evident that they had to do farm chores just to keep the colony going, the enthusiasm waned. By 1881 many of them had left.[10]

By then their debt had risen again to over $7,000 and their Corning shops had shut down. Western Iowa, especially from January to March, seemed more than ever oppressive and bleak. Armand Dehay lamented that, "seeing that we cannot realize a beautiful and great community in Iowa because of the climate and topographic situation," the only option was to look elsewhere. He did. Early in 1881, having read glowing accounts of the popularity of socialism in San Francisco, he took his family there and lived temporarily with his brother Theodore. Dehay met with Emile Bée, a leader of the Socialist Labor Party. Bée encouraged him to relocate the community in the area, where they would find strong support for Icarian doctrines and ready markets for their products and produce. Dehay wrote back to the Leroux brothers, Paul and Pierre, and encouraged them, and others, to come to California.[11]

That spring the Lerouxs joined Dehay. After inspecting several sites in the Napa Valley they decided to transplant the young Icaria, or what was left of it, to Cloverdale, a small town eighty miles north of San Francisco. They purchased on credit, with their Iowa property as collateral, an 885-acre ranch on the Russian River for $15,000. They called their new utopia "Speranza," after the masthead of Jules Leroux's defunct newspaper *L'Espérance*. On October 15, 1884, twenty-four adults affixed their names to a Certificate of Co-Partnership and filed it in the county courthouse at Santa Rosa.[12]

Their first concern was how to pay the mortgage. They built a sawmill and prepared forty-five acres for grape plants. They put in one hundred acres of wheat and a five-acre orchard of peach trees. Three hundred acres were set aside as pasture. By 1883, with the sale of their Iowa lands, they had reduced the debt to about $6,000. But their goal of a self-sufficient community eluded the tiny band. Péron, still in Iowa, lamented that "their dream of an ideal society is beyond their capacity" and that they probably "must disavow" their most cherished convictions. Péron was right. They just did not have enough Icarians to operate a community, and, worse still, they were unable to recruit new members.

But size was only one of a litany of problems that fell, one after another, upon Icaria Speranza. For example, they tried renting shops in Cloverdale to sell their produce, but this venture fell through. Although the Iowa land initially had brought in substantial cash, by 1884 what remained attracted nothing like the $8.00 an acre Dehay had counted on. Back in Corning the Conservatives filed lawsuits for unpaid indemnity. Then, to top it off, Péron and Fugier went to France on a hair-brained scheme to purchase expensive purebred Percheron horses for a stud farm at the community.[13]

In 1885, San Francisco socialists who had loaned them money suspected trouble and sued before the colony went into bankruptcy. The suit was transferred to Adams County, where the society's tangible assets, unsold land, were located. There, on August 3, 1886, the Adams County Circuit Court dissolved Icaria Speranza and appointed a receiver to sell its remaining real estate and reimburse all creditors. The following summer, Armand Dehay ruminated sadly to young Alex Marchand that the community was "crushed like a house built on sand." Alex's father, in Corning, sarcastically commented that "they are finally punished for their sins."[14]

The sin to which the elder Marchand referred was Icaria Speranza's almost total abandonment of the Icarian rules of the "community of goods." Their charter, the "Contract and Articles of Agreement," adopted late in 1883, governed the colony mainly on the principles of Fourier and Saint-Simon. For example, they had a scheme of profit sharing. All assets and income were deposited in a community fund, and each year after expenses were met the extra income was to be distributed among the members of Icaria. They also had a plan of "work premiums," by which all members over the age of sixteen would receive from fifty cents to a dollar-and-a-half each month as an incentive if they performed their assigned job well. They permitted unrestricted ownership of private possessions. An Icarian could own a wardrobe, furniture, household implements, and any gifts valued under fifty dollars. The document had little to say about education of the children; education was not as important to them as it had been in the other communities.[15]

Still, old habits persisted. They built and used a refectory, just as they had done in Iowa. They said that marriage was indispensable to personal happiness and community solidarity. They embraced Cabet's Christian morality and discussed his writings on brotherhood and love of mankind. They stiffened the admissions requirements and insisted that all members be fully versed in Cabet's ideas. They stipulated that "Each and every applicant . . . should sufficiently know the French language to speak it and read it fluently." They doubled the probation period to one year. Once admitted the person had to stay put. All members had "to reside in the place where the commune is located, in houses furnished for that purpose; and said residences shall only be used for their legitimate destination, viz: exclusively as dwellings for said members." Article 52 stated that any Icarian who "having sojourned for more than three consecutive days" from the colony could be expelled at the written request of only five voting members of the Assembly. Such rules, for a small community barely on its feet, were prohibitive. No new candidates for Icaria Speranza ever rapped on their door.[16]

Back in Iowa the Conservatives continued on as "New Icaria." Although "timid and timorous" because of the disruption, they were not discouraged. They were determined to learn from past mistakes. In their minds, the root of all the squabbles, bickering, and acrimony had been the vagueness of their constitution. And so they drafted an elaborate new document of twenty-nine articles. They now called themselves an "association," not a corporation, "freely and willfully made, signed and accepted," known as the "New Icarian Community of Adams County (Iowa)."[17]

They transferred all property to the association and pledged to it future possessions "of all kinds." They renounced later claims against the association either for property donated, for work done, or services rendered. They swore "to give all of our time, strength, and abilities to the service of the association during all the time that we are members of it, and to obey at all times and in all circumstances, without either opposition or murmur, the laws and regulations which would be adopted."

The constitution created a president, secretary-treasurer, and directors of industry, agriculture, and clothing, all elected on February 3 for one-year terms. Women were given a limited franchise. They still could not "vote on all decisions" but could have the franchise on matters such as admissions, constitutional revision, and questions involving morals, education, amusements, and propaganda. As before, a woman could serve as a director of clothing, and women could vote for that individual.

The Conservatives made admission to New Icaria extremely difficult. A provisional member had to get a nine-tenths majority. After a year's probation adults had to contribute $100 apiece and $20 for each child. If they passed this inspection and received another nine-tenths vote, at year's end they were full members of New Icaria. Anyone could leave the association by notifying the Assembly in writing fifteen days in advance. They would get back the entrance fee, and this amount could be increased by a vote of three-fourths of the Assembly. No stranger could stay in their utopia for more than two weeks without a nine-tenths vote of approval.

Everyone had to "obey the directors and execute the work that would be assigned to them," and they had to work all the time and to the best of their abilities. Anyone could be expelled by the nine-tenths vote for not complying with the constitution or the orders of the directors, or if an individual "revolted against" the association's authority or "fomented an isolated party" in the workshops. Communal products could be distributed only by the President with approval of the Assembly. New Icaria would be a tightly knit family. With only a few days of discussion they approved the document on May 1, 1879.[18]

Their first priority was to build a refectory with some of the $1,500 promised from the Progressives. The remainder of the indemnity was to be used to cover the costs of moving eight frame homes to the new location, high on a bluff about a mile from the old village, with a commanding view of the rolling countryside. The first floor of the thirty-by-fifteen-foot building had a dining area with five round tables and fifty chairs, a cupboard, books, a grandfather clock, and a small organ. The second floor, accessed by a central staircase, had two rooms for bachelors and an apartment. The eight houses, rolled on logs to the new site, were laid out in a rectangle on either side of the refectory to form the border of a community garden in which they planted shrubs and trees. A brick walkway and bright flower beds surrounded the family homes. One of the structures served as a nursery and a shoe shop; another was designated for the blacksmith and carpenter.[19]

The New Icarians lived in Spartan simplicity with no rugs and only a few essential pieces of furniture. Yet "these neat and tidy French women," one visitor observed, "had managed to give an air of decency and even of comfort to their little homes." In the spring of 1883 Shaw described a community of thirty-four French-speaking people (twelve men, ten women, twelve children) dressed plainly in white and blue cloth and straw hats who enjoyed a calm, bucolic life. They had a tailor and shoemaker but no crafts or industry. They had abandoned the saw and flour mill. These once enthusiastic, idealistic utopians had become more than ever a comfortable farm clan related by experience and ideology rather than by blood.[20]

Only on Sundays, a day when farm work could be set aside for a while, did they enjoy a quiet picnic on the Nodaway River or gather in the refectory for a bit of singing or to watch a small skit. The library was seldom used. Marchand published a monthly newspaper, *La Revue Icarienne*, in a small print shop on the second floor of his home. It kept them apprised of world happenings and, to their own private satisfaction, of the quick failure of the Young Icarians in California. They ignored all political questions except to vote, regularly, for Republican candidates. Sometimes neighbors from nearby farms stopped for visits, but mostly the Icarians just kept to themselves.[21]

New Icaria stagnated and gradually died. They reduced the number of directors from four to two because, Jules Gentry said, supervision was superfluous in their small, well-functioning Icarian family. Women could now vote without any restrictions. By 1883 *La Revue Icarienne* listed departures, each notice accompanied by a testimonial about how much they had contributed to Icaria. Sauva in the spring of 1884 returned to Paris with a departure claim of $584. Charles Levy moved away the next year, followed by Léon Bettannier. Léoncio Cubells went away. Frémont, a Parisian who had joined in 1878, abandoned the colony. Valmor Caillé and Armel Marchand just gave up. In May 1888 Jules Maillon, sometime editor of their newspaper, left to return to France to die. And, of course, there were no new members.

By the end of the decade New Icaria consisted of nine men, and six of them were between sixty-one and seventy-four years old. *La Revue Icarienne* published mundane accounts of weather, crops planted, birthdays, and the health of remaining Icarians, a litany of the daily life of aging idealists living on the Iowa knoll. Marie Marchand Ross, when she returned to Icaria for a brief visit, was overwhelmed by the melancholy spectacle. "The community really did not exist any more," she wrote, "since there were only a few people left and most of them very old and not able to do the heavy work of the farm."[22]

These Icarians knew what was happening. They sensed their isolation and decay. But they accepted it because life then had its own reward, tranquility. A quiet, undisturbed routine was solace to those who had been uplifted, uprooted, castigated, and displaced, but who had remained true, so they believed, to Cabet's dream.

In their twilight years they became preoccupied with what they ate and what they wore. Marchand caught this sense of *temps perdu* in the March–April 1884 edition of *La Revue Icarienne:* "There was nothing new to report," he lamented, only the "daily occupations and what our food, housing, and clothing consists of." "The oldest are trusted with the most sedentary work, . . . the youngest do the heaviest work. . . . the women and young girls are entrusted with the making and keeping of the clothing." "At breakfast we have vegetable soup, coffee with milk, butter or cheese, and often eggs." "At dinner, a dish of meat and one or two dishes of vegetables . . . at supper, soup, a dish of vegetables, stewed apples or jam . . . for beverage, at dinner and supper, milk for those who want it and an unlimited supply of very wholesome water. On holidays, we have been indulging ourselves with wine." From the material point of view, he concluded, "we do not lack anything. . . . among us the most scrupulous equality prevails in everything."[23]

It was February 3, 1895, just three years shy of the fiftieth anniversary of the departure of the First Advance Guard. On that glorious, uplifting morning almost fifty years ago the "Soldiers of Humanity," intoning the *Chant du Départ* on the foredeck of their steamship *Rome,* slipped out of Le Havre to the cheers of Cabet and hundreds of witnesses on the dock. They were going to spearhead the planting of the "community of goods" in the New World. It would become a beacon for liberty, fraternity, and equality. Not one Icarian doubted then the success of their mission.

But now, on this cold, dreary February day, eight old people sat down for dinner at one of the tables in the refectory. The other four tables were empty, chairs turned up. They gathered to commemorate the anniversary, long before hailed with so much gaiety, song, and dance, with a somber repast of meat and vegetables and water. The conversation was sparse and muted, brief glimpses of the past. Marchand, in his eighty-first year, recalled how he had endured those awful days in Texas. Eugène Bettannier, president of New Icaria every year but one since the split, boasted of how his father had helped to lead the Majority at Nauvoo to claim their democratic rights against the usurpations of the Minority. Hippolite Claudy talked of Nauvoo, of Cabet's departure for St. Louis that bright October afternoon. Jules Gentry laughed about that July 4 celebration

The last Icarians at New Icaria about 1888. Prudhommeaux, *Icarie et son Fondateur,* 605.

twenty years ago when, the day before the big trip into Corning, his son Jules Jr., filled with youthful enthusiasm, had asked to get permission from the Assembly to earn money as a field hand so that he could celebrate like the Americans.[24]

After dinner they turned to the serious business of electing new officers for the coming year. The four men and four women stared at each other. Who would be president? Who would fill the two directorships? Silence. Marchand refused. He said he was too old. Claudy was not interested, never had been, he said. Gentry complained that he was too sick to do much of anything, let alone be president of Icaria. Bettannier mumbled that he was weary; he had been president long enough. It was someone else's turn. So Icaria had come to that. Only four men to fill three offices, and not one would serve. Everybody, without saying a word, understood what had happened. It was late, though, and time to go to bed.[25]

On February 16 they gathered in the vacant refectory again, briefly, for the last time as the General Assembly of New Icaria. Madame Gentry pleaded not to take the final step, but she was ignored. Bettannier called for the vote that would officially dissolve the community. It was affirmative, unanimous. Marchand then suggested that Bettannier go to Corning and ask the Circuit Court to appoint him as Receiver in charge of dissolution. There was no trouble from any quarter.

Over the following three years the details were slowly, systematically agreed upon. The eight survivors consented to share all the colony's assets with the twenty-one Icarians who had signed the 1879 "Contract." It was merely a question of how they would be distributed. Some took cash, some land, others accepted a written guarantee of a lifetime annuity of housing, food, clothing, and medical care in exchange for the value of their share. Sixteen adults and ten children received their portion of the $16,000 net assets.[26]

On Saturday morning, October 22, 1898, with everything in order Bettannier appeared before the regular session of the Adams County District Court. Judge M. Towner, without hesitation, signed the order that pronounced the community, the last Icaria, legally dissolved. The lamp of mystical idealism, lit by Cabet's imagination in the Reading Room of the British Museum some sixty years before, had gone out.[27]

Epilogue

After 1898 the aged Icarians dispersed and went to live in other locations, some of them in or near the town of Corning. Bettannier and his wife were the only ones to stay on at the communal site until he was killed in 1905 in an accident while visiting relatives in Tropica, California. The Gentry and Claudy families spent the rest of their days in Adams County. Fugier became a farmer of sorts. He bought a 350-acre tract near the town of Creston where he raised horses. The Mourots moved to California to be close to the Lerouxs and the Dehays, and they all are buried on a hillside cemetery overlooking the Russian River. Marchand went to stay with his daughter Marie and son-in-law at Columbus, Georgia.[1]

Three months after the Icarians buried Cabet in St. Louis's Old Picker Cemetery, they exhumed the remains and reinterred them in a better location in the same cemetery. On November 12, 1906, his remains were again exhumed and placed in the New St. Marcus Evangelical Cemetery, with an obelisk granite monument to mark the spot. But fifty years later the monument had crumbled to such an extent that the cemetery officials decided to bury what was left of it next to the coffin. In 1962, members of the French Society of St. Louis, urged by Professor Jacques C. Chicoineau of Webster University, restored the monument at the head of the grave. It reads "Etienne Cabet. Born Dijon France 1788. Died St. Louis, Mo. 1856. Founder of the Icarian Colony."[2]

For all their dedication and dogged devotion to the ideal society of the *Voyage en Icarie,* the Icarians, except for the small band at Corning after 1876, never found their dream. More than any other perfectionist community in America, they were perpetual seekers. Icaria was always something that receded, as Pascal said, with an eternal flight.

The Promised Land, when entered, evaporated. Once they found Icaria they discovered no fruit to pick, no salutary climate to enjoy, no life without drudgery. Always dissatisfied pilgrims, they were unable to enjoy their utopia because the realities were so disappointing. Yet in their quest for the elusive "community of goods," their feeling of self-sacrifice made their frustrations durable, almost rewarding. They accepted on faith what Cabet told them when in May 1847 he wrote, "They will be workers full of courage, intelligence, and learning, elite men, examined and tested who, as one man, afire with dedication and enthusiasm, will go out to win happiness for their posterity, their country, and all of humanity, even more than for themselves."

The first Icarians came to America for asylum. They saw in France, in exaggerated terms to be sure, a society twisted by economic oppression, disease, egotistical bureaucrats, and brutal police. To these victims of surveillance, unemployment, immorality, accidents, and harassment their country was, wrote Jacques Rancière, a "haunting reality of an intolerable world." Their conscience and their pride would not allow them to accept even a perception of misery. They would not submit, as they saw so many of their countrymen doing (the obtuse, unskilled worker and the docile bourgeois), to the intolerable. Yet France was too riddled with "godless men, idlers, plunderers" to hope for change. There was no alternative but a bittersweet expatriation to establish the "community of goods" as a refuge for their unhappiness and then to use it as a sanctuary from which they could save humanity.

But actual conditions in America confounded their dream. Nevertheless, most of the First Advance Guard in Texas, experiencing awful heat, desolation, and disease, wrote bizarre, absolutely false descriptions of fecundity and comfort. At New Orleans, after the Texas calamity, most Icarians still believed Cabet's promises. Others hated him for lying. And so it went later, in Nauvoo, Cheltenham, and Corning. Icarians on one side accused their opponents of selfishness and materialism. The other side denounced their enemies for calumny, despotism, and abandonment of ideals. Time and again all of them lamented that everything had changed, heaven had become hell, the other fellow was to blame. At that point—in New Orleans, Nauvoo, Cheltenham, and Corning—it was time to start over. In the face of the destruction of their community neither side in these confrontations walked away from their dream. True enough, in each case the particular community as it had functioned economically and politically ceased to exist. Work was stopped or sabotaged, dialogue degenerated into name-calling battles, fraternal sharing turned into silence.

But at that juncture, when their utopia was disintegrating, they reasserted themselves. They reorganized into smaller units, grasped hold of what they thought was Cabet's vision of a perfect society without money and property, and impatiently, sometimes impulsively, gathered for another effort. One more time they discarded concerns about comfort and personal health and pursued farther away a new fraternal order.

And, inevitably, the refuge did not materialize. The "organic Icaria," as Bourg called it in 1850, was never found. It was, in the original meaning of the Greek word *utopia,* a "no place."

The Icarian communities did not last because they were built primarily upon ideals and morality and only secondarily upon sensible community rules, efficient economic production, and physical well-being. Their constitutional principles, essentially the maxims of the *Voyage en Icarie,* were at once too lofty and too cumbersome and invited endless bickering. Their economic plan was mostly a daydream. They could not keep accurate business records, find an income to match expenses, or resolve labor disputes. Except for the brief period of prosperity at Corning during the decade after the Civil War, and New Icaria's stability at the end, only a Dr. Pangloss's enthusiasm justified a belief in Icaria's financial stability and progress.

What sustained the Icarian quest? The question is crucial because once the initial oppressors and oppression were left behind in France, what enemy, so important a uniting force in any community, could take its place? In America Icaria's nemesis was vanity, materialism, and selfishness. Virtue and dedication marked the "true Icarian" from the conceit of the apostate. So always one group of Icarians saw itself as Soldiers of Humanity, as giving everything to the community, laboring not for themselves but for mankind. Always they felt themselves victims of perfidious brothers and sisters who came to Icaria for all the wrong reasons: comfort, influence, respect, even power. These late-coming Icarians (the Nauvoo Majority, Cheltenham dissidents, Young Icarians), had their own ideas—against Cabet when he was alive or his writings later on—about how things ought to be done. And so it went, each side indicting the other. The original band of Icarians saw in their enemies vainglory, sensualism (tobacco and whiskey, for example), and arrogance: egotism in its most malignant form. The newcomers saw docile, subservient minions of Cabet or Mercadier, or at Corning lazy, dull-witted farmers whose self-centered complacency made them oblivious to how far the community had drifted from its original goals.

The Icarians also fought constantly for legitimacy, for the maintenance or the restoration of righteous principles and viable authority. Consequently, even small differences quickly escalated into showdowns that meant crushing the opposition. When they fought they had no room for compromise and mediation, only schism and separation. Cabet set out, when challenged, to squash his opponents. At Cheltenham, Mercadier expelled his adversaries. Marchand, although mild-mannered, could not tolerate the reforms demanded even by his own son. Dehay, at Icaria Speranza, in the name of legitimacy, increased the admission requirements until the small community was frozen in its tracks and doomed to a fleeting existence. Only during the last years of New Icaria, when the old folks at that communal farm seemed no longer to care much who was in charge, did harmony and fraternity settle in. So, the Icarians, at the core, were idealistic but intolerant romantics whose attitudes changed little in over half a century. Always impatient with human nature, they could not endure for long the proposition that morality can survive only with accommodation, that sin and repentance go together. They could not allow a whittling away of sacred precepts, always writ large on their refectory walls like so many Stations of the Cross in a French cathedral.

Perhaps, in the final analysis, they clung to their dream of the "community of goods" because they knew that it could never be achieved. Their commitment rested upon the *expectation* of success, someday. The voyage itself counted the most. They were gratified by the awareness that they were moving toward Cabet's "second Promised Land, an Eden, an Elysium, a new Earthly Paradise." At times of dissension and crisis they were rejuvenated by the hope of improving upon the most recent, and failed, pathway to utopia.

The Icarians—Majority and Cabetists, Stalwarts and Dissidents, Conservatives and Progressives—were comforted by a naive certainty that they, more than any people on earth, were on the right track. They believed Cabet when he wrote that they could "realize Equality and Fraternity, prevent covetousness and ambition, suppress rivalries and antagonism, destroy jealousy and hatred, render vice and crime almost impossible, assure concord and peace, finally give happiness to a regenerated Humanity." And when they were on the journey, however small in number, while they persevered, they were confident that they had kept the faith. Perhaps they did.[3]

Notes

Introduction

1. Johnson, *Utopian Communism,* 16.
2. Ibid., 18.
3. Rancière, *La nuit des prolétaires,* 356–426. In 1989 the book was translated into English by John Drury and published by Temple University Press as *The Nights of Labor: The Worker's Dream in Nineteenth-Century France.*

Chapter 1: Origins

1. Carle and Beluze, *Biographie,* 1–18; Cabet, *Biographie,* 1–2.
2. Carle and Beluze, *Biographie,* 18. Jacotot gave Cabet a copy of Fenelon's *Télémaque,* and Cabet claimed to have discovered in this work the basic tenet of his adult utopian scheme, the total uselessness of money.
3. Ibid., 27.
4. Cabet, *Biographie,* 2–3; Prudhommeaux, *Icarie,* 11.
5. The move was not entirely impulsive. Cabet had made preliminary plans to relocate there as early as 1816, when he visited the capital and established contacts with important liberal politicians. C. Proudhon to Cabet, 17 May 1826; Piogy to Cabet, 5 May 1839, Archief Cabet, Internationaal Instituut voor Sociale Geschiedenis, Amsterdam (IISG); Carle and Beluze, *Biographie,* 58–59. The term *Charbonnerie* was derived from an Italian political organization called the "Carbonari" that had created radical, anti-monarchy cadres in Abruzzes, Naples, and the Papal States.
6. Johnson, *Utopian Communism,* 24.
7. Dézamy, *Calomnies,* 7; Dubois, "Etienne Cabet," 321–23.
8. "Exposé d'une révolution nécessaire dans le gouvernement de France," 1, 6, 3–4, 39, 42–43, 70–83, Archief Cabet, IISG.
9. Carle and Beluze, *Biographie,* 66–77; Cabet, *Biographie,* 3; Cabet, *Lettre de M. Cabet, ex procureur-général,* 34. Cabet said that he quit his legal practice in Paris in 1827 because of "ill health," but by December 1829 his health had returned and he requested to be admitted to the Paris bar. In this same letter he briefly described his unsuccessful banking activities. Cabet to Balonnier, 12 Dec. 1829, Cabet Collection, Southern Illinois University-Edwardsville (SIUE), folder 1, no. 6.

10. Cabet most likely felt homesick for Paris while in Corsica, but he was not disappointed with the appointment, as Prudhommeaux claimed (*Icarie*, 38). See Cabet to Mme. Nicod, 20 Nov. 1830, Archief Cabet, IISG, in which his only complaint was about the weather and that his "work had him exhausted." His house, though, was "the most beautiful one in the country." Cabet's brochure, *Au duc d'Orléans* (Paris: A. Mie, 1830), dated 7 Aug. 1830, is in the Archief Cabet, IISG.

11. Carle and Beluze, *Biographie*, 114-15; letter of 12 Nov. 1830 to Dupont quoted in Prudhommeaux, *Icarie*, 41-42.

12. Cabet, *Correspondance*, 4, 23, 35, 38-41. On February 17, 1831, he wrote to Lafayette from Bastia, expressing grave concern about a conservative backlash in France. Cabet to Lafayette (Mon cher General), 17 Feb. 1831, Cabet Collection, SIUE, folder 1, no. 4. On February 19, 1831, Decruzy wrote in detail to Cabet about the political problems in Paris. See Decruzy to Cabet, 19 Feb. 1831, Cabet Collection, SIUE, folder 2, no. 23. On March 12 Cabet wrote to a Dijon politician named Mauquin to state his qualifications and eligibility to run against "MdC" (Mauquin de Chauvelin) in the upcoming election for delegates to the Chamber of Deputies. Cabet to Mauquin, 12 Mar. 1831, Cabet Collection, SIUE, folder 1, no. 4. See also Cabet to Decruzy, 12 May 1831, Cabet Collection, SIUE, folder 1, no. 7.

13. Carle and Beluze, *Biographie*, 164-68; Cabet, *Lettre de M. Cabet, ex procureur-général*, 24, 36-37.

14. *Journal politique et littéraire de la Côte-d'Or*, 24 Apr. 1831, Archief Cabet, IISG. In a letter to Jourdon, Cabet confided his plans to run for office in Dijon. Cabet to Jourdon, 17 May 1831. Then, the next day, he drafted a letter to Mauquin wherein he identified his opponent. Cabet to Mauquin, 12 May 1831, Cabet Collection, SIUE, folder 1, nos. 1 and 2; Cabet, *Discours d'installation*, 5.

15. Carle and Beluze, *Biographie*, 164-65; Cabet, "Aux electeurs," Archief Cabet, IISG.

16. Cabet, *Lettre de M. Cabet, député*, 4. French law required that a member of the Chamber of Deputies own property in his home district worth 500 francs in taxes. Cabet, though, had paid taxes of only forty-six francs on a small tract of land outside Dijon that he had purchased in the early 1820s. His friends quickly transferred to Cabet's name some real estate worth 509 francs in taxes. He then opened his campaign.

17. Ibid., 4, 10-11; Cabet, *Biographie*, 6. An account of Cabet's activities while Prefect as well as the reaction to his re-entry into radical politics is found in *L'aviso de la Méditerrané, journal de Toulon et du Var*, 8 June 1851, Archief Cabet, IISG. Vote returns are found in the Centre d'Accueil et de Recherche des Archives Nationales (CARN), BB[18] 1194 (Côte d'Or).

18. Guarneri, *The Utopian Alternative*, 23.

19. Fotion, "Cabet and Icarian Communism," 33-42.

20. Ibid., 34-35; Pinckney, *The French Revolution*, 366-67; Johnson, *Utopian Communism*, 31n39; Prudhommeaux, *Icarie*, 45-47.

21. Cabet, *Correspondance,* 48-49.

22. Cabet, *Histoire de la révolution,* première partie, 58-60, 157-255; troisième partie, 193-240. The book went through two more printings in May and November, 1833.

23. Ibid., 32-34, 96-98, 100-102, 148, 165-72, 196, 386. A December 26, 1833, order from the Paris Préfet de Police accused the society of violating French press laws and demanded an immediate report on their activities.

24. Cabet, *Biographie,* 9; Fotion, "Cabet and Icarian Communism," 51.

25. The publications of the "Association Libre"—petitions, pamphlets, subscription lists—are located in the Archief Cabet, IISG. Cabet, *Faits préliminaires,* 4-5. See also Cabet, *Association libre*.

26. Cabet, *Biographie,* 9-10; Cabet, *Le Populaire, prospectus* (24 June 1833). A second prospectus issued in September just before the first printing of the newspaper was distributed throughout Paris by twenty-five sellers dressed in tricolor uniforms of the Revolution. See Prudhommeaux, *Icarie,* 86-87; Johnson, *Utopian Communism,* 37.

27. Cabet, *Biographie,* 11; Cabet, *Le "National,"* 69-70. The two articles were specifically discussed and defended at his trial. See Cabet, *Poursuites,* première partie, 14-25.

28. Collins, *The Government and Newspaper Press,* 77.

29. Cabet, *La République du Populaire,* 6, 11. See Cabet's marginal notes against the government in Ministère de la Guerre, *Développements*.

30. Cabet, *Moyens d'améliorer,* 4, 6. The same emphasis upon education as a weapon in resisting police repression was seen in Cabet's address when he was installed as a member of the Association Libre. Cabet, *Association libre.*

31. Association Libre, "Dossier," Archief Cabet, IISG; *Surveillance, de l'Association libre pour l'éducation du peuple,* CARN, BB[18] 1338 dos 9306, BB[18] 1472 dos 6733; The banquet is described in *Republican banquet at Dijon* (1833), CARN, F6779 dos 20; Cour de Paris, *Affaire,* 1:93.

32. Cabet, *Le "National,"* 69-70.

33. Cabet, *Faits préliminaires,* deuxième partie. Prudhommeaux describes the trial in *Icarie,* 96-97.

34. Cabet, *Poursuites,* 41-56; Dupin, *Mémoires,* 3:160. Official documents on Cabet's trial are found in CARN, BB[18] 1214 dos 8792, BB[18] 1215 dos 9177, BB[18] 1221 dos 193, F[7] 6783 dos 4, BB[18] 753 dos 5, BB[18] 760 dos 5.

35. Cabet, *Le "National,"* 71-72. For a detailed account of the situation regarding Delphine LeSage see Johnson, *Utopian Communism,* 41n65. For Cabet's own explanation, written in 1848, see Cabet, *Biographie,* 7.

36. Fotion, "Cabet," 59.

Chapter 2: Icaria Conceived

1. Cabet, Le *"National,"* 71–72; Cabet, *Biographie,* 13. The official order to leave Belgium, "Leopold, roi des Belges . . . enjoint au sieur *Etienne Cabet, étranger actuellement à Bruxelles, de quitter le territoire de la Belgique . . . ,"* is in the Archief Cabet, IISG.

2. Cabet's attitudes toward exile are reflected in Cabet to [his mother], 4 Sept. 1834; Cabet to Nicod, 16 Jan., 10 Feb. 1836, Archief Cabet, IISG. In *Toute la vérité au peuple,* 20–21, he later recounted his contacts there with Louis Napoleon. Cabet, *Biographie de M. Cabet,* 14. On Berrier-Fontaine see Cabet's thirty-nine letters to Berrier-Fontaine, 1843–48, Cabet Collection, SIUE, folder 2, no. 29; "Berrier-Fontaine-Cabet Correspondance" in the Papiers Cabet, Bibliothèque Historique de la Ville de Paris (BHVP); Christopher Johnson "Etienne Cabet and the Icarian Communist Movement," 101–4. Cabet identified his living quarters with Berrier-Fontaine in a letter to Owen in 1847. Cabet to Owen, 15 Aug. 1847, letter no. 1053, University of Wisconsin Microfilm, Illinois Historical Survey, University Library, University of Illinois at Urbana-Champaign.

3. Cabet to Nicod, 16 Jan. 1836, Archief Cabet, IISG. Cabet's financial situation is discussed in a letter sent to him from a friend in Belgium named Emile Pickering. Pickering to Cabet, March 1838. Cabet Collection, SIUE, folder 12.

4. *Toute la vérité,* 88; Dézamy, *Calomnies,* 32.

5. Cabet, *La justice d'avril.* See manuscript note on Cabet's writing of the tract in the Archief Cabet, IISG.

6. Cabet, *Histoire populaire,* 1:vii. This work was published in two more editions, in 1845 (as six volumes) and in 1851 (as five volumes).

7. Ibid., 4:91–127.

8. Ibid., 2:539–40.

9. Ibid., 4:633.

10. The earliest mention of his writing the novel is in a letter from Laurie in Brussels [?] to Cabet in London, 1 Sept. 1837, Cabet Collection, SIUE, folder 12. Cabet, *Comment je suis communiste et mon crédo communiste,* 4th ed., 3–5. He wrote, "There [in London] during these five years, working eighteen hours a day, studying history, composing the elements for a history for the people, a universal history, a history of England, a history of France, a history of the French Revolution, seeing only everywhere calamities, believing to see the evil in the vices of social organization, searching for the remedy, thinking to find it in the Democratic Republic, looking to organize it in its perfection, I came to the conclusion that Communism was the only means to completely realize Democracy and the Republic, . . . I drafted my *Travels in Icaria.*" Cabet, "Histoire de la communauté icarienne colonie-persécution contre M. Cabet et le communisme, Nauvoo, April 24, 1851," Cabet Collection, SIUE, folder 4, no. 6.

11. Carle and Beluze, *Biographie,* 8; Prudhommeaux, *Icarie,* 3; Henri

Desroche, Preface, 24; Piotrowski, *Etienne Cabet*, 53; Fotion, "Cabet," 76, 83-88; Cabet, *Toute la vérité*, 85.

12. Cabet, *Toute la vérité*, 93.

13. Mercier, born in 1740, was a teacher who became a Girondist in the first years of the Revolution. Later, under Napoleon, his earlier radical associations caused the government to place him under surveillance. Nothing came of the harrassment, however, and he died peacefully at Bicetre in 1815. Mercier, *L'an deux mille quatre cent quarante*, 11, 84, 136, 262-64, 311-12, 316. For other utopian ideas prevalent at the time of Cabet's writing see Manuel and Manual, eds., *French Utopias*, especially their remarks on nineteenth-century utopias, 7-16. Cabet is included on pp. 329-44.

14. Cabet, *Travels in Icaria*, 735. Cabet in a letter to Owen from Paris in August 1847 revealed that the two men had visited frequently at Owen's home and at Berrier-Fontaine's place. Cabet to Owen, 15 Aug. 1847, Owen Papers, no. 1503. See Prudhommeaux, *Icarie*, 133-35. See also Owen's letter to Cabet of 10 Aug. 1851, published in *Le Populaire*, 15 July 1851.

15. Cabet, Travels in Icaria, 519, 740.

16. Angrand, *Etienne Cabet*, 14. Janice Fotion in her dissertation discounted the degree to which Cabet had to face hard times. She thought that he only had to budget his money and to live frugally but not in distress. There is no doubt, though, that Cabet came down from his accustomed life style. And, several times, "in order to escape the misery" of this poverty, he had to borrow money from his brother Louis, by then a prosperous Dijon businessman.

17. Dunham, *The Industrial Revolution*, 350-51, 425.

18. Cabet, *Toute la vérité*, 84-85. On the year and a half it took Cabet to write *Voyage en Icarie*, see Johnson, "Etienne Cabet," 122-24.

19. Fotion, "Cabet," 118; Piotrowski, *Etienne Cabet*, 76-77; Cabet, *Travels in Icaria*, 422, 463-76; Cabet, *Voyage en Icarie*, 2d ed., 308, 337-47.

20. Cabet, *Travels in Icaria*, 349-66, 418-41, 461-501, 508; Cabet, *Voyage en Icarie*, 254-67, 305-22, 336-65.

21. Cabet, *Travels in Icaria*, 51, 53; Cabet, *Voyage en Icarie*, 37, 39.

22. Cabet, *Travels in Icaria*, 66, 76-80, 87; Cabet, *Voyage en Icarie*, 48, 56-60, 64.

23. Cabet, *Travels in Icaria*, 137; Cabet, *Voyage en Icarie*, 100-101.

24. Cabet, *Travels in Icaria*, 209, 219-28; Cabet, *Voyage en Icarie*, 153, 161-66. Prudhommeaux thought that Cabet was also influenced by Rousseau, whose *La Nouvelle Héloïse* served in part as a model for the *Voyage en Icarie*. Prudhommeaux, *Icarie*, 144.

25. Cabet, *Travels in Icaria*, 76-77, 80-81; Cabet, *Voyage en Icarie*, 56-57, 59-60.

26. Cabet, *Travels in Icaria*, 251; Cabet, *Voyage en Icarie*, 184.

27. Cabet, *Travels in Icaria*, 105; Cabet, *Voyage en Icarie*, 77.

28. Cabet, *Travels in Icaria*, 111, 113-17, 129; Cabet, *Voyage en Icarie*, 82-86, 95.

29. Cabet, *Travels in Icaria*, 360-66; Cabet, *Voyage en Icarie*, 262-66.
30. Cabet, *Travels in Icaria*, 278-79, 301-4, 373; Cabet, *Voyage en Icarie*, 203-4, 220-22, 271-72.
31. Cabet, *Travels in Icaria*, 131; Cabet, *Voyage en Icarie*, 97.
32. Cabet, *Travels in Icaria*, 231-33; Cabet, *Voyage en Icarie*, 169-71.
33. Cabet, *Travels in Icaria*, 57, 136, 799.
34. Ibid, 141-42; Prudhommeaux, *Icarie*, 320.
35. Prudhommeaux, *Icarie*, 31. Lux is quoted in Piotrowski, *Etienne Cabet*, 81. Carré, *Cabet*, 8, 98, 106; Roberts, "Etienne Cabet," 89, 93.
36. de Tocqueville, *Democracy in America*, 1:208-9; 2:13, 131, 146.

Chapter 3: Icarianism in France

1. Cabet to Altroche, Apr. 1838; Lamennais to Cabet 29 Apr. 1838; Nicod to Cabet, 1838; Voyer d'Argenson to Cabet, 15 May 1838; Archief Cabet, IISG; Cabet, *Toute la vérité*, 9. Of the *Voyage en Icarie*, Cabet wrote in the spring of 1851 that "I published it on my return from exile in 1840 while publishing at the same time in *Le Populaire* successively more than 40 writings to develop and defend my system of Icarian Communism." "Histoire de la communauté icarienne . . . ," Cabet Collection, SIUE, folder 4, no. 6. Dufruit, a professional translator who lived in Paris, was mentioned in a letter to Cabet from Benoit. Benoit to Cabet, n.d. [probably 1840], Papiers Cabet, BHVP. Cabet's concern that his idea about dictatorial power being necessary in France in the event of a revolution would frighten off support for publishing the *Voyage* is in "Note à X," 22 Aug. 1839, 1-4, Archief Cabet, IISG.
2. Cabet, *Voyage et aventures*, preface; Prudhommeaux, *Icarie*, 194*n2*.
3. "Note à X," 1-4, Archief Cabet, IISG.
4. Blanc, *Organisation du travail;* Proudhon, *What Is Property?;* Jean Jacques Pillot's newspapers *La tribune du peuple* (1838-39), *Ni châteaux ni chaumières* (1840), Bibliothèque Nationale. Johnson, *Utopian Communism*, 66, 69-70, 72-75, 79, 110, 115-16, 126, 145, 231-32.
5. Tellier to Cabet, 12 May 1842; Boitel to Cabet, 21 Aug. 1844, Papiers Cabet, BHVP. For an account of the turn toward violence in 1841 see the extant copies of *La Fraternité*, Dec. 1841-Feb. 1842, Archief Cabet, IISG; Johnson, *Utopian Communism*, 66, 75, 79.
6. Cabet, *Ma ligne droite*, 17.
7. The first run of *Le Populaire*, 3 July 1833-8 Oct. 1835, was subtitled "newspaper of the political, material, and moral interests of the people." Copies are in the Bibliothèque Nationale.
8. *Le Populaire*, 14 Mar. 1841. On the divisions between "Communists" and "Reformists" see Johnson, *Utopian Communism*, 66-82.
9. In this social section of *Le Populaire* Cabet fell into the habit of printing elaborate praise of himself sent in by subscribers.
10. Boitel to Cabet, 21 Aug. 1844, Papiers Cabet, BHVP. For the appeal

of Cabet's message of Christian morality to the French middle-class merchant, see the letters from Charles Chameroy in the Cabet Collection, SIUE; and Desmoulin to Cabet, 26 Apr. 1843, 26 Nov. 1846; Laty to Cabet, 4 May 1848; Ellena to Cabet, 12 Sept. 1847, Papiers Cabet, BHVP.

11. Cabet, *La Femme*, 49–60, also elaborated upon the feminism articles of *Le Populaire*. Some of Cabet's appeal to women came from his call for pacifism or "civil courage." See the letters praising Cabet's leadership in the Communist camp from Mme. Anne Buissan, a "femme proletaire" and flower shop worker from Lyon. Mme Buissan to Cabet, 29 Oct. 1842, 18 Feb. 1844, and two undated letters, Papiers Cabet, BHVP.

12. *Le Populaire*, 11 Sept. 1842.

13. *Le Populaire* 16 Apr., 15 Nov., 23 Dec. 1841; 30 Jan. 1842; Cabet, *L'ouvrier.*

14. Cabet, *Voyage*, 37–39, 176–97; Cabet, *Travels*, 50–53, 240–69.

15. Johnson, *Utopian Communism*, 93–95.

16. Ibid., 100, 147, 149.

17. Chapius to Cabet, 6 Oct., 31 Oct. 1844, Papiers Cabet, BHVP.

18. Johnson, *Utopian Communism*, 105. Because of Chameroy's fear of being arrested as an agent-provocateur he signed the letters with the pseudonym of Chaville. See the letters of Chameroy to Cabet in the Cabet Collection, SIUE, folder 12. Chameroy was instrumental in convincing Cabet to start publication of the *Almanach icarien*, an extremely popular practical advice manual peppered with Icarian doctrines, which ran each year from 1843 to 1848. Cabet's handwritten contract for the publication of the almanac, dated 25 Nov. 1843, is in the Cabet Collection, SIUE, folder 1, no. 15. *Le Populaire*, 3 July 1842, 20 July 1843. Especially important are Chameroy's views in "Un Commis-voyageur" of the reaction to the publication of the *Voyage en Icarie* and the early growth of the new run of *Le Populaire*. A typescript of "Un Commis-voyageur," signed by Prudhommeaux, is in the Cabet Collection, SIUE, folder 12, no. 20. Johnson, *Utopian Communism*, 72n46.

19. Johnson, *Utopian Communism*, 105. Icarianism spread through *Le Populaire* and, by word of mouth, beyond France. There was a large contingent in Barcelona, and *Voyage en Icarie* was translated into Spanish. Cabet's close friend Louis Krolikowski was the correspondent for the German principalities, where a German translation of the book was published. Berrier-Fontaine remained as the principal contact in London. See "Biographie Louis Krolikowski," *L'Etoile du Kansas et de l'Iowa*, Aug. 1879. For a detailed account of how these Icarian chapters, or "clubs" as they were called, functioned see the undated letter, Caulon to Cabet, Papiers Cabet, BHVP. On the Barcelona community see Ventura, "'Icaria' vida," 139–251. The Spanish translation of *Voyage en Icarie* appeared in Barcelona in 1848 as *Viaje por Icaria ... traducida al castellano por D. Francisco J. Orellana*, 2d ed. (Barcelona: Imprenta y Liberia Oriental de Martin Carlé, 1848).

20. Cabet, *Ma ligne droite*, 36.

21. *Le Populaire*, 8 May 1842.

22. On the early trouble in Lyons see Chapius to Cher Citoyen, 31 Oct. 1844; Dézamy to Cabet, n.d.; Vincent, Gerret, and others to Dézamy, n.d., Papiers Cabet, BHVP. Johnson, *Utopian Communism,* 115-16.

23. Johnson, *Utopian Communism,* 144.

24. Ibid., 145-49.

25. Ibid., 153-54, 305-6.

26. Ibid., 153.

27. Ibid., 157.

28. Ibid., 165.

29. Ibid., 165-68.

30. Rancière, *La nuit des prolétaires,* 364, 387; Turgard to Cabet, 8 Feb. 1848, Papiers Cabet, BHVP.

31. *Le Populaire,* 6 June, 7 Nov. 1848.

32. Ibid., 13 Nov. 1842, 31 Oct. 1846, 5 Sept. 1847.

33. In April 1844 he had confided to Berrier-Fontaine, "I am going to occupy myself with True Christianity and I believe that this work will result in the greatest happiness for our doctrine." Cabet to Berrier-Fontaine, 7 Apr. 1844, Cabet Collection, SIUE, folder 2, no. 29; *La Fraternité* Jan. 1846; Johnson, *Utopian Communism,* 231-33.

34. Cabet, *Le vrai Christianisme,* preface, 619-20; Cabet, *Colonie Icarienne aux Etats-Unis,* 131.

35. Cabet, *Le vrai Christianisme,* 165-96, 495.

36. Ibid., 160, 234-50, 267, 386, 622, 627-29. Typical of the impact of *Le vrai Christianisme* on some of his followers, elevating Cabet's stature beyond that of a political leader to a savior of mankind, is an undated "Hail to citizen Cabet," signed by "Encontre." Here, after lofty testimonies to Cabet's greatness, Encontre ends, "Hail to citizen Cabet who has understood the sublime mission! Hail to the apostle of eternal truths! Hail to the stringent supporter of democracy! Hail to the father of the worker! Hail to the continuator of *true Christianity!* Hail to the creator of blessed Icaria! Hail to the champion of justice, to the defender of the rights of men, to the hero of fraternity! Hail to citizen Cabet." Encontre au citoyen Cabet, Papiers Cabet, BHVP.

Chapter 4: The Exodus

1. "Cabet to the French Democratic Society of London," 1843, Archief Cabet, IISG; Cabet to Berrier-Fontaine, 7 Apr. 1844, Cabet Collection, SIUE, folder 2, no. 29.

2. The religious imagery employed by many Cabet disciples by 1847 can be seen in a letter of Etienne Dubeau to Cabet on 26 July 1847, Papiers Cabet, BHVP. Such imagery also can be seen in printed letters in *Le Populaire* of 26 Feb., 26 Mar., 26 May, 27 June, and 28 Aug. 1846. A very negative initial reaction to Cabet's announcement of leaving France, and to his charging his followers six hundred francs for the privilege of accompanying him, is

seen in a letter of F. Lechapt, an extremely disappointed Icarian, to Cabet, dated 27 May 1847, Papiers Cabet, BHVP.

3. Johnson, *Utopian Communism,* 235–36. Cabet confided his deep pessimism about the future of Icarianism in the increasingly hostile political environment of France in a letter to Berrier-Fontaine, 7 Jan. 1847, Cabet Collection, SIUE, folder 2, no. 29.

4. Desmoulins to Cabet, 26 Nov. 1846; Jules de Beaufort to Cabet, 4 Mar. 1846, Papiers Cabet, BHVP.

5. Faucheux and Morauzeau, "Les débuts du communisme," 74–76; Maitron, ed., *Dictionaire Biographique,* 334, mentions the Madeline affair and its connection with Cabet. Johnson, *Utopian Communism,* 237.

6. Johnson, *Utopian Communism,* 240–42; Taschereau, *Revue rétrospective,* 95.

7. *Le Populaire,* 8 May 1847.

8. Cabet to Berrier-Fontaine, 19 Mar. 1847, Cabet Collection, SIUE, folder 2, no. 29. Cabet to Berrier-Fontaine, exchange of letters of April 1847, especially the letter of 13 April 1847. Berrier-Fontaine also told Cabet that there was little support in London for the emigration project. Berrier-Fontaine to Cabet, 27 Apr. 1847, in Papiers Cabet, BHVP. *Le Populaire,* 20 Apr., 30 May, 26 Sept., 28 Nov. 1847,

9. Charles Sully to Robert Owen, 17 Aug. 1847; T. W. Thorton to Owen, 25 Jan., 5 July 1847, Owen Papers, nos. 1445, 1472. The full story of the Peters Company and the role of William Smalling Peters and his sons in the operation is in Connor, *The Peters Colony of Texas.* Cabet and the Icarians were the last group to agree to settle on the land that had been contracted out by the company between February 1841 and July 1, 1848. See Begos, "'Icaria,'" 84–85. The Owen Papers reveal that he was in London only from September 22, 1837, to early January 1838 and could have met with Cabet only during that time. Otherwise, Owen was not in the capital while Cabet was anchored there throughout his exile. William Cligg to Robert Owen, 8 June 1837; William Dare to Robert Owen, 20 Dec. 1837, Owen Papers, nos. 901, 976.

10. W. S. Peters to Robert Dale Owen, 7 June 1847, Owen Papers, no. 1457. William Smalling Peters's shares in the "Texas Emigration and Land Company" were considerable. According to Connor, Peters, as an "original member" of the company, owned 500 shares valued at $250 a share. Moreover, his sons W. C., Henry J., and John each owned 500 shares. Connor, *Peters Colony,* 74–75, 162.

11. T. W. Thornton to Robert Owen, 6 Aug. 1847; Charles Sully to Robert Owen, 14 Aug. 1847; Cabet to Robert Owen, 18 Aug. 1847; W. S. Peters to Robert Owen, 9 July 1847, Owen Papers, nos. 1497, 1502, 1503, 1534. The *Prospectus* was mentioned in a letter dated 2 Nov. 1847, W. S. Peters to Robert Owen, Owen Papers, no. 1529.

12. George C. Peters to Robert Owen, 17 Oct. 1847, Owen Papers, no. 1515.

13. *Le Populaire*, 14 Nov. 1847. Prudhommeaux offered the excuse that Cabet's poor command of the English language accounted for his misunderstanding of the terms of the Peters Concession. Prudhommeaux also argued that since Cabet never signed an agreement it had no legal authority. See Prudhommeaux, *Icarie*, 203–15, 219–23. See Cabet to Berrier-Fontaine, 20 Jan., 25 Jan., 6 Feb., 21 Feb. 1848, Cabet Collection, SIUE, folder 2, no. 29, for contradictory evidence that Cabet had plenty of time to consider the terms of the Peters Concession because he did not accept the offer in writing until January 3, 1848. In any event, the document was given to Cabet *in French* and he kept this copy in his files until the departure of the First Advance Guard the next month. He gave the "Peeters [sic] Concession" to Gouhenant, head of the Advance Guard, to present to Henry O. Hedcoxe, president of the Peters Company in Texas, as confirmation of their settlement rights on the Trinity River. Hedcoxe's English copy, sent to him by W. S. Peters, was lost in July 1852 when his home and office were raided by outraged Mexican settlers and his records destroyed. See Connor, *Peters Colony*, 142, 149. The French copy of the Concession clearly states that there were sections reserved by the government as belonging to the Company "that Cabet might later acquire" either by exchanging some of his own granted sections "at the mutual agreement of the two parties" or by purchase at two dollars an acre. Prudhommeaux, *Icarie*, 613–14. On September 2, Berrier-Fontaine specifically warned Cabet that "the majority of the Democratic Society of London appears in effect to be totally opposed to the project." Berrier-Fontaine to Cabet, 2 Sept. 1847, Papiers Cabet, BHVP; Cabet to Berrier-Fontaine, 16 Jan. 1848, Cabet Collection, SIUE, folder 2, no. 29. Cabet to Robert Owen, 7 Nov. 1847, Owen Papers, no. 1527, mentions the appointment of Sully.

14. Berrier-Fontaine to Cabet, 1 Oct. 1847, Papiers Cabet, BHVP.

15. Cabet, *Prospectus: Grande émigration*, 2.

16. The initiation fee of 600 francs or 120 dollars was well beyond the average weekly pay of twelve francs for an unskilled worker. Some workers felt they had betrayed Cabet in not being able to pay the 600 francs and offered to contribute whatever portion they could afford. One such unfortunate, named Bruere, lamented that his resources would only spare a total of 220 francs. Bruere to Cabet, 28 Aug. 1847, Papiers Cabet, BHVP. *Le Populaire*, 11 Apr., 4 July, 15 July, 29 Aug., 10 Oct., 31 Oct., 18 Nov., 21 Nov. 1847. The letter from F. Lechapt, a Parisian typesetter, to Cabet, 27 May 1847, Papiers Cabet, BHVP, did not appear in *Le Populaire*.

17. Cabet, *Réalisation d'Icarie*, 6:262. Typical of the support Cabet received in the mail was the "Lettre sur la réforme sociale." In it the author, Aimey, condemned all the oppression and repression emerging in France and stated that it "gives the strongest testimony and sympathy in repeating the rallying call of let's go to Icaria." Aimey, "Lettre sur la réforme sociale," 5 Aug. 1847, Papiers Cabet, BHVP.

18. *Le Populaire*, 19 Sept. 1847.

19. Ibid., 28 Nov. 1847.

20. Ibid., Jan.-Feb. 1848. The story was later recounted by Cabet in *Notre procès en escroquerie*. Prudhommeaux, *Icarie*, 217n1. Cabet had been questioned by the police sometime in the middle of December 1847 about the emigration plans, but nothing further came of this event until his arrest on January 5, 1848. *Le Populaire*, 9 Jan. 1848.

21. Cabet, "Adresse de la 1re avant-garde," in *Opinions et sentiments*, 13-14. For the only surviving first-hand reaction to the departure by one of the members of the First Advance Guard, see the letter of Pierre Grillas to Rose Grillas, Le Havre, 28 Jan. 1848, Grillas Papers, Center for Icarian Studies (CIS). A handwritten note from A. Bertrand to Cabet dated 15 Aug. 1847 contains the words of the "Chant du premier départ, air de la Marseillaise," Cabet Collection, SIUE, folder 8, no. 11. By the time of the departure of the Third Advance Guard on September 26, 1848, Cabet required each person to sign a formal "engagement" of fidelity and "submission to the director of the *Gérance*," i.e., Cabet. See "Engagement de la troisième avant-garde", 26 Sept. 1848, Archief Cabet, IISG. See Prudhommeaux, *Icarie*, 611-12, for the full text of the "Chant du départ icarien."

22. Cabet, *Bien et mal*. The reaction to Cabet's position, especially on the National Guard issue, is expressed in an undated letter from Felix Lambre in the Papiers Cabet, BHVP.

23. Shaw, *Icaria*, 30; Johnson, *Utopian Communism*, 269-70.

24. Quoted in Johnson, *Utopian Communism*, 278-79. A description of the complicated political situation at the time of the spring elections is found in a letter from Leopold Domart to Cabet, 22 Mar. 1848, Papiers Cabet, BHVP. A poster campaign against the Communists on April 10 was discussed in a letter, Vigner to Cabet, 10 Apr. 1848, Papiers Cabet, BHVP.

25. Chevalier to Cabet, 22 Apr. 1848, Papiers Cabet, BHVP; Prudhommeaux, *Icarie*, 221n2. Louis Ménard was an associate of Louis Blanc and his defense of the victims of the anticommunist hysteria in *Prologue d'une révolution* forced him into exile in London.

26. Cabet, *Société fraternelle centrale*. Letters to Cabet reinforced a growing sense of hostilities against Icarians by the provincial government. Marie Esnault to Cabet, 2 May 1848; Forestier to Cabet, 26 Mar. 1848, Papiers Cabet, BHVP. On Cabet's feeble attempt to get elected to the national legislature see "Aux électeurs de Paris sur les candidatures des citoyens Cabet, Proudhon, Pierre Leroux," dated 11 Apr. 1848, Papiers Cabet, BHVP.

27. *Le Populaire*, 22 May, 28 May 1848; Autun Laty to Cabet, 2 May, 4 May 1848; Paquet to Cabet, 19 June 1848, Papiers Cabet, BHVP.

28. Johnson, *Utopian Communism*, 284n71.

29. Cabet, *Insurrection du 23 juin*, 17-18, 25.

30. Ibid. On the crackdown by the police see Despierres to Cabet, "Police Correctionnelle," 17 Nov. 1848; Julien Lecerf to Cabet, 22 Aug. 1848, Papiers Cabet, BHVP.

31. The names of the Icarians, outside of those in the Advance Guards,

who emigrated between February and December 1848 (the passengers on the "Grand Departures" one through four) have been compiled by Jules Renaud of Alexandria, Virginia, from the Manifest Lists in the National Archives, Washington, D.C. Renaud Collection, CIS, folders 1 and 2. The Beluze quotation is from a 2 Sept. 1905 letter printed in Prudhommeaux, *Icarie*, 222n1. A total of 310 people came to New Orleans on these Departures. On the rumor of an epidemic, probably cholera, that was raging in America causing cancellation of commitments to emigrate see Victor Rebout to Cabet, 21 Aug. 1848, Papiers Cabet, BHVP. Each Icarian who met the financial requirements received a personal letter signed by Cabet formally admitting him or her to Icaria. The letter also specified the time and place of departure. Such a document is found in the Papiers Cabet, BHVP, dated 16 Nov. 1848.

32. Shaw, *Icaria*, 39-40. In the fourth edition of Cabet's *L'ouvrier*, 46-47, Cabet was still pushing the Texas utopia. But by then other Icarians in France received contradictory reports from relatives and friends involved in the American expedition. They wrote to the Ministry of Justice to demand a full judicial inquiry into what was going on. One such complaint, a letter of Charles Hoiret of Rouen, insisted upon an investigation into the "foundation, administration, and direction of the Colony Icarian Community of M. Cabet." Hoiret, ouvrier tisseraud d'à Rouen à monsieur l'Ministère de la Justice, 22 Dec. 1848, Cabet Collection, SIUE, folder 8, no. 13.

33. See the map in Prudhommeaux, *Icarie*, 222.

34. Johnson, *Utopian Communism*, 289, 296.

35. Guarneri, *The Utopian Alternative*, 21, 23; Beecher, *Charles Fourier*, 433, 448.

Chapter 5: The First American Icarias

1. Cabet's last weeks in France were devoted to locating whatever recruits he could find and dispatching them to New Orleans. By the end of November he had arranged seven more departures to America, amounting to a total of 445 men, women, and children. One more departure of 40 Icarians, the "Quatrième grand départ," left Le Havre after Cabet, on December 18, 1848. Prudhommeaux, *Icarie*, 241-43.

2. Cabet, *Colonie icarienne aux Etats-Unis*, 134.

3. The letter to Beluze is mentioned by Cabet in Prudhommeaux, *Icarie*, 241. Prudhommeaux, *Icarie*, 239-43; Etienne Cabet Papers, "Correspondance et documents divers concernant les communautés icariennes au Texas, 1847-1898," Bibliothèque Nationale, Département des Manuscrits, boxes 3-8; Cabet, *Défense*, 12-13. For a detailed account of the journey of the First Advance Guard from New Orleans to Shreveport to Sulphur Prairie and then to the Peters Tract, see the letter of Levy of Reims to his family, dated 2 June 1848. It was reprinted by J. B. Gérard in *L'Observateur*, 4 Dec. 1880. This same issue also printed Alexis Armel Marchand's first impression of "the middle of the forests of the New World" in a letter to his brother in Paris.

More accounts of the Texas episode were printed in the same newspaper in January 1881. Prudent to Beluze, 1 Oct. 1849, Archief Cabet, IISG, recounts the difficulties of the Texas debacle. Similar stories are to be found in "Correspondance et documents divers concernant les communautés icariennes au Texas, 1847–1898," Bibliothèque Nationale, Département des Manuscrits, (1847–98).

4. *Le Populaire*, 11 July, 20 Aug., 1 Oct. 1848; Conner's study of the settlement pattern of the Peters Tract shows that it was not as desolate as some of the Icarians perceived it to be. The tract contained 1700 adult males, most of whom had families by January 1843. These settlers, mainly from the South and the state of Illinois, were farmers. Only six families were described as hunters or traders. They did, however, settle in clumps, and large parts of the tract were without inhabitants. The location of the Icarian land, just north of Dallas along the Elm Fork of the Trinity River near the junction of the Denton and Oliver creeks, was one of these unsettled areas. Connor, *Peters Colony*, 47–48, 86–89, 120–21, 135.

5. *L'Observateur*, 4 Dec. 1880, Jan. 1881.

6. *Le Populaire*, 1 July 1849. One Icarian, a tailor from Lyons named Gluntz, wrote that if Sully had been in charge and not Gouhenant, "Icaria today would be really prosperous [and] it is probable that we would not have lost a person." The original land grant to the Icarians is in the General Land Office, Austin, Texas.

7. *Colonie Icarienne*, 2 Aug. 1854. For the first accounts of the colony on the Red River see *Le Populaire*, 11 July 1848; *L'Observateur*, Aug. 1880.

8. *Le Populaire*, 12 Nov., 3 Dec. 1848; *Northern Standard*, Clarksville, Texas, 20 Jan. 1849. On the charges against Gouhenant see *Colonie Icarienne*, 2 Aug. 1854.

9. On the final disposition of the Icarian land see Begos, "'Icaria,'" 89–92.

10. "Lettre de la Nouvelle Orléans," dated 13 Nov. 1848, appeared in *Le Populaire*, 17 Dec. 1848. See also *Le Populaire*, 18 Feb. 1849, on the exploratory commissions, and Prudhommeaux, *Icarie*, 243n2.

11. Quoted in Shaw, *Icaria*, 40.

12. Cabet, "Influence et manoeuvres des Jésuites," Cabet Collection, SIUE, folder 8, no. 15; *Le Populaire*, 17 Dec. 1848. Cabet's letter of 22 Jan. 1849 was printed in *Le Populaire* on April 15, 1849, and had a full account of Cabet's version of the Texas disaster and of events at New Orleans. For a detailed description of the prevailing disillusionment at New Orleans just before Cabet's arrival, see the letter of Auguste Roiné to his brother, 10 Dec. 1848, *The Center for Icarian Studies Newsletter* May 1981: 6–7. The letter of a *"femme"* to Ernestine Grillas, n.d., Grillas Papers, CIS, folder 1, depicts the reaction of the Icarian women to conditions at St. Ferdinand Street. See also the strong endorsement that most of the First Advance Guard adopted on January 22 in "Protestations des membres du premier avant-gard restés fidèles" and "Adresse des Icariens restés fidèles, janvier 22, 1849," in the

Cabet Collection, SIUE, folder 8, nos. 1 and 2. "There at New Orleans," Cabet wrote, "I found the debris of a routed army. But I rallied them; and after long explanations in the General Assembly, I proposed to continue the enterprise," in "Histoire de la colonie icarienne," Cabet Collection, SIUE, folder 9, no. 4.

13. Cabet, *Voyage de M. Cabet*; A. Bourg to Robert Owen, 13 Dec., 15 Dec. 1848, Owen Papers, nos. 1722, 1726, informed Owen of Cabet's arrival from Paris and arranged a meeting between the two men.

14. *Le Populaire*, 19 Sept. 1847; Cabet, *Réalisation de la communauté d'Icarie*, 4:84.

15. Cabet, *Réalisation de la communauté d'Icarie*, 4:163; 8:370-71; *Le Populaire*, 5 Sept. 1847.

16. Cabet, *Icarie: Les Icariens d'Amérique* gives a picture of the situation in New Orleans. Of special interest is the long letter of Pierre Bourg reprinted on pages 4-11 of the pamphlet. It gives almost a diary of events from December 27, 1848, to February 16, 1849. See also the New Orleans *Daily Orleanian*, 27 Jan. 1849; the *Louisiana Courier*, 28 Nov. 1848, 16 Apr. 1849. Cabet gives a brief account of the split in *Colonie icarienne aux Etats-Unis*, 136.

17. Rancière, *La nuit des prolétaires*, 369; *Le Populaire*, 21 Jan. 1849.

18. *Gazette des Tribunaux*, 25 July 1851.

19. *Le Populaire*, 18 Feb., 15 Apr. 1849.

20. Ibid., 1 July 1849. As late as February 5 Pierre Grillas wrote to his wife from New Orleans, "I can't give you any details on the place or the plan where we will be going to from here to form our new Icaria." Grillas Papers, CIS.

21. "Choix de Nauvoo," *Le Populaire*, 1 July 1849, discusses the reaction of the Witzig commission to Nauvoo. The commission summarized it again in a written report to the officers of the Nauvoo Icaria, dated 14 Apr. 1849. See "Rapport de Durond et Witzig," Cabet Collection, SIUE, folder 8, no. 16.

22. Cabet, *Voyage en Icarie*, 7; *Travels in Icaria*, 10.

23. Cabet, Lettre de M. Cabet, Nauvoo, March 25, 1849, Cabet Collection, SIUE, folder 8, no. 17; *Le Populaire*, 20 May 1849.

24. Ibid., 9 Oct. 1849; Prudent, "Extract d'une lettre du Prudent à ses amis, Nauvoo, Illinois, Etats Unis d'Amérique, August 10, 1849," Archief Cabet, IISG.

25. *Le Populaire*, 1 July 1849, lists the casualties as three men—Boulat, age 32, Chuallier, age 65, and Coutellier, age 61—and two infants, Blanc and Fayard. But during the next two weeks fifteen others died at Nauvoo from cholera and fever. By April 13 their number was down to 260 Icarians. Cabet, *Réalisation de la Communauté*, 4:60; Cabet, *Colonie icarienne aux Etats-Unis*, 15, 136.

26. Job, *Voyage*, 109.

27. The records housed in the Historical Department of the Church of Jesus Christ of Latter-day Saints, Salt Lake City, show that the three trustees

were Joseph L. Heywood, David Fullmer, and Almon W. Babbitt. David Le Baron, Babbitt's brother-in-law, acted on power of attorney for the trustees. Hancock County, Deeds, 1849, pp. 562 and 2909. Le Baron to Cabet, recorded Apr. 1849; *Le Populaire*, 7 Oct. 1849; Holinski, "Cabet et les Icariens," 542–50; Cabet, *Colonie icarienne aux Etats-Unis*, 135–36. The deed for the property containing the mill and distillery is in the Iowa State Historical Library Collection, CIS. It was between Cabet and George Edwards, Jr., and his wife, dated 8 Apr. 1850. Cabet paid $3,000 for the property. Another deed dated 15 Sept. 1849 between Cabet and Freeman Elliot and Sarah Elliot, his wife, for lot 7 block 3 of Kimball's first addition of two-and-a-half acres on Ripley Street was for $100. Both handwritten documents are in box 5, folder 3. By August the Icarians were well enough established at Nauvoo to hold a formal welcoming ceremony in which mutual pledges of friendship were exchanged between Cabet and Malgar Couchman, the Hancock County sheriff, and N. C. Philips, a "municipal lawyer and secretary." See "Assemblée des citoyens à Nauvoo à l'établissement des Icariens," Cabet Collection, SIUE, folder 8, no. 15.

28. *Le Populaire*, 25 Mar., 20 May, 1 July 1849; Bourg, "Arrivée à Nauvoo des Icariens partis sur le *Callender* May 21, 1850," Cabet Collection, SIUE, folder 7, no. 9. For a sense of the high idealism and optimism of these first months at Nauvoo see the letter of Pierre Grillas to his wife, 11 Apr. 1849, Grillas Papers, CIS.

29. *Le Populaire*, 7 Oct. 1849.

30. Bourg, "Déstruction du temple de Nauvoo par un orage," 29 May 1850, Cabet Collection, SIUE, folder 9, nos. 9 and 10; *Colonie Icarienne*, Oct. 1854; Shaw, *Icaria*, 49; "Réponse des Icariens de Nauvoo aux dissidents de St. Louis," 1 June 1850, Cabet Papers, ms 486, Harold B. Lee Library Archives and Manuscripts, Brigham Young University, Provo.

31. Cabet's enthusiasm and confidence despite his worries over illnesses and deaths were revealed in his letters to his daughter Céline of 21 June 1850, 17 Aug. 1850, and 14 Aug. 1852, and letters to Beluze of 29 Mar. and 15 Apr. 1850, Cabet Collection, SIUE, folder 3, nos. 1 and 2. Cabet, *Prospectus de la colonie icarienne*, 3–5. Cabet, *Colonie icarienne aux Etats-Unis*, 143–64. *Le Populaire*, 1 July 1849, estimated the cost of the ocean trip to America to be about 200 francs. Prudhommeaux, *Icarie*, 292n3.

32. Cabet, *Colonie icarienne aux Etats-Unis*, 144–62. Barnes, "An Icarian in Nauvoo," discusses the letters of Pierre Roux, a visitor to the Nauvoo Icaria from March 1849 to April 1851. Pierre Grillas, in a letter to his wife, 7 July 1849, Grillas Papers, CIS, folder 1, describes the frantic activity at Nauvoo during the early months there. The type of food and times of meals served in the refectory are listed on a handwritten but unsigned manuscript, "Nourriture des Icariens à Nauvoo," Cabet Collection, SIUE, folder 8, no. 14.

33. *Le Populaire*, 19 Sept. 1847; "Social Contract or Act of Association of the Icarian Community, November 8, 1848," Illinois State Historical Library. Cabet, *Colonie icarienne aux Etats-Unis*, 44–48. There was a movement as

early as April 1849 to get Cabet to relinquish his control. See "Discussions intérieures" and "Adresse de communistes icariens à Nauvoo à la Gérance d'Icarie, avril 18, 1849," Cabet Collection, SIUE, folder 8, no. 18, and "Adresse des Icariens de Nauvoo mai 18, 1849," Cabet Collection, SIUE, folder 7, no. 4.

34. "An Act to Incorporate the Icarian Community," in Prudhommeaux, *Icarie*, 618-20.

35. The constitution was first printed in *Le Populaire*, 3 Feb. 1850. See Cabet, *Colonie icarienne aux Etats-Unis*, 49-68. The first officers chosen under the 1850 constitution were Cabet (president), Prudent (food and finances), Favard (clothing and lodging), Montaldo (education and health), Witzig, senior, (industry and agriculture), Bourg (secretary). See *Le Populaire*, 7 Apr. 1850.

36. Job, *Voyage*, 126-27, 131-32. The charges against Cabet were printed in P. J. Proudhon's newspaper *La Voix du Peuple*, 17 Apr. 1850, and reprinted in *Le Populaire*, 18 July 1847.

37. Job, *Voyage*, 130; Cabet, *Adresses des Icariens*; Cabet, *Adresse des Icariens . . . Protestation.*

38. Cabet, *Progrès de la colonie icarienne*, 4; Marchand, "Adresse des Icariens de Nauvoo au cit. Cabet en réponse à la protestation de quelques dissidents, mars 6, 1851," Cabet Collection, SIUE, folder 7, no. 5.

39. Cabet, *Aux Icariens de France*; United States Census, Population Schedules, 1850, Hancock County, Illinois.

40. Job, *Voyage*, 110.

41. Cabet to Beluze, 6 Aug. 1849, quoted in Prudhommeaux, *Icarie*, 256*n3*; Cabet, "Influence et manoeuvres des Jésuites," Cabet Collection, SIUE, folder 8, no. 15.

42. *Colonie Icarienne*, 9 Aug. 1854; Cabet, *Colonie icarienne aux Etats-Unis*, 140, 162-66; Prudent to Beluze, 1 Mar. 1853, Cabet Collection, SIUE, folder 5, no. 1, mentions the earlier idea of the Texas plan. Cabet, *Progrès de la colonie icarienne*, 21-22; Cabet, *Colonie icarienne. Situation dans l'Iowa.* The land lay on either side of the Nodaway River about one mile east of the future Adams County seat of the town of Corning. The first transfer of land was not made until 1855. It was of 182.83 acres by "Franklin Pierce, President to Etine [sic] Cabet," dated 15 Oct. at $1.25 an acre. Over the next year supplemental transfers, at the same price, conveyed 3,225 acres to the "Nauvoo Society" in Cabet's name.

43. *Le Populaire* 4 Nov. 1849, 5 Aug. 1851; Cabet, *Réalisation d'Icarie*, 4:68, 80. A member of the First Advance Guard, Thurel, had obtained a personal judgment against Cabet for 650 francs, his entrance fee, from the Commercial Court of Paris. Cabet, *Colonie icarienne aux Etats-Unis*, 18-22; Prudhommeaux, *Icarie*, 238-64.

44. Cabet, "Protestation du cit. Cabet contre la 2eme condemnation par défaut," May or June 1850; Cabet, "Au président de la cour d'appel de Paris, chambre correctionnelle," Paris, 17 Apr. 1851; Cabet, "Citoyen Cabet au

monsieur le président de la chambre correctionnelle de la cour d'appel de Paris," n.d.; "3eme lettre de citoyen Cabet à Louis Napoléon," 2 Apr. 1850, Cabet Collection, SIUE, folder 3, nos. 3, 4, 7, 8. The unanimous resolution of the General Assembly against Cabet's going to France, dated 17 Oct. 1856, is also in the Cabet Collection, SIUE, folder 7, no. 7, entitled "Les Icariens de Nauvoo du citoyen Cabet." Cabet and Krolikowski, *Système de Fraternité*, 1:56-58, reprinted the letter to Napoleon. Another letter to him from Cabet of 12 Nov. 1849, and printed in *Le Populaire*, 6 June 1856, outlined what was to be Cabet's defense. The first discussion of the suit against Cabet was seen in *Le Populaire*, 7 Oct. 1849. See *Le Populaire*, 7 Apr. 1850, for the judgment by default claim, and 22 Nov. 1850 for Cabet's request for a continuance. Cabet, *Colonie icarienne aux Etats-Unis*, 20. Cabet's private thoughts just before leaving Nauvoo for Paris were revealed in "Départ du cit. Cabet," 17 May 1851, Cabet Collection, SIUE, folder 7, no. 13.

45. Owen to Cabet, 15 July 1851, printed in *Le Populaire*, 10 Aug. 1851.

46. *Le Populaire*, 27 June 1851; Cabet, *Colonie icarienne aux Etats-Unis*, 20-21; Cabet, "Départ de Nauvoo," in *Opinions et Sentiments*, 26-27; CARN BB18 1473 dos. 6817, BB18 1550 dos. 6556.

47. Cabet, *Colonie icarienne aux Etats-Unis*, 21. Beluze's account of the trial is in a letter to Prudent, 14 Aug. 1851. See Beluze, "Nouvelle victoire du cit. Cabet," Cabet Collection, SIUE, folder 9, no. 19.

48. Cabet to Céline, 27 Jan. 1852, was written from the Dépôt de la Préfecture de Police. He confided to her that his arrest was a mistake. Cabet Collection, SIUE, folder 3, no. 2. Cabet, *Colonie icarienne aux Etats-Unis*, 22-23; *Nouvel organe de la démocratie par L. Blanc, Cabet, P. Leroux, et par un grand nombre de démocrates. Prospectus; Project d'une communauté en Angleterre, par Cabet fondateur de la colonie icarienne en Amérique;* and Cabet's correspondence, Mar.-Aug. 1851, with L. Blanc in the Archief Cabet, IISG. Teakle, "History and Constitution," maintained that "Cabet would have tried it in England, taking all necessary precautions, if he had been able to remain three or four months longer in 1852 to prepare for the enterprise." He returned by steamboat to St. Louis, then by stage to Jacksonville, Carthage, and finally to Nauvoo.

Chapter 6: The *Communauté de Biens* at Nauvoo

1. The most detailed description of the layout of the Nauvoo Icaria is found in Rogers, "Housing and Family Life." A contemporary description was published in *Le Populaire* in August 1850 by Pierre Bourg, the community secretary.

2. Cabet, *Colonie icarienne aux Etats-Unis;* Rogers, "Housing and Family Life," 40-46; Rude, *Voyage en Icarie*, 257-66. Much of the information about the community comes from Cabet's writings. A frantic scribbler, he wrote annual reports, pamphlets, brochures, addresses, and a stream of letters. He operated a newspaper first called *The Poular Tribune* and later

changed to *Colonie Icarienne*. For a short time in 1850 he also printed with the help of Witzig a German-language newspaper called *Der Communist*.

3. *Le Populaire*, 31 Jan. 1851; Rude, *Voyage en Icarie*, 150–51.

4. Three of the living quarters buildings were located on the southeast corner of the square. The rest were placed across the street on the north side.

5. Rude, *Voyage en Icarie*, 149–50.

6. Ibid., 42, 151.

7. Cabet, *Colonie icarienne aux Etats-Unis*, 156–57; Prudhommeaux, *Icarie*, 308.

8. Cabet, *Compte-rendu*, 9.

9. Cabet's most detailed summary of daily life at Nauvoo is found in his *Progrès de la colonie icarienne*. *Revue Icarienne*, Feb. 1855; Prudhommeaux, *Icarie*, 302n2.

10. Rude, *Voyage en Icarie*, 152.

11. *Le Populaire*, 23 May 1851. The first farm cost Cabet $400, and the second one was bought for $210. Cabet leased the three smaller units for a total of $300 annually.

12. Cabet, *Colonie icarienne aux Etats-Unis*, 157.

13. Ibid., 144–62; Miller, "Icarian Community," 106.

14. *Le Populaire*, 11 Apr. 1851.

15. Holinski, "Cabet et les Icariens"; *New York Tribune* 2 July 1853; Cabet, *Colonie icarienne aux Etats-Unis*, 181–82. For a comprehensive account of Icarian medicine and medical theory see Hausheer, "Icarian Medicine."

16. Prudhommeaux, *Icarie*, 277–84, 303–5.

17. *Colonie Icarienne*, 29 Nov. 1854; Cabet, *Défense*, 6; Cabet, *Colonie icarienne aux Etats-Unis*, 137–38, 141–45, 166–68; Sutton and Gundy, "Icarian Embarkation," 19–33.

18. Cabet-Baxter letters, 1854–1855, CIS; Sutton and Smithson, " 'Mon Cher Emile,' " 20–37; Prudhommeaux, *Icarie*, 292n3; Cabet, *Colonie icarienne aux Etats-Unis*, 143; State of Illinois, Census 1855, Hancock County, 49–56.

19. *Colonie Icarienne*, 27 Sept. 1854; *Center for Icarian Studies Newsletter*, 4, no. 2 (Spring 1982): 7; Rude, *Voyage en Icarie*, 46; Cabet, *Colonie icarienne aux Etats-Unis*, 160. The musical scores and lyrics of Icarian songs are found in the Iowa Historical Library Collection, CIS, box 1, folder 1. Cabet's restrictions on the Americans is in "Icarian Concerts," Archief Cabet, IISG.

20. Rude, *Voyage en Icarie*, 155.

21. Prudhommeaux, *Icarie*, 336.

22. Rude, *Voyage en Icarie*, 154; P. Bourg, "Une soirée de dimanche en Icarie," 12 Jan. 1850, Cabet Collection, SIUE, folder 9, no. 14.

23. *Le Populaire*, 2 Dec. 1849; Sutton, "Utopian Fraternity," 23–38; P. Bourg and E. Cabet, "Célébration en Icarie de l'anniversaire de la fev. 3, 1850," Cabet Collection, SIUE, folder 9, no. 5.

24. Cabet, *Colonie icarienne aux Etats-Unis*, 159–60; Vallet, *Communism*, 19.

25. Cabet, *Colonie icarienne aux Etats-Unis*, 161; Rude, *Voyage en Icarie*, 46. This kind of Sunday afternoon meeting with discussions of political and social questions was common among French workers. Cabet, though, turned the focus from politics to morals and ethics, giving it a much more elevated tone than the rough-and-tumble exchanges seen in France. See Vallet, *Communism*, 19.

26. Cabet, *Voyage en Icarie*, 35, 73–74, 94–95; *Travels in Icaria*, 49, 100–101, 127–28; Cabet, *Progrès de la colonie icarienne*, 15–18; Cabet, *Colonie icarienne aux Etats-Unis*, 59–60, 92–99.

27. Cabet, *Colonie icarienne aux Etats-Unis*, 92–99.

28. Rude, *Voyage en Icarie*, 44–45, 158.

29. Vallet, *Communism*, 18–19. The Icarian school apparently enjoyed a high reputation among the Americans in Hancock County, some of whom wrote to Cabet to try to have their children admitted. Cabet, pleading a shortage of space and anticipating large numbers of new Icarian arrivals from France, refused. One such refusal is in a letter of Cabet to Homer Brown of Hamilton, Illinois, 14 Dec. 1855, in the Illinois State Historical Library, Springfield.

30. Cabet to Beluze, 11 Jan. 1853, Cabet Collection, SIUE, folder 5, no. 1.

31. Cabet, *Colonie icarienne aux Etats-Unis*, 34, 118–19; Cabet, *Crédo communiste*, 7; Cabet, *La femme*, 49–60. Cabet's version of the events of 1853 can be seen in his letters to Beluze, 4 Jan. 1853–24 Jan. 1854, Cabet-Beluze Correspondence, Cabet Collection, SIUE, folder 5, no. 1.

32. "Décision de l'Assemblée Générale contre la femme C. et E. G." in Prudhommeaux, *Icarie*, 340.

33. Ibid., 341–42.

34. Cabet, *Inventaire*, 27–31.

35. Cabet to Beluze, 20 Mar., 26 June 1855, quoted in Prudhommeaux, *Icarie*, 321n1.

36. Cabet, *Colonie icarienne. Réforme icarienne*, 122; Cabet, *Lettre sur la réforme*, 13.

37. *Le Populaire*, 2 Dec. 1849; Prudhommeaux, *Icarie*, 325.

38. Cabet to Denise, 4 Oct. 1853, Cabet Collection, SIUE, folder 3, no. 2; Cabet, *Colonie icarienne aux Etats-Unis*, 189–90. Prudent had warned Cabet as early as April 17, 1852, that his absence was causing serious disruptions in discipline at Nauvoo. He told Cabet that his presence was "absolutely necessary." They were "paralyzed," and if Cabet stayed alway, in place of "order and harmony, concord and faith in the [Icarian] way" there would be "defiance and discouragement." See Prudent to Beluze, Nauvoo, 20 Apr. 1852, in Cabet, *Opinions et Sentiments*, 29.

39. Prudhommeaux, *Icarie*, 346–48.

40. Ibid., 348–61.

Chapter 7: The Schism

1. Cabet, *Colonie icarienne aux Etats-Unis*, 210-11; Rude, *Voyage en Icarie*, 50-62; Bush, "Communism," 409-28; King, "M. Cabet and the Icarians," 289-98.

2. Cabet, *Guerre de l'opposition*, 5-13. Cabet privately sensed the paradox facing his utopia as early as the summer of 1852: namely that to survive Icaria needed a large and steady influx of new members, yet its capacity to absorb them was severely limited. In a letter to his daughter he instructed her to tell Beluze not to send over so many Icarians as the previous year and to send only "strong men with their contributions." Cabet to Céline, 14 Aug. 1852, Cabet Collection, SIUE, folder 3, no. 2.

3. Cabet, *Colonie icarienne aux Etats-Unis*, 208-12.

4. Ibid., 123, 211. Prudhommeaux, *Icarie*, 368n1, comments on Cabet's strokes.

5. Cabet, *Colonie icarienne aux Etats-Unis*, 222-26; "Proposition of M. Cabet as it was read to the General Assembly on the 16th of December, 1855," signed by Gérard, Iowa State Historical Library Collection, CIS, box 5, folder 3.

6. Cabet, *Colonie icarienne aux Etats-Unis*, 226-33.

7. *Revue Icarienne* 5 Jan., 19 Jan. 1856.

8. Ibid., 10 Mar. 1856; The new editor of the *Revue Icarienne*, named Naville, wrote in the October 1856 issue that "the colony is dividing into two camps, almost equal in number. The one having at its head M. Cabet, composed in large part of old people, of men having a large family, who out of fear stayed by his side; the other, composed in large part of young men, robust, workers, without charges and all the more independent. It is necessary to have only one president and this evening they have two of them!" (p. 4). The letters to Beluze, 4 Jan. 1853-27 Nov. 1854, are in the Cabet Collection, SIUE, folders 5 and 6. *Le Populaire*, 2 Dec. 1849.

9. *Revue Icarienne*, 19 Jan. 1856, devoted the entire issue, fourteen pages, to the controversy.

10. *Le Populaire*, 6 Sept., 13 Sept. 1851; *Colonie Icarienne*, 11 Oct. 1854; *Revue Icarienne*, 1 Apr. 1857; Gérard's handwritten essay "On the discussion which took place in our Meeting of February 6th . . ." is in Iowa State Historical Library Collection, CIS, box 5, folder 3.

11. Cabet, *Guerre de l'opposition*, 3-4; Cabet, *Adresse du Fondateur*; Cabet, *Manifestations*.

12. Cabet, *Guerre de l'opposition*, 6-9.

13. Ibid., 23-33; Cabet, *Rapport de la commission de surveillance*, 1-3; Cabet, *Rapport de la commission d'examen*.

14. Cabet, *Guerre de l'opposition*, 12-14.

15. Cabet, *Toute la vérité*, 20-24; Céline Cabet (Widow Favard) to M. R. Roiné, 29 Mar. 1856, Konesman Collection, CIS. In this letter Cabet's daughter castigates the revolt against her father and blames Roiné, a Cabetist, for not destroying it at the inception. "All [French] Icarians think that

you . . . are wrong not to ask the expulsion of the first nucleus of the dissidents." She predicted that after the community was dissolved "they will cut each others' throats, for they will have to live with their own resources, not one [French] Icarian will give them assistance." Cabet's relationship with his wife Denise was distant. The surviving letters to her are brief, cursory accounts of the weather and inquiries into health matters. His letters to his daughter, Céline, on the other hand, are full of revelations about his plans, hopes, and concerns about Icaria. See the letters to his wife and daughter, 1850–53, in Cabet Collection, SIUE, folder 3, nos. 1 and 2. Prudhommeaux, *Icarie,* 395–96.

16. A full account of this session appeared in Cabet's *Guerre de l'opposition,* 10–33. See also Bonnaud, *Etienne Cabet et son oeuvre,* 175.

17. Cabet later claimed as an excuse for the $1,600 being found in his office that the money was set aside by him for some potential Icarians for safe keeping when they decided not to enter the community. Prudhommeaux, *Icarie,* 397n1.

18. Cabet, *Guerre de l'opposition,* 14–38; *Revue Icarienne* 26 July 1854; *Courrier des Etats-Unis,* 13 Aug. 1856.

19. Cabet, *Guerre de l'opposition,* 38–56.

20. Cabet, *Actual Situation; To the Icarian Community, July 14, 1856; To the Public,* Iowa State Historical Library Collection, CIS, box 5, folder 3. Cabet wrote to the "Icarian Colony in Iowa" on May 21, 1856. Montaldo Collection, CIS, folder 1. On the twenty-four-hour body guard, Cabet identified Mercadier and Chavant who "slept with me." "I am very happy with them" he confided to his daughter. Cabet to Céline, 20 June 1856, Cabet Collection, SIUE, folder 3, no. 2.

21. Cabet, *Deuxième déclaration de la minorité à la majorité, Nauvoo, 2 août 1856,* in Prudhommeaux, *Icarie,* 402.

22. Cabet might well have chosen St. Louis because the social and political environment of that city caused other communal societies, such as the Communia and Sociality colonies, to locate there. An organization called the *St. Louis Communisten-Verein,* consisting of seventy members, encouraged groups of Socialists and Communists to settle in the city. The society had received in 1847 Hermann Ewerbeck's German translation of Cabet's *Voyage en Icarie.* See Petermann, "Communia and Socialty Colonies." *Revue Icarienne,* 2 Oct. 1856, 15 Apr. 1857; Beluze, *Lettre sur la colonie icarienne,* 1–11; Cabet, *Manifestes,* 15; Prudhommeaux, *Icarie,* 404–7; Vallet, *Communism,* 23–25.

23. Beluze, *Lettre sur la colonie icarienne,* 30–34. A handwritten unsigned document, "Mémorial," written in late August or early September, refers to "doors broken into with axes," "locks picked," and the "Minority with women and children deprived of food," in Iowa State Historical Library Collection, CIS, box 5, folder 3. Cabet, *Guerre de l'opposition,* 33–64; Cabet, *Manifestations,* 1–11.

24. *Revue Icarienne,* 2 Oct. 1856. The action was not binding according

to the 1850 constitution. This document, article 32 on the Laws on Admissions, Retreat, and Exclusion, requires that nine-tenths of the members be present and that three-fourths of them vote to exclude. Cabet, *Colonie icarienne aux Etats-Unis*, 72. In the *Revue Icarienne* of October 1856, editor J. B. Gérard published the "Proposition of the General Assembly of the Icaria Community for the exclusion of M. Etienne Cabet," 34.

25. *Nouvelle Revue Icarienne*, 12 Oct. 1856.

26. Cabet, *Départ de Nauvoo*, 6–7, 8–9.

27. Ibid., 18.

28. Cabet, "Addresse de citoyen Cabet aux Icariens en France sur la séparation et le départ pour St. Louis," in *Départ de Nauvoo*, 20–21.

29. "A Resolution of the General Assembly of the Icarian Community for the Expulsion of E. Cabet," Illinois State Historical Library, Springfield.

30. A typescript copy of the account of Cabet's death and burial, written by Josephine Gobel, daughter of George Gobel, a member of the funeral cortege, is located in the Missouri Historical Society Collection, CIS, folder 3. The exact location of "The Town of New Bremen" is identified by an unsigned manuscript description and transcription of St. Louis City Council records, 1845–1905, in the Missouri Historical Society Collection, CIS, folder 5. Sutton, " 'Earthly Paradise,' " 48–49.

31. Beluze, *Aux Icariens*, 1; *Nouvelle Revue Icarienne*, 1 Jan. 1857; Chicoineau, "Etienne Cabet," 19n17; Sutton, " 'Earthly Paradise,' " 48–49.

32. *Le Populaire*, 7 Apr. 1850.

33. Ibid., 2 Sept. 1849.

34. Ibid.

35. Cabet, *Réalisation d'Icarie*, 86.

36. Guarneri, *Utopian Alternative*, 206, 211.

37. The term "Associanism" was given by Guarneri to the adaptation of Fourierism to America's "democratic politics and a free-wheeling capitalist economy." Guarneri, *Utopian Alternative*, 175.

38. Kanter, *Commitment and Community*.

39. Guarneri, *Utopian Alternative*, 162.

40. Ibid., 198–99, 325–26, 387–88, 392.

Chapter 8: Cheltenham

1. Mercadier, *Compte-rendu de la Gérance*, 14–17, 20–21; Beluze, *La colonie icarienne à Saint-Louis*, 1–21. Although 180 Icarians, including Cabet, left Nauvoo by 1857, one had committed suicide and three men had died. By March 1 the Jalageas family of seven had left and one man, Lemoine, was expelled. For Beluze's promise of support, see Prudhommeaux, *Icarie*, 427.

2. Mercadier, *Compte-rendu de la Gérance*, 7.

3. Ibid., 1–21.

4. Ibid., 1–21. Mercadier's full enumeration of occupations is on pages

13-14. The term "philosophical people" was used by Mercadier in his pamphlet *Inauguration du cours icarien*.

5. *Compte-rendu de la Gérance*, 8-9.

6. Ibid., 9.

7. They had unsuccessfully petitioned the state of Illinois to repeal the Nauvoo charter and to return to them their share of communal property. Originally they expected the Hancock County Court, petitioned earlier by Cabet, to dissolve the Nauvoo Icaria immediately and to order a reassignment of assets. The court first delayed the petition until March 1857, then denied the request. Shaw, *Icaria*, 59.

8. Ibid., 10.

9. Ibid., 11. The other men were Grubert, Bossay, and Bauer.

10. Ibid., 14-17; Shaw, *Icaria*, 59. Mercadier estimated a net of $7,700 from the Nauvoo holdings, after expenses. He expected to realize about half that amount, based upon the relative sizes of the Majority and Minority, in a final settlement. Prudhommeaux, *Icarie*, 472-75.

11. Prudhommeaux, *Icarie*, 382-85. *Nouvelle Revue Icarienne*, 15 Feb. 1851, has the resolution and the gestures of conciliation and cooperation sent to St. Louis by the Cabet women and by Beluze.

12. Beluze, *Notre Situation à Saint-Louis*, 5, 10.

13. Ibid., 10-11.

14. Ibid., 12.

15. Brooks, "Some New Views," 32-34; Queen and Carpenter, *The American City*, 129-30.

16. Beluze, *Deuxième lettre à Maximilien*, 53-54.

17. "Beluze to Members of the Icarian Colony at Cheltenham," n.d., Cabet Collection, SIUE, folder 8, no. 12; Beluze, *Lettres icariennes*, 1:264; Beluze, *Notre situation à Saint-Louis*, 12-13; Mercadier, *Compte-rendu de la situation morale*, 6, 8; Prudhommeaux, *Icarie*, 441n3. A myriad of new, unanticipated expenses was involved in starting a community of that size. For example, the first year they paid $550 for a steam engine, $650 for lumber, $125 to equip the pharmacy, and $300 for miscellaneous items such as a horse, leather, wool, and iron, for a total outlay of $1,625. Added to that amount was the first installment on the mortgage of $500 due on June 1, followed by another $1,000 set for February 1, 1859. Prudhommeaux, *Icarie*, 441n3.

18. Beluze, *Inauguration du cours icarien*, 43-56. Beluze's reaction to the publication of the *Inauguration* and his account of the condition of the colony by 1858 was in a circular letter from Paris dated 5 Oct. 1858. Cabet Collection, SIUE, folder 8, no. 1.

19. Lauer and Lauer, "Cheltenham," 181.

20. The December debates are summarized in Loiseau to My dear Parents, 19 Apr. 1859, Cabet Collection, SIUE, folder 12, no. 45. Prudhommeaux, *Icarie*, 443-46.

21. Beluze, *Lettres icariennes*, 2:81-88. For a different view of the crisis

than that offered by Beluze, see Loiseau to My dear Parents, 19 Apr. 1859, and Loiseau to My dear Gérard, 2 July 1859, Cabet Collection, SIUE, folder 12, nos. 45 and 46.

22. Prudhommeaux, *Icarie*, 445-46.

23. Ibid., 446-47; *Nouvelle Review Icarienne*, 15 Apr., 15 July 1859.

24. Beluze, *Lettres icariennes*, 2:6-7, 14-16, 90.

25. Beluze, *Cheltenham*, 14.

26. Blick and Grant, "French Icarians," 20-21.

27. *Compte rendu . . . d'août 1857 . . . février 1858*, p. 10; Blick and Grant, "French Icarians," 24.

28. Beluze, *Lettres icariennes*, 1:36-37; Beluze, *Cheltenham*, 16, 20; Beluze, *Célébration à Saint-Louis*, 19-20.

29. Blick and Grant, "French Icarians," 19.

30. Ibid, 19, 22; Mercadier, *Inauguration du cours icarien*, 13.

31. Blick and Grant, "French Icarians," 17.

32. Ibid., 25.

33. Prudhommeaux, *Icarie*, 447-54.

34. Ibid.

35. Beluze, *Lettres icariennes*, 6:270-80, 8:352, 9:403. One of the men, Joseph Loiseau, blamed their plight on the close proximity to St. Louis and on the excessive material demands of the young women who, he stated, regard the community as "an inexhaustible mine." Loiseau to My dear Parents, 19 Apr. 1859, Cabet Collection SIUE, folder 12, no. 45.

36. Beluze, *Lettres icariennes*, 1:341-43. Loiseau detailed their precarious economic circumstances in his letter to Beluze, 4 June 1860, Cabet Collection SIUE, folder 12, no. 49. Prudhommeaux, *Icarie*, 452n2.

37. Mercadier to Beluze, 3 Jan., 12 Jan. 1860, quoted in Prudhommeaux, *Icarie*, 452n2. Loiseau to Beluze, 30 Apr. 1860, Cabet Collection SIUE, folder 12, no. 29 gives a dreary account of daily life by that spring. He told Beluze that the community did not even have enough money for clothing. See "Lettres de Benjamin Mercadier à Jean-Pierre Beluze, 1857-1862," Etienne Cabet Papiers, Bibliothèque Nationale, Département des Manuscrits, VIII (18153).

38. Beluze, *Lettres icariennes*, 9:409-11; Loiseau to Beluze, 30 Apr., 4 June, 9 Oct. 1860, Cabet Collection, SIUE, folder 12, nos. 48, 49, 50; Prudhommeaux, *Icarie*, 455.

39. Mercadier left Arsène Sauva, who had joined Cheltenham in July 1860, temporarily in charge. Prudhommeaux, *Icarie*, 456. Mercadier, "Mémoire à M. le Procureur impérial, sur les plaintes en escroquerie, portés à Paris, contre M. Beluze par M. Lertzellman et les époux Coeffe, décembre 3, 1862," Cabet Collection, SIUE, folder 8, no. 6. Beluze was kept informed about the deterioration in Cheltenham by other members of the colony. Barbot wrote him a long account in the summer of 1861. See Barbot to Beluze, 2 July 1861, Cabet Collection, SIUE, folder 12, no. 8. Barbot stated that his letter "had to make [Beluze] comprehend the wretched situation and

disorder in the community." Madame Flaig to Beluze, 29 Sept. 1862, Cabet Collection, SIUE, folder 12, no. 2, wrote of the death of the colony coinciding with the death of her husband. A similar distressing picture of the war's impact on Cheltenham is found in the letters of Charles Raynaud, senior, to Beluze in the spring and fall of 1861. Raynaud used phrases like "the most grave situation." Raynaud to Beluze, 19 May, 3 Oct. 1861, Cabet Collection, SIUE, folder 12, no. 21. Beluze, *Lettres icariennes,* 12:99, 112; 13:129; 15:180.

40. Beluze, *Lettres icariennes,* 19:290; Shaw, *Icaria,* 71–72; Beluze, *Lettre pour annoncer;* "A l'assemblée générale de la colonie icarienne de Cheltenham, janvier 6, 1863," Cabet Collection, SIUE, folder 8, no. 5. The last statement is quoted in Prudhommeaux, *Icarie,* 463–64. See Joseph Loiseau to Beluze, 9 Nov. 1863, Archief Cabet, IISG. Beluze and the two Cabet women lived in Paris with their pension reduced by 1,000 francs. Madame Cabet died at the age of 86 at Saint-Mande on August 26, 1877. Her daughter, Céline, had married Beluze in June 1862. Céline's first husband, Firman Favard, died in 1847. She died without children on April 15, 1866. Beluze stayed on in Paris until his death in 1905. He published "Un précurser du collectivisme: Etienne Cabet" in the journal *Acacia.* He also started the short-lived "Workers Credit Bureau" to provide financing for consumer co-ops. In 1863 he published a pamphlet that outlined his glorification of the common worker. Pamphlets from Beluze's "Crédit du Travail" are found in the Archief Cabet, IISG, under the title *Les associations conséquences du progrès . . .* and in "Société du credit au travail," Bibliothèque Nationale, Département des Manuscrits, Etienne Cabet, Papiers, XXI (18166). Beluze was succeeded as the head of what remained of the French Icarians by Charles Raynaud, to whom he turned over his documents and papers. On the condition of the Icarians in France after Cabet's death see Johnson, *Utopian Communism,* 290–300. The bad feelings were mutual. Icarians at Cheltenham charged Beluze with financial mismanagement and not sending the money he promised. They also said that Beluze failed to send over "tested Icarians devoted to the popular cause." Instead he gave them "stupid men" and "prostitutes." Clèdes to Monsieur, 12 Nov. 1862, Cabet Collection, SIUE, folder 11, no. 2. Beluze's account of the split is detailed in an 1863 pamphlet, published in Paris, *Ch. Raynaud, rapport de la commission nominée le 1*er *novembre 1862, pour vérifier la gestation du cit. Beluze . . . ,* Archief Cabet, IISG. The steady departure of individuals from Cheltenham in 1862–63 was discussed by Raynaud in a letter to Beluze, 1 Apr. 1863, Cabet Collection, SIUE, folder 12, no. 31. The Mercadier-Beluze split is well covered in "Lettres . . . Mercadier à Beluze," Etienne Cabet, Papiers, Bibliothèque Nationale, Département des Manuscrits, VII (18153).

41. Raynaud, writing from St. Louis, not Cheltenham, in December 1863 told Beluze what happened to the members of the Cheltenham community in the months after its demise. Charles Raynaud to Beluze, 2 Dec., 15 Dec. 1863, Cabet Collection, SIUE, folder 12, no. 21.

Chapter 9: Corning: The Commune

1. *Revue Icarienne,* 4 Feb. 1857. The officers still standing or newly elected in the September election were Gérard (president), Marchand (secretary), Mourot (lodging and clothing), Katz (health and education), Ferrandon (agriculture), and Schroeder (finance). *Réalisation du communisme,* 6-9.

2. *Revue Icarienne,* 4 Feb. 1857.

3. Ibid., Apr. 1857. The cost of just one lawyer in the fight to defend the charter in the Illinois legislature was $1,000. See also Prudhommeaux, *Icarie,* 470-77.

4. The previous summer they filed the papers, in the name of Cabet, for the "Articles of Association" for the "Icarian Society" in the Adams County Recorder's Office. See the articles dated 4 Aug. 1854 in the Adams County Recorder's Office, book D, 116-18. Cabet, *Colonie icarienne aux Etats-Unis,* 162-66. Rogers, "Housing and Family Life," 58, names Jules Renaud as the Icarian agent. He was so listed in the second (1854) Adams County tax records. The full title search of the land on which the community was to be built from June 15, 1855, on lands located in Sections 29, 32, including all judgments, taxes, mortgages, releases, and other legal matters are in a typescript copy, sixty pages, abstract numbers 3894, 2827, 3876, dated 22 Jan., Gauthier Collection, CIS, folders 1 and 2. The letter of 4 Sept. 1853 was reprinted in Prudhommeaux, *Icarie,* 319n1. Cabet, *Colonie icarienne. Situation dans l'Iowa,* 6; Prevos, "History," 239; Gallaher, "Icaria." Renaud made purchases in several land offices in the area, whose exact locations are unknown, but all of the purchases were located in Adams County. See *Abstract of Land Entries 1851-1859: Adair and Adams County,* A V, III, 20, Iowa Historical Department of Museums and Archives, Historical Building, Des Moines, Iowa.

5. *The Representative,* 20 Aug. 1859; Gauthier, *"Quest for Utopia,"* 43-44; Shaw, *Icaria,* 76-77, 158-61. The debt of about $30,000 included an allocation of sums that Mercadier claimed were due to the Cabetists as well as actual outstanding obligations. See Prudhommeaux, *Icarie,* 480-82. Mortgage of A. Marchand, President of the Icarian Community to William Shephard, August 15, 1859, Adams County Deeds.

6. Gauthier, *"Quest for Utopia,"* 44, 58-60; "Articles of Incorporation," 10 Sept. 1860, Adams County Recorder's Office, book D, 472-44; Prudhommeaux, *Icarie,* 480-81; Shaw, *Icaria,* 77-78; United States Census, Population Schedules, Adams County Iowa, 1860.

7. The Fugier letter is quoted in Prudhommeaux, *Icarie,* 485n1.

8. Cabet, *Colonie icarienne. Situation dans l'Iowa,* 6; Prevos, "History," 239; Gallaher, "Icaria," 103-5.

9. Gauthier, *"Quest for Utopia,"* 50-52.

10. Quoted in Ibid., 57.

11. Rogers, "Housing and Family Life," 62; Ross, *Child of Icaria,* 7.

"Minutes of proceedings of the Icarian Community translated from the French language into the English; to wit: Book Exhibit 1, November 1, 1860; U. Blanche, Director"; A. Gauvain, Secretary, to Cher ami, 10 July 1860; A. Gauvain to Cher ami, 30 July, 17 Aug. 1860, University of Nebraska-Omaha, Institute for Icarian Investigations Collection, CIS, box 1, folders 1 and 2. United States Census, Population Schedules, Adams County, Iowa, 1860.

12. "Statement of Revenue of Agriculture Since 1860," Iowa Historical Library Collection, CIS, box 5, folder 1; Prudhommeaux, *Icarie,* 486; Shaw, *Icaria,* 81–82; Rogers, "Housing and Family Life," 63*n185;* Prevos, "History," 244; *The Communist,* July 1867: 1, Iowa Historical Library Collection, CIS, box 3, folder 1. For the crucial role that Shephard played in extending them credit during the first lean years see Gauthier, *"Quest for Utopia,"* 59–60.

13. Accounts of visitors include those of a Missouri Communist, Alexander Longley, who came there in 1866. A state archaeologist, C. A. White, visited that same year. M. A. Massoulard arrived in the spring of 1875 from a Shaker colony in Kentucky. Charles Nordoff, a sociologist, arrived in 1874. He published a brief section on the Icarians in his *Communistic Societies of the United States.* In 1876 William Hinds, an Oneida communitarian, visited the colony and published his observations in a 1908 book entitled *American Communities and Cooperative Colonies.* See also Moorehead, "Icaria," 161–68. Marie Marchand's reminiscence, *Child of Icaria,* was published in 1938.

14. Rogers, "Housing and Family Life," 64; Smith, "The Story of Icaria," 45. A pamphlet, *Situation of the Icarian Community, September 1877,* in the Iowa State Historical Library Collection, CIS, box 5, folder 3, states that the library contained "about 2,000 books." An inventory of the remnants of the Corning library was made from the extant books that in 1971 were stored in the University of Nebraska-Omaha, Institute for Icarian Investigations. This twelve-page typescript inventory of June 1971 is in the University of Nebraska-Omaha, Institute for Icarian Investigations, CIS, box 1, folder 2.

15. Any adult leaving the colony would get $100 plus $20 for each year they had lived in Icaria. In 1869 J. Montaldo was elected president; in 1870, J. C. Schroeder; and in 1871, Antoine Gauvan. Shaw, *Icaria,* 116–17; Hinds, "The Icarians," 382–83. See "Election of Officers of the Icarian Community 1860–1878" and A. Gauvain to Dear Friend, 24 Aug. 1860, University of Nebraska-Omaha, Institute for Icarian Investigations, box 1, folders 2 and 3. The first manuscript lists all colony officers. The second letter discusses the debates over the new constitution. "The Act of Incorporation of the Icarian Community of Corning" is reprinted in Prudhommeaux, *Icarie,* 638–40. It lists the powers of the officers.

16. Shaw, *Icaria,* 158; "Resolutions Passed at a Meeting of the Stockholders of the Icarian Community, November 1st 1860," Iowa Historical Library Collection, CIS, box 3, folder 1.

17. Ross, *Child of Icaria,* 108, 125–27; Shaw, *Icaria,* 86.

18. Rogers, "Housing and Family Life," 151–53, 155–59, 163; Shaw,

Icaria, 86. They kept their livestock in barns located well away from the living area, and the mill was about a mile away on the Nodaway River.

19. Rogers, "Housing and Family Life," 72-78.

20. Ibid., 77-78; Prudhommeaux, *Icarie*, 495; Prevos, "History," 247.

21. Shaw, *Icaria*, 119.

22. Ross, *Child of Icaria*, 25-26.

23. Clark, "Cultural and Historical Geography," 121.

24. Shambaugh, *Amana*, 175.

25. Hinds, "The Icarians," 69.

26. Ross, *Child of Icaria*, 28-30.

27. Ibid., 34-35.

28. Ibid., 13.

29. Ibid., 13-14; Prevos, "History," 280n58.

30. Ross, *Child of Icaria*, 97.

31. Ibid., 97-98.

32. Ibid., 122, 125, 127.

33. Ibid., 95, 101; Hinds, "Icarian Community," 85.

34. Ross, *Child of Icaria*, 56.

35. Gérard, *Quelques vérités*, 21.

36. Sauva, *La crise icarienne, 1877-1878*, 2-5. Accounts of the New York-Corning contacts and reasons for the former communists moving to Icaria are described in *L'Etoile du Kansas et de l'Iowa*, 1 Apr., 1 May 1880.

37. Gentry, *Journal et manuscrits inédits*, 45, 53, 118.

38. Sauva, *La crise icarienne, 1877-1878*, 2-3; Prudhommeaux, *Icarie*, 526, 545-46, 598; Savage, "Jules Leroux." The earliest account of the fight over Jules Leroux's admission is in *L'Etoile du Kansas et de l'Iowa*, 23 June, 1 Sept. 1877.

39. Sauva, *La crise icarienne, 1877-1878*, 5.

40. Ibid., 6, 8.

41. Ibid., 5-6; Péron, in "Project of Contract" written in September 1877, declared that "the two groups . . . of the Icarian family can no longer live together." See this manuscript and holograph copy of "Proposition to the General Assembly Concerning the Function of a Branch of the Icarian Community," 26 Sept. 1877, Iowa Historical Library Collection, CIS, box 3, folder 1.

42. *La Jeune Icarie*, 1 May 1878.

43. On the Conservative side were Marchand, Léon Bettannier, and Eugène Bettannier; the Progressives were Dereure, Fugier, and Gauvin.

44. Gentry, *Journal et manuscrits inédits*, 36, 39, 41, 45, 55, 82, 119-22, 142. See the Progressives' account of withholding food and clothing during the winter months by the Conservatives in an article signed by E. Péron, A. Gauvain, E. Fugier, and A. Marchand, published in the Corning *Union*, Iowa Historical Library Collections, CIS, box 1, folder 5. Another article in the same newspaper of 22 Nov. 1877, "Trouble in Icaria," signed by Theo. Gorham, substantiates the Progressives' charges. A transcript copy of the following four articles published in the Corning *Union* are found in the

University of Nebraska-Omaha, Institute for Icarian Investigations Collection, CIS, box 2, folder 5: Theo. Gorham, "Trouble in Icaria," 22 Nov. 1877; Eugène Bettannier, "To the Editor of the Union," 29 Nov. 1877; A. Gauvain, E. Fugier, A. Marchand, "We have read in your paper an interesting article by Mr. Theo. Gorham," 1877.

45. Sauva, *La crise icarienne, 1877–1878,* 7.

46. Ibid., 8. The details of the following court proceedings are found in the land records, Adams County, Iowa, abstract numbers 2827, 3876, 3894, in the Gauthier Collection, CIS, folders 1 and 2.

47. Ibid., 10.

48. Ibid.

49. The complete handwritten transcripts of the court proceedings, "State of Iowa vs. Icarian Community," from February 14 to October 31, 1877 is in the University of Nebraska-Omaha, Institute for Icarian Investigations, CIS, box 1, folder 1.

50. Gentry, *Journal et manuscrits inédits,* 185; Shaw, *Icaria,* 108; Prudhommeaux, *Icarie,* 542. The Progressives, in a manuscript of thirty-five questions, asked the judge to submit to the jury reasons why the charter should be revoked. Iowa Historical Library Collection, CIS, box 5, folder 1. Sauva's pamphlet *La Crise icarienne. No. 2,* dated August 1878, contains extracts from the trial.

51. Hinds, "Icarian Community," 370–79.

Chapter 10: The Final Icarias: Young, Speranza, and New

1. Shaw, *Icaria,* 113–52.

2. *La Revue Icarienne,* Mar. 1879; *La Jeune Icarie,* 22 Feb. 1879. The estimated value of the East was $22,462, and that of the West was $25,260. Gauthier, *"Quest for Utopia,"* 85–87.

3. *La Revue Icarienne,* Apr. 1879; *Réalisation du communisme,* 8–13. For lingering hostilities between the two groups see "D'une lettre de B. Malon, membre de la Commune," *L'Etoile du Kansas et de l'Iowa,* Oct. 1879.

4. *La Jeune Icarie,* 15 Mar. 1879. A French version of the contract is found in a three-page, undated broadside, "Contrat de la nouvelle communauté icarienne d'Adams County, Iowa," Iowa Historical Library Collection, CIS, box 3, folder 3.

5. "Icarian Constitution," in *Réalisation du communisme,* 14–24.

6. Ibid., 24–40. "Law upon Admission into the Icarian Community," "Law upon Withdrawal and Expulsion from the Icarian Community," "Articles of Incorporation of the Icarian Community," "Act of Donation to the Icarian Community," in *Réalisation du communisme,* 24–40.

7. In 1880 Péron changed the title of the newspaper to *Le Communiste-Libertaire Organe de la Communauté Icarienne, Succédant à La Jeune Icarie.* The prospectus, in the Archief Cabet, IISG, explains the change as necessary to "sum up our socialist aspirations."

8. Hine, *California's Utopian Colonies,* 63. In addition to *La Jeune Icarie,* begun in May 1878, the Progressives also were discussed in Jules Leroux's *L'Etoile du Kansas et de l'Iowa.* For further discussion of the newspapers published in the two communities after 1878, and of written communiqués circulated by the Conservatives, see Prevos, "History," 281–82. The "Personnel of Icaria" designating both full members and provisional members was published in *Réalisation du communisme,* 41–42.

9. Shaw, *Icaria,* 134.

10. *La Jeune Icarie,* 31 Dec. 1880; Prudhommeaux, *Icarie,* 570–74.

11. Biographical sketch of Armand Dehay by Mrs. Lorraine Berry, *Center for Icarian Studies Newsletter,* Spring 1984: 4–5; Hine, *California's Utopian Colonies,* 63–65. F. Giacobi was another San Francisco resident and strong supporter of the Icarians. See his letters to Jules Leroux printed in *L'Etoile des Pauvres et des Souffrants,* 1 Feb. 1881. Dehay's glorious image of California's climate and its economic opportunities was printed in Leroux's *L'Etoile des Pauvres et des Souffrants* on May 1, 1881, and was no doubt read by Young Icarians back in Corning. Cloverdale and Sonoma County were specifically discussed in the 1 Aug. 1881 issue.

12. Hine, *California's Utopian Colonies,* 58, 64–67; Prudhommeaux, *Icarie,* 574–79; *L'Etoile des Pauvres et des Souffrants,* 1 Dec. 1881.

13. *La Revue Icarienne,* May–June 1886, discusses in detail the Péron-Fugier scheme. The complicated, confusing story of the fight between Péron-Fugier and the Cloverdale Icarians, including an abortive attempt to merge Icaria Speranza with Young Icaria, is found in Gauthier, *"Quest for Utopia,"* 94–96.

14. *La Revue Icarienne,* July–Aug. 1886, June 1887; E. Péron to A. Marchand, 9 Aug. 1882, Marchand Papers, CIS. A legal technicality allowed for the change of venue. The contract of Icaria Speranza had specifically cited the "Act of Donation of the Icarian Community," a document adopted by the Corning Icaria and filed on April 28, 1879, in the office of the Adams County Recorder of Deeds; A. Dehay to A. Marchand, 4 June 1888, Marchand Papers, CIS; "Act of Donation to the Icarian Community," qtd. in *Réalisation du communisme,* 24–25. *La Revue Icarienne* stated that the court awarded $13,000 to the San Francisco men and $7,000 to cover all remaining claims.

15. The text of the "Contract and Articles of Agreement" is printed in Shaw, *Icaria,* 204–16. Kagan, *New World Utopias,* 36–48. Hine, *California's Utopian Colonies,* 71; "Contract and Articles of Agreement of the Icaria-Speranza Commune," section 14, article 50, reprinted in Shaw, *Icaria,* 213.

16. "Contract and Articles," section 15, articles 51 and 52, in Shaw, *Icaria,* 213–14.

17. *La Revue Icarienne,* Mar. 1879.

18. "Icarian Constitution," in *Réalisation du communisme,* 14–23; *Contrat de la nouvelle communauté icarienne d'Adams County, Iowa,* 1–16. On the hesitant members see *La Revue Icarienne,* Mar. and Sept. 1879.

19. Ross, *Child of Icaria*, 105-9; Rogers, "Housing and Family Life," 93-95, 165-77; Shaw, *Icaria*, 114.

20. Ross, *Child of Icaria*, 105-9, 114; Rogers, "Housing and Family Life," 165-69; Smith, "The Story of Icaria," 55-59; Shaw, *Icaria*, 115. The thirty-four person community owned 1,100 acres on which they grew corn and oats and grazed cattle and sheep and raised hogs. With the sale of some acreage they stabilized their finances by the mid-eighties with debts at $5,797 and assets of over $28,000.

21. Ross, *Child of Icaria*, chs. 26, 32; Blick and Grant, "Life in New Icaria"; "A Part of the Library of the Icarian Colony, Adams County Iowa," gift of Eugene Bettannier in Iowa State Historical Library Collection, CIS, box 5, folder 2; Shaw, *Icaria*, 115-20; *La Revue Icarienne*, Feb. 1888.

22. Ibid., Apr. 1884-Feb. 1888; Ross, *Child of Icaria*, 142.

23. *La Revue Icarienne*, Mar.-Apr. 1885, Feb. 1888; Prevos, "History," 285n108; Ross, *Child of Icaria*, 130-33.

24. Smith, "Story of Icaria," 48; Shaw, *Icaria*, 162.

25. Prudhommeaux, *Icarie*, 601-2.

26. Smith, "Story of Icaria," 47-48; Prevos, "History," 285n110, on the financial distribution; Hinds, *American Communities*, 353; Prudhommeaux, *Icarie*, 603-4.

27. *Adams County Union Republican*, 27 Oct. 1898; Ross, *Child of Icaria*, 142.

Epilogue

1. Professor Michel Cordillot of the Université de Paris-Nord is compiling a biographical dictionary of French émigrés to the United States entitled *Dictionnaire biographique des émigrés politques et des militants ouvriers et socialistes Français aux Etats-Unis (1848-1917)*. When published it will include entries for 497 Icarians that this author has collaborated with Cordillot in compiling. The data so far on the Icarians shows a pattern of easy assimilation into American life after they left the community. They were able, with rare exception, to find comfortable jobs that matched their varied occupational skills in cities and towns. Rarely, as in the case of Gérard for instance, did they venture into agriculture. "Article of Agreement . . . between Jules Maillon . . . and E. F. Bettannier, February 23, 1895," Iowa State Historical Library Collection, CIS, box 5, folder 3; Santa Rosa *Free Democrat*, 16 June 1975, 14 Sept. 1976; Dale Ross, "Homesteading on the Big Bend—A Chapter in the History of Icarian Assimilation in America," National Icarian Heritage Association Symposium, July 8-10, 1988, Nauvoo, Illinois, typescript on file in CIS; Gray, "The Icarian Community," 113-14; Prudhommeaux, *Icarie*, 598n1; Shaw, *Icaria*, 155-70. The final disposition of the Iowa Icarian property after 1898 was traced by Paul Gauthier of Corning, Iowa, from information found in the Adams County Land Records 1895-1954. Gauthier, *"Quest for Utopia,"* 101-3, discusses the last years of New Icaria.

A typescript of the inventory is in the Gauthier Collection, CIS, folders 1 and 2.

2. "Décision de l'assemblée générale concernant les restes de Cabet, janvier 19, 1857," "Nouvelle inhumation des restes du fondateur d'Icarie," "Procès verbal d'inhumation des restes du fondateur d'Icarie," Cabet Collection, SIUE, folders 9 and 10, no. 20; Photograph of Cabet's 1962 tombstone in New St. Marcus Evangelical Cemetery, CIS, Photographic Collections. A sketch of the 1906 tombstone in the Old Riddle Cemetery and a newspaper article on Cabet's death and internment published in the St. Louis *Globe*, 1888, is in the Missouri Historical Society Collection, CIS, folder 3. Mercadier's entries in the St. Louis *City Directory*, 1866-96, are found in a manuscript transcription in the Missouri Historical Society Collections, CIS, folder 5.

3. *Le Populaire*, 9 May 1847, 7 Apr. 1850; Chapius and Poncet to Cabet, 6 Nov. 1844, Papiers Cabet, BHVP; Cabet, *Voyage en Icarie*, preface; Jacques Rancière, *La nuit des prolétaires*, 367-68, 374. Grant, "Icarians"; Grant, "Utopias that Failed"; Sargent, "English and American Utopias," 16-22; Sutton, "Experiments," 60-63.

Bibliography

Special Collections

The main sources of information for this book in the United States are the collections of the Center for Icarian Studies at Western Illinois University. These materials, all identified by Finding Aids and most summarized by Descriptive Inventories, constitute the largest single depository of Icarian data this side of the Atlantic. The Center has all extant Icarian newspapers, listed separately in this bibliography, including the complete run of *Le Populaire*. It houses manuscripts, diaries, musical scores, public documents (land records, vital statistics, census data), dissertations and theses, oral history tapes, videotapes, photographs, rare books (including the first edition of Cabet's *Voyage et aventures de Lord William Carisdall en Icarie*), monographs, and articles published in scholarly journals. Copies of many of the large Icarian holdings of other institutions are available at the Center, such as the Cabet Collection of Southern Illinois University–Edwardsville and the Icarian files of the Iowa State Historical Library at Des Moines.

My research is also based upon archival, manuscript, and print sources found in Paris at the Centre d'Accueil et de Recherche des Archives Nationales (CARN), Bibliothèque Nationale, and Bibliothèque Historique de la Ville de Paris (BHVP); in Amsterdam at the Internationaal Instituut voor Sociale Geschiedenis (IISG); and in London at the British Museum. The complete collection of the Robert Owen Correspondence, located in the Manchester Co-operative Union Library, Manchester, England, is on microfilm at the Illinois Historical Survey, University Library, University of Illinois at Urbana-Champaign.

The manuscript materials in Europe are extensive. The Bibliothèque Nationale, Etienne Cabet, Papiers, (18146-18166) comprise correspondence to and from Cabet (1830-56), communications concerning the Texas disaster, and letters between Mercadier and Beluze (1852-62). The Papiers Cabet (BHVP) (Folders 329-395) contain correspondence mainly from the 1840s, covering the growth of Icarianism after Cabet's return to Paris, up to and including the story of the early emigration to America. The Archives Nationales hold files dealing with Cabet's two appearances in court in 1834 and 1851 (files BB[18] 1214-1221, 1473, and 1550). The Archief Cabet (IISG) has materials relating to the Icarians in Europe and America. Of special significance is the correspondence to and from Beluze while he was head of the

Paris Bureau and during the years immediately after his separation from the American communities. The Instituut has also recently acquired Icarian manuscripts from Stanford University and other American institutions.

The most significant American manuscript collection is "Cabet and his Icarian Colony," of Southern Illinois University–Edwardsville. Available on microfilm at the Center for Icarian Studies, it includes about 1,600 pages of original manuscripts and 46 printed pieces covering the period from 1831 to 1898. The "Iowa Historical Library Collection" at the Center has Cabet's letters to and from Beluze, correspondence of Icarians at the colonies of Nauvoo, Cheltenham, and Corning, materials dealing with the 1877–78 split of the last community, and materials concerning the dissolution of New Icaria in 1898.

Other collections of particular importance at the Center for Icarian Studies are the Marchand Collection, the Lillian M. Snyder Collection, the Dale Larsen Collection, the Renaud Collection, and the collection of vital statistics. The Marchand Collection, donated by Dale Ross, the great-grandson of Marie Marchand Ross, includes extensive correspondence concerning the split of the Corning Icaria and the establishment of Icaria Speranza. The Dale Larsen Collection has forty-nine items relating to the unfortunate Texas experiment and the stay of the Icarians at New Orleans in 1848–49. The Renaud Collection has transcriptions from the National Archives in Washington, D.C., that detail the Grand Departures from Le Havre between February and December 1848. The lists of data in the vital statistics file are census manuscripts, both national and state, mortality schedules, cemetery records, and naturalization records.

Cabet's Publications

The first listing of Cabet's published works appeared in Prudhommeaux, *Icarie*, xiv–xl. An updated version, to 1967, can be seen in Johnson, "Etienne Cabet and the Icarian Communist Movement." The works cited below can be found either in the Center for Icarian Studies, the Bibliothèque Nationale, Archives Nationales, the Bibliothèque Historique de la Ville de Paris, the Instituut voor Sociale Geschiedenis, or the British Museum. An extensive collection of Icarian pamphlets and brochures is also housed in the St. Louis Public Library and the New York Public Library.

Newspapers

The most valuable newspaper source on the Icarians is *Le Populaire*, 1833–35 and 1841–51, available on microfilm in the Center for Icarian Studies or in original copy at the Bibliothèque Nationale, Lc^2 1360. The other newspapers listed below cover almost exclusively the American utopias. Extant copies are also in the Center for Icarian Studies.

Adams County Republican
Colonie Icarienne
Der Communist

The Communist
Le Communist Libertaire
L'Etoile du Kansas et de l'Iowa
L'Etoile des Pauvres et des Souffrants
La Jeune Icarie
Nouvelle Revue Icarienne
The Nauvoo Tribune
L'Observateur
The Popular Tribune
Revue Icarienne (Nauvoo)
La Revue Icarienne (Corning)

Primary Sources

Beluze, Jean Pierre. *Aux Icariens.* Paris: 3 rue Baillet, 1856.
———. *Célébration à Saint-Louis du 9ᵐᵉ anniversaire de la fondation d'Icarie.* Paris: 3 rue Baillet, 1857.
———. *Célébration du premier anniversaire de la naissance du fondateur d'Icarie.* Paris: 3 rue Baillet, 1857.
———. *Cheltenham.* Paris: 3 rue Baillet, 1858.
———. *Deuxième lettre à Maximilien.* Paris: 3 rue Baillet, 1858.
———. *La colonie icarienne à Saint-Louis.* Paris: 3 rue Baillet, 1857.
———. *Lettre à Maximilien sur la colonie icarienne.* Paris: 3 rue Baillet, 1858.
———. *Lettre circulaire sur la situation de la colonie icarienne de Cheltenham.* Paris: Malteste, 1859.
———. *Lettre pour announcer ma démission de gérant du bureau icarien.* Paris: Malteste, 1863.
———. *Lettres icariennes à mon ami Eugène.* 2 vols. Paris: 3 rue Baillet, 1859-62.
———. *Lettre sur la colonie icarienne par un Icarien.* Paris: 3 rue Baillet, 1856.
———. *Mort du fondateur d'Icarie.* Paris: 3 rue Baillet, 1856.
———. *Notre situation à Saint-Louis.* Paris: 3 rue Baillet, 1857.
———. *Organisation du travail.* Paris: Malteste, 1866.
———. *Qu'est-ce que la société du crédit au travail?* Paris: Guillaumin, 1863.
———. *Rapport de la commission nominée le 1ᵉʳ novembre 1862 pour vérifier la question du citoyen Beluze, représentant de la colonie icarienne en France.* Paris: 3 rue Baillet, 1863.
Blanc, Louis. *Histoire de dix ans.* 13th ed. 5 vols. Paris: Germer Baillière, 1883.
———. *Organisation du travail.* Paris: Pagnerre, 1848.
Cabet, Etienne. *Au duc d'Orléans.* Paris: A. Mie, 1830.
———. "Aux électeurs de l'arrondissement de Dijon." *Journal politique et littéraire de la Côte d'Or,* 24 Apr. 1831.
———. *A bas les communistes!* Paris: Malteste, 1848.
———. *Adresse des Icariens de Nauvoo au citoyen Cabet, protestation de*

quelques dissidents et réponse du citoyen Cabet. Paris: Bureau du *Populaire,*
1851.

——. *Adresse du fondateur d'Icarie aux Icariens.* Paris: 3 rue Baillet, 1856.

——. *Adresses des Icariens de Nauvoo au citoyen Cabet.* Paris: Bureau du
Populaire, 1851.

——. *Almanach icarien, astronomique, scientifique, pratique, industriel,
statistique.* Paris: Bureau du *Populaire,* 1843–48.

——. *Arrestations illégales des crieurs publics.* Paris: L. E. Herhan, 1833.

——. *Association libre pour l'éducation du peuple. Discours de M. Cabet.*
Paris: Demonville, 1833.

——. *Aux Icariens de France.* Paris: Malteste, 1852.

——. *Au peuple.—République démocratique et sociale.* Paris: Malteste,
1848.

——. *Aux membres du gouvernement provisoire.* Paris: Malteste, 1848.

——. *Bien et mal, danger et salut après la révolution de février 1848.* Paris:
Bureau du *Populaire,* 1848.

——. *Biographie de M. Cabet, ancien procureur général, ancien député,
directeur du "Populaire," et réponse aux ennemis du communisme.* Paris:
Bureau du *Populaire,* 1846.

——. *Ce que je ferais si j'avais 500,000 dollars.* Paris: 3 rue Baillet, 1854.

——. *Célébration à Nauvoo du septième anniversaire du départ de la
première avant-garde icarienne (3 fév. 1848).* Paris: 3 rue Baillet, 1855.

——. *Colonie icarienne aux Etats-Unis d'Amérique. Sa constitution, ses lois,
sa situation matérielle et morale après le premier semestre de 1855.*
Paris: 3 rue Baillet, 1856.

——. *Colonie icarienne. Réforme icarienne du 21 novembre 1853.* Paris: 3
rue Baillet, 1853.

——. *Colonie icarienne. Situation dans l'Iowa au 15 octobre 1853.* Paris: 3
rue Baillet, 1853.

——. *Colonie icarienne. Tempérance. Tabac et whiskey.* Nauvoo: Imprimerie
Icarienne, 1853.

——. *Colonie ou république icarienne dans les Etats-Unis d'Amérique. Son
histoire.* Paris: Bureau de l'Emigration Icarienne, 3 rue Baillet, 1854.

——. *Comment je suis communiste et mon crédo communiste.* Paris: Bureau
du *Populaire,* 1841.

——. *Comment je suis communiste.* Paris: Bourgogne et Martinet, 1841.

——. *Communauté icarienne. Prospectus. Conditions d'admission.* Nauvoo:
Imprimerie Icarienne, 1854.

——. *Compte-rendu par le président de la communauté sur l'état de la
colonie icarienne après le premier semestre de 1854.* Paris: 3 rue Baillet,
1854.

——. *Constitution of the Icarian Community.* Nauvoo: Icarian Printing
Office, 1854.

——. *Correspondance avec Louis-Philippe, Dupont de l'Eure, Barthe, etc., sur
la marche du gouvernement depuis le 1ᵉʳ août 1830.* Paris: Rouanet, 1831.

———. *Credo communiste*. Paris: Prévot, 1841.

———. *Curieuse lettre du citoyen Cabet à Louis-Napoléon*. Paris: Bureau du *Républicain populaire et social*, 1851.

———. *Défense du citoyen Cabet accusé d'escroquerie devant la cour d'appel de Paris*. Paris: Bureau du *Populaire*, 1851.

———. *Départ de Nauvoo du fondateur d'Icarie avec les vrais Icariens*. Paris: 3 rue Baillet, 1856.

———. *Deuxième lettre à Louis-Napoléon*. Paris: Bureau du *Républicain populaire et social*, 1851.

———. *Dialogue entre un garde national républicain et un garde national juste-milieu*. Paris: L. E. Herhan, 1833.

———. *Discours d'installation de M. Cabet*. Paris: L. E. Herhan, 1833.

———. *Discours prononcé le 1er mars 1831 à l'occasion du rétablissement du jury en Corse*. Bastia, Corsica: J. Fabiani, 1831.

———. *Faits préliminaires au procès devant la cour d'assises contre M. Cabet, député de la Côte-d'Or*. Paris: Rouanet, 1833.

———. *La femme, ses qualités, ses titres, ses droits; son malheureux sort dans la présente société; causes du mal; remède; son bonheur dans la communauté*. 4th ed. Paris: Bureau du *Populaire*, 1844.

———. *Guerre de l'opposition contre le citoyen Cabet, fondateur d'Icarie*. Paris: 3 rue Baillet, 1856.

———. *Histoire de la révolution de 1830 et situation présente (sept. 1832) expliquées et éclairées par les révolutions de 1792, 1799 et 1804 et par la restauration*. Paris: A. Mie, 1832.

———. *Histoire populaire de la révolution française, de 1789 à 1830, précedée d'une introduction contenant le précis de l'histoire des Français depuis leur origine jusqu'aux Etats Généraux*. 4 vols. Paris: Pagnerre, 1839–1840.

———. *Icarie: Les Icariens d'Amérique*. Paris: Bureau du *Populaire*, 1849.

———. *Insurrection du 23 juin 1848 avec ses causes, son caractère et ses suites, expliquée par la marche et les fautes de la révolution du 24 février*. Paris: Bureau du *Populaire*, 1848.

———. *Inventaire de la colonie icarienne, 1853. Célébration de l'anniversaire du 3 février 1848. Un jugement en Icarie*. Paris: 3 rue Baillet, 1853.

———. *La justice d'avril. Lettre à M. Guizot*. Paris: Pagnerre, 1835.

———. *Lettre de M. Cabet, député, aux électeurs du deuxième arrondissement de Dijon et à ses concitoyens*. Dijon: Douiller, 1831.

———. *Lettre de M. Cabet, ex-procureur-général en Corse, aux électeurs du deuxième arrondissement de Dijon (Côte d'Or)*. Dijon: Douiller, 1831.

———. *Lettre sur la réforme icarienne du 21 novembre 1853. Réponse du citoyen Cabet à quelques objections sur cette réforme*. Paris: 3 rue Baillet, 1854.

———. *Ma ligne droite, ou le vrai chemin du salut pour le peuple*. Paris: Prévot, 1841.

———. *Manifestations et adresses par les Icariens de Nauvoo au fondateur d'Icarie*. Paris: 3 rue Baillet, 1856.

———. *Manifestes de l'opposition et réponse du citoyen Cabet.* Paris: 3 rue Baillet, 1856.

———. *Moyens d'améliorer l'état déplorable des ouvriers.* Paris: L. E. Herhan, 1833.

———. *Le "National" traduit devant le tribunal de l'opinion publique et M. Cabet accusé par le "National."* Paris: Prévot, 1841.

———. *Nécessité de populariser les journaux républicains.* Paris: L. E. Herhan, 1833.

———. *Notre procès en escroquerie ou poursuites dirigées contre les citoyens Cabet et Krolikowski à l'occasion de la fondation d'Icarie.* Paris: Bureau du *Populaire,* 1849.

———. *Nouvelle biographie générale.* Paris: Firmin-Didot, 1855.

———. *Opinion icarienne sur le mariage. Organisation icarienne. Naturalisation des Icariens.* Paris: 3 rue Baillet, 1855.

———. *Opinions et sentiments publiquement exprimés concernant le fondateur d'Icarie.* Paris: 3 rue Baillet, 1856.

———. *L'ouvrier; ses misères actuelles; leur cause et leur remède; son futur bonheur dans la communauté; moyens de l'établir.* 4th ed. Paris: Bureau du *Populaire,* 1848.

———. *Péril de la situation présente. Compte à mes commettants.* Paris: A. Mie, 1831.

———. *Le Populaire, prospectus.* Paris: L. E. Herhan, 1833.

———. *Poursuites du gouvernement contre M. Cabet.* Paris: Bureau du *Populaire,* 1834.

———. *Procès du "Propagateur de Pas-de-Calais."* Paris: Bureau du *Populaire,* 1833.

———. *Procès du journal républicain "Le Patriote" de la Côte-d'Or et de l'association dijonnaise contre les impôts antipopulaires sur les boissons et le sel.* Paris: Bureau du *Populaire,* 1833.

———. *Procès et acquittement de Cabet accusé d'escroquerie au sujet de l'émigration icarienne. Histoire d'Icarie.* Paris: Bureau du *Républicain populaire et social,* 1851.

———. *Progrès de la colonie icarienne établie à Nauvoo (Etats-Unis d'Amérique). M. Cabet à Julien, Icarien disposé à venir en Icarie.* Paris: 3 rue Baillet, 1854.

———. *Prospectus de la colonie icarienne. Conditions d'admission.* Paris: 3 rue Baillet, 1855.

———. *Prospectus de la colonie icarienne.* Paris: 3 rue Baillet, 1855.

———. *Prospectus. Emigration icarienne. Conditions d'admission. Rapport de la Gérance à l'assemblée générale.* Paris: 3 rue Baillet, 1852.

———. *Prospectus: Grande émigration au Texas, en Amérique, pour réaliser la communauté d'Icarie.* Paris: Bureau du *Populaire,* 1848.

———. *Rapport de la commission d'examen des publications et imprimés fait du 30 septembre 1855 au 22 mars 1856.* Nauvoo: Imprimerie Icarienne, 1856.

———. *Rapport de la commission de surveillance et de vérification des comptes à l'assemblée générale de la communauté icarienne.* Nauvoo: Imprimerie Icarienne, 1856.

———. *Réalisation d'Icarie, grande émigration en Amérique.* Paris: Bureau du *Populaire*, 1849-1850.

———. *Réalisation de la communauté d'Icarie—Nouvelles de Nauvoo.* Paris: Bureau du *Populaire*, 1847.

———. *Réception et admission dans la communauté icarienne des 38 Icariens partis du Hâvre le 8 septembre 1853.* Paris: 3 rue Baillet, 1854.

———. *Réponse d'un républicain aux calomnies des pamphlétaires de la police.* Paris: L. E. Herhan, 1833.

———. *La république du populaire.* Paris: Bureau du *Populaire*, 1833.

———. *Societé fraternelle centrale.—Discours du citoyen Cabet, 10ᵐᵉ discours, mai 1848. Exposé rapide sur la doctrine et la marche du communisme icarien.* Paris: Bureau du *Populaire*, 1848.

———. *Toute la vérité au peuple ou réfutation d'un pamphlet calomniateur.* Paris: Prévot, 1842.

———. *Toute la vérité.* Nauvoo: Imprimerie Icarienne, 1856.

———. *Travels in Icaria.* Trans. Robert P. Sutton. Macomb: Western Illinois University Press, 1985.

———. *Voyage de M. Cabet (New York, 6 janv. 1849).* Paris: F. Malteste, 1849.

———. *Voyage en Icarie.* Paris: Matlet, 1842.

———. *Voyage et aventures de Lord William Carisdall en Icarie.* Paris: Hippolyte Souverain, 1839.

———. *Le vrai Christianisme suivant Jésus-Christ.* Paris: Bureau du *Populaire*, 1846.

Cabet, Etienne, and Louis Krolikowski. *Système de fraternité.* 6 vols. Paris: Bureau du *Populaire*, 1849-50.

Carle, Henry, and J. P. Beluze. *Biographie de Etienne Cabet, fondateur de l'école icarienne.* Paris: 3 rue Baillet, 1861-62.

Considérant, Victor. *Le socialisme devant le vieux monde.* Paris: Librairie Phalanstérienne, 1848.

Cour de Paris. *Affaire du mois d'avril: rapport fait à la cour par M. Girod (de l'Ain).* Paris: Imprimé royale, 1834.

Dézamy, Théodore. *Calomnies et politique de M. Cabet; réfutation par des faits et par sa biographie.* Paris: Prévot, 1842.

Dupin, André. *Mémoires.* 3 vols. Paris: H. Plon, 1860.

Gentry, Jules. *Journal et manuscrits inédits, 1876-1879.* Corning, Iowa: n.p., 1880.

Gérard, J. B. *Quelques vérités sur la dernière crise icarienne.* Corning, Iowa: n.p., 1880.

Holinski, A., "Cabet et les Icariens." *La revue socialiste* 1891: 539-50; 1892: 40-49, 201-4, 315-21, 449-56; 1893: 296-307.

Job [Frédrich Olinet]. *Voyage d'un autunois en Icarie à la suite de Cabet.* Autun: Dejussieu, 1898.

King, Henry. "M. Cabet and the Icarians." *The Lakeside Monthly* Oct. 1871: 289-98.

Leroux, Pierre. *La grève de Samarez.* 2 vols. Paris: Dentu, 1863-64.

Lux, Heinrich. *Etienne Cabet und der ikarische Kommunismus: mit einer historischen Einleitung.* Stuttgart: Dietz, 1894.

Ménard, Louis. *Prologue d'une révolution.* Paris: Cahiers de la Quinzaine, 1848.

Mercadier, Benjamin. *Compte-rendu de la Gérance à la communauté icarienne à Saint Louis, sur la situation morale et matérielle de la communauté pendant les mois de novembre et décembre 1856 et les mois de janvier et février 1857.* Paris: 3 rue Baillet, 1857.

———. *Compte-rendu de la situation morale et matérielle de la communauté icarienne du mois d'avril 1857 au mois de février 1858.* Paris: 3 rue Baillet, 1858.

———. *Contrat social ou acte de société de la communauté icarienne. Lois sur l'admission.* Paris: 3 rue Baillet, 1857.

———. *Inauguration du cours icarien.* Paris: 3 rue Baillet, 1858.

———. *Organisation du travail dans la communauté icarienne. Loi du 2 février 1857 sur le tabac.* Paris: 3 rue Baillet, 1857.

Mercier, Louis Sebastian. *L'an deux mille quatre cent quarante.* Philadelphia: T. Dobson, 1795.

Ministère de la Guerre. *Développements et justification à l'appui du projet de loi concernant les fortifications de Paris.* Paris: Imprimé royale, 1833.

Moorehead, S. W. "Icaria and the Icarians." *The Western Magazine* July 1877: 161-68.

Nordoff, Charles. *The Communistic Societies of the United States.* London: J. Murray, 1875.

Péron, Emile. "Histoire d'Icarie." *Revue socialiste* July 1880: 448.

Proudhon, Pierre-Joseph. *What Is Property? An Enquiry into the Principle of Right and of Government.* Trans. Benjamin R. Tucker. New York: H. Fertig, 1966.

Réalisation du communisme. Précis sur Icarie. Constitution, lois et règlements de la communauté icarienne. Corning, Iowa: n.p., 1880.

Ross, Marie Marchand. *Child of Icaria.* New York: City Printing Co., 1938.

Sauva, Arsène. *La crise icarienne, 1877-1878.* Corning, Iowa: n.p., 1878.

———. *La crise icarienne, no. 2. Une manoeuvre perfide.* Corning, Iowa: n.p., 1878.

———. *Icarie.* Corning, Iowa: n.p., 1877.

Taschereau, J. *Revue rétrospective; ou, Archives secrètes du dernier gouvernement.* Paris: Paulin, 1848.

de Tocqueville, Alexis. *Democracy in America.* 2 vols. New York: Vintage Books, 1945.

Vallet, Emile. *Communism: History of the Experiment at Nauvoo of the Icarian Settlement.* Nauvoo, 1917.

Wick, Barthinius. "The Icarian Community—Story of Etienne Cabet's Experiment in Communism." *The Midland Monthly* Apr. 1895: 370-76.

Secondary Sources

Agulhon, Maurice. *Une ville ouvrière au temps du socialisme utopique: Toulon, 1815-1851.* Paris: Nathan, 1970.

Albertson, Ralph. "A Survey of Mutualistic Communities in America." *The Iowa Journal of History and Politics* Oct. 1936: 375-444.

Allain, Mathe. *France and North America: Utopias and Utopians.* Lafayette: University of Southwestern Louisiana, 1978.

Angle, Paul. "An Illinois Paradise: The Icarians at Nauvoo." *Chicago History* Spring 1965: 199-209.

Angrand, Pierre. *Etienne Cabet et la république de 1848.* Paris: Presses Universitaires de France, 1848.

Barnes, Sherman B. "An Icarian in Nauvoo," *Journal of the Illinois State Historical Society* June 1941: 233-44.

Beecher, Jonathan. *Charles Fourier: The Visionary and His World.* Berkeley: University of California Press, 1986.

Begos, Jane Dupree. "'Icaria,' a Footnote to the Peters Colony." *Communal Societies* 1986: 84-91.

Blick, Boris, and H. Roger Grant. "French Icarians in St. Louis." *Bulletin,* Missouri Historical Society, Oct. 1973: 3-28.

——. "Life in New Icaria, Iowa: Nineteenth-Century Utopia." *Annals of Iowa* Winter 1974: 198-204.

Bonnaud, Félix. *Etienne Cabet et son oeuvre: appel à tous les socialistes.* Paris: Société Libre d'Editions des Gens des Lettres, 1900.

Brooks, George R. "Some New Views of Old Cheltenham." *Bulletin,* Missouri Historical Society, Oct. 1965: 32-34.

Bush, Robert D. "Communism, Community and Charisma: The Crisis in Icaria at Nauvoo." *The Old Northwest* Dec. 1977: 499-528.

Carré, Paul. *Cabet: De la démocratie au comunisme.* Lille: Imprimerie le Bigot Frères, 1903.

Charléty, Sebastien. *Histoire du Saint-Simonisme (1825-1846).* Paris: Gauthier, 1965.

Chicoineau, Jacques C. "Etienne Cabet and the Icarians." *Western Illinois Regional Studies* Spring 1979: 5-19.

Clark, Robert E. "A Cultural and Historical Geography of the Amana Colony, Iowa." Ph.D. diss., University of Nebraska-Lincoln, 1974.

Cole, Margaret I. *Robert Owen of New Lanark.* New York: A. M. Kelley, 1969.

Collins, Irene, *The Government and Newspaper Press in France, 1814-1884.* Oxford: Oxford University Press, 1959.

Connor, Seymour. *The Peters Colony of Texas: A History and Biographical Sketches of the Early Settlers.* Austin: The Texas State Historical Association, 1959.

Desroche, Henri. Preface. *Voyage en Icarie,* by Etienne Cabet. 1848; rpt. Paris: Editions Anthropos, 1970.

Dubois, Paul-François. "Etienne Cabet." *Revue bleue* Mar. 1908: 321-25.

Dunham, Arthur L. *The Industrial Revolution in France, 1815-1848.* New York: Exposition Press, 1955.

Duveau, Georges. *1848.* Paris: Gallimard, 1965.

Eisenstein, Elizabeth. *The First Professional Revolutionary: Filippo Michele Buonarotti.* Cambridge: Harvard University Press, 1958.

Evans, D. O. *Le socialisme romantique: Pierre Leroux et ses contemporains.* Paris: Rivière, 1948.

Faucheux, L., and L. Morauzeau. "Les débuts du communisme en Vendée: L'affaire Madeline." *Etudes: Bibliothèque de la révolution de 1848* 1953: 77-88.

Fotion, Janis Clark. "Cabet and Icarian Communism." Ph.D. diss., University of Iowa, 1966.

Gallaher, Ruth A. "Icaria and the Icarians." *The Palimpsest* Apr. 1921: 97-112.

Gauthier, Paul S. *"Quest for Utopia": The Icarians of Adams County, Iowa.* Corning, Iowa: Gauthier Publishing Co., 1992.

Grant, H. Roger. "Icarians and American Utopianism." *Illinois Quarterly* Feb. 1972: 5-15.

———. "Utopias that Failed: The Antebellum Years." *Western Illinois Regional Studies* Spring 1979: 38-51.

Gray, Charles. "The Icarian Community." *Annals of Iowa* July 1903: 107-14.

Guarneri, Carl J. *The Utopian Alternative: Fourierism in Nineteenth-Century America.* Ithaca: Cornell University Press, 1991.

Hammen, Oscar J. "1848 et 'le Spectre du Communisme.'" *Le contrat social* 1958: 191-200.

Hausheer, Herman. "Icarian Medicine: Etienne Cabet's Utopia and Its French Medical Background." *Bulletin of the History of Medicine* May 1941: 294-331, 401-35, 517-29.

Hayded, Dolores. *Seven American Utopias: The Architecture of Communitarian Socialism, 1790-1975.* Cambridge: Harvard University Press, 1976.

Hinds, William Alfred. "The Icarians." *American Communities and Cooperative Colonies.* Chicago: Charles H. Kerr & Co., 1908. 361-96.

Hine, Robert V. *California's Utopian Colonies.* San Marino, Calif.: Henry E. Huntingdon Library and Art Gallery, 1953.

Holloway, Mark. "Icaria." *Heaven on Earth: Utopian Communities in America, 1680-1880.* New York: Dover Press, 1960. 198-211.

Johnson, Christopher H. "Communism and the Working Class Before Marx: The Icarian Experience." *American Historical Review* June 1971: 642-89.

———. "Etienne Cabet and the Icarian Communist Movement in France, 1839-1848." Ph.D. diss., University of Wisconsin, 1968.

———. "Etienne Cabet and the Problem of Class Antagonism." *International Review of Social History* 1966: 403-43.

———. *Utopian Communism in France: Cabet and the Icarians, 1839-1851.* Ithaca: Cornell University Press, 1974.

Kagan, Paul. *New World Utopias.* New York: Penguin Books, 1975.

Kanter, Rosabeth Moss. *Commitment and Community: Communes and Utopias in Sociological Perspective.* Cambridge: Harvard University Press, 1972.

Labrousse, Ernest. *Le mouvement ouvrier et les théories sociales en France de 1815 à 1840.* Paris: Centre de Documentation Universitaire, 1961.

Lauer, Jeanette, and Robert H. Lauer. "Cheltenham: The Search for Bliss in Missouri." *Missouri Historical Quarterly* Jan. 1987: 173-83.

Lehning, A. "Discussions à Londres sur le communisme icarien." *Bulletin of the International Institute of Social History* 1952: 87-109.

Loubere, Leo A. *Louis Blanc: His Life and His Contribution to the Rise of Jacobin Socialism.* Evanston: Northwestern University Press, 1961.

Luke, Kenneth O. "Nauvoo, Illinois, Since the Exodus of the Mormons, 1846-1873." Ph.D. diss., Saint Louis University, 1973.

Maitron, Jean, ed. *Dictionnaire biographique du mouvement ouvrier français.* Paris: Editions Ouvrières, 1964.

Manuel, Frank. *The New World of Henri de Saint-Simon.* South Bend: Notre Dame University Press, 1965.

———, and Fritzie P. Manuel, eds. *French Utopias: An Anthology of Ideal Societies.* New York: Schocken Books, 1971.

Mathe, Allain, ed. *France and North America: Utopias and Utopians.* Lafayette: University of Southwest Louisiana, 1978.

Miller, I. G. "The Icarian Community of Nauvoo, Illinois." *Transactions of the Illinois State Historical Society* 1906: 103-7.

Petermann, Gerd Alfred. "The Communia and Sociality Colonies and their Roots in the German Social-Reform Movement of St. Louis, 1846-47." *Communal Societies* 1990: 1-23.

Pinckney, David H. *The French Revolution of 1830.* Princeton: Princeton University Press, 1972.

Piotrowski, Sylvester A. *Etienne Cabet and the "Voyage en Icarie": A Study in the History of Social Thought.* Washington, D.C.: Catholic University Press, 1935.

Prevos, Andre. "A History of the French in Iowa." Ph.D. diss., University of Iowa, 1981.

Prudhommeaux, Jules. *Icarie et son fondateur Etienne Cabet.* Paris: Edouard Cornély et Cie, 1907.

Queen, Stuart A., and David Carpenter. *The American City.* New York: McGraw-Hill, 1953.

Rancière, Jacques. *La nuit des prolétaires.* Paris: Fayard, 1981.

Rees, Thomas. "Nauvoo, Illinois, Under Mormon and Icarian Occupation." *Journal of the Illinois State Historical Society* Jan. 1929: 514-21.

Roberts, Leslie J. "Etienne Cabet and his *Voyage en Icarie*, 1840." *Utopian Studies* 1991: 77-94.

Rogers, Elizabeth Ann. "Housing and Family Life of the Icarian Colonies." M.A. thesis, University of Iowa, 1973.

Rude, Fernand. *Voyage en Icarie: deux ouvriers viennois aux Etats-Unis en 1855.* Paris: Presses Universitaires de France, 1955.

Sargent, Lyman Tower. "English and American Utopias: Similarities and Differences." *The Journal of General Education* Spring 1976: 16-22.

Savage, Nadine Dormoy. "Jules Leroux in Icaria." *The French Review* May 1976: 1025-40.

Sewell, William, Jr. *Work and Revolution in France: The Language of Labor from the Old Regime to 1848.* New York: Cambridge University Press, 1980.

Shambaugh, Bertha M. H. *Amana that Was and Amana that Is.* New York: Benjamin Blom, Inc., 1971.

Shaw, Albert. *Icaria, a Chapter in the History of Communism.* New York: G. P. Putnam, 1884.

Smith, Martha Browning. "The Story of Icaria." *Annals of Iowa* Summer 1965: 36-64.

Smithson, Rulon N., with Robert P. Sutton. " 'Mon Cher Emile': The Cabet-Baxter Letters, 1854-1855." *Western Illinois Regional Studies* Spring 1979: 20-37.

———. *Augustin Thierry: Social and Political Consciousness in the Evolution of a Historical Method.* Geneva: Librairie Droz, 1972.

Spitzer, Alan B. *Old Hatreds and Young Hopes: The French Carbonari Against the Bourbon Restoration.* Cambridge: Harvard University Press, 1971.

Sutton, Robert P. "Alfred Henry Piquenard, 1825-1876." *Hayes Historical Journal* Fall 1992: 44-46.

———. " 'Earthly Paradise': The Icarian Experiment in St. Louis." *Gateway Heritage: Quarterly Magazine of the Missouri Historical Society–St. Louis* Spring 1992: 48-59.

———. "Etienne Cabet and the Nauvoo Icarians." *Illinois Magazine* Mar.-Apr. 1985: 7-12.

———. "Experiments in Communitarianism." *Illinois: Its History and Legacy,* ed. Roger O. Bridges and Rodney O. Davis. St. Louis: River City Publishers Limited, 1984. 57-68.

———. "The Icarian Communities in America, 1848-1898." *Communities: Journal of Cooperation* Winter 1985: 42-50.

———. "Utopian Fraternity: Ideal and Reality in Icarian Recreation." *Western Illinois Regional Studies* Spring 1983: 23-38.

Sutton, Robert P., and Lloyd and Wilma Gundy. "Icarian Embarkation: Le Havre to Nauvoo, 1854." *Western Illinois Regional Studies* Spring 1986: 19-33.

Teakle, Thomas. "History and Constitution of the Icarian Community." *Iowa Journal of History and Politics* April 1917: 214-86.

Ventura, Jordi. " 'Icaria' vida, teorías y obra de Etienne Cabet, sus seguidores catalones y experimentos comunistas icarianos." *Cuadernos de Historia Económica de Cataluña* June 1972: 139–251.

Zablocki, Benjamin D. *Alienation and Charisma: A Study of Contemporary American Communes.* New York: Free Press, 1981.

Index

ROBERT P. SUTTON is professor of history at Western Illinois University, where he is also the director of the Center for Icarian Studies. He has published numerous articles on the Icarian communities in leading historical journals. He was co-author and narrator of the 1992–93 public television series *Illinois: A Historical Panorama*. His five books include *Rivers, Railways, and Roads: A History of Henderson County, Illinois,* which was awarded the Certificate of Excellence by the Illinois State Historical Society. He is currently co-authoring a new translation of Cabet's *Voyage en Icarie* and co-editing the "Dictionnaire biographique des émigres politiques et des militants ouvriers et socialistes Français aux Etats-Unis 1848–1917," scheduled to appear as volume 45 of Jean Maitron's *Dictionnaire biographique du mouvement ouvrier Français*. Western Illinois University has presented him Faculty Excellence Awards ten times for outstanding achievement in teaching and scholarship, and in the spring of 1993 its College of Arts and Sciences presented him the Outstanding Research Award for career excellence in scholarly publication. He serves on the Board of Directors for the Communal Societies Association.

Books in the Statue of Liberty–Ellis Island Centennial Series